TABLE ◇OF◇ CONTENTS

DOWNLOAD YOUR FILES

Downloading your files is simple. To access your digital files, please go to the last page of this book and follow the instructions.

For technical assistance, please email: info@vaulteditions.com

Copyright
Copyright © Vault Editions Ltd 2023.

Bibliographical Note
This book is a new work created by Vault Editions Ltd.

ISBN: 978-1-922966-48-3

HOW TO DRAW TATTOO FLASH

VOID DOOR

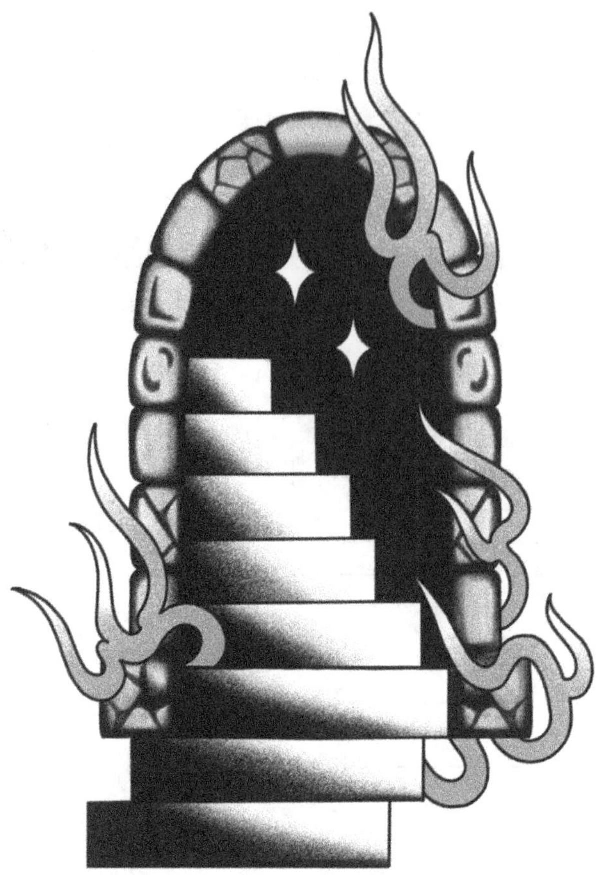

A void door tattoo symbolises mystery, transition, and the unknown, often representing the passage between different realms or states of being, and carrying themes of introspection, change and exploration.

01

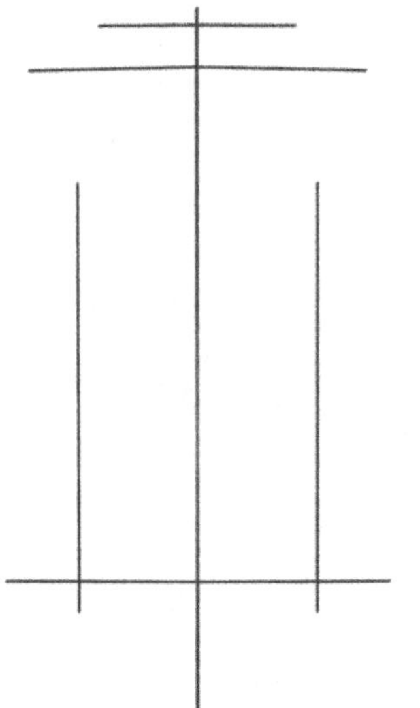

02

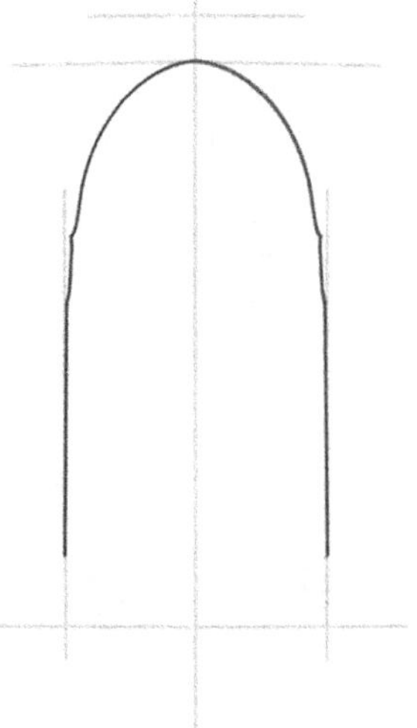

03

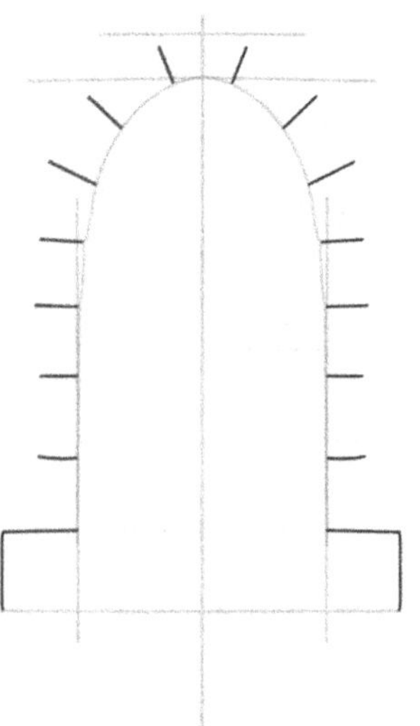

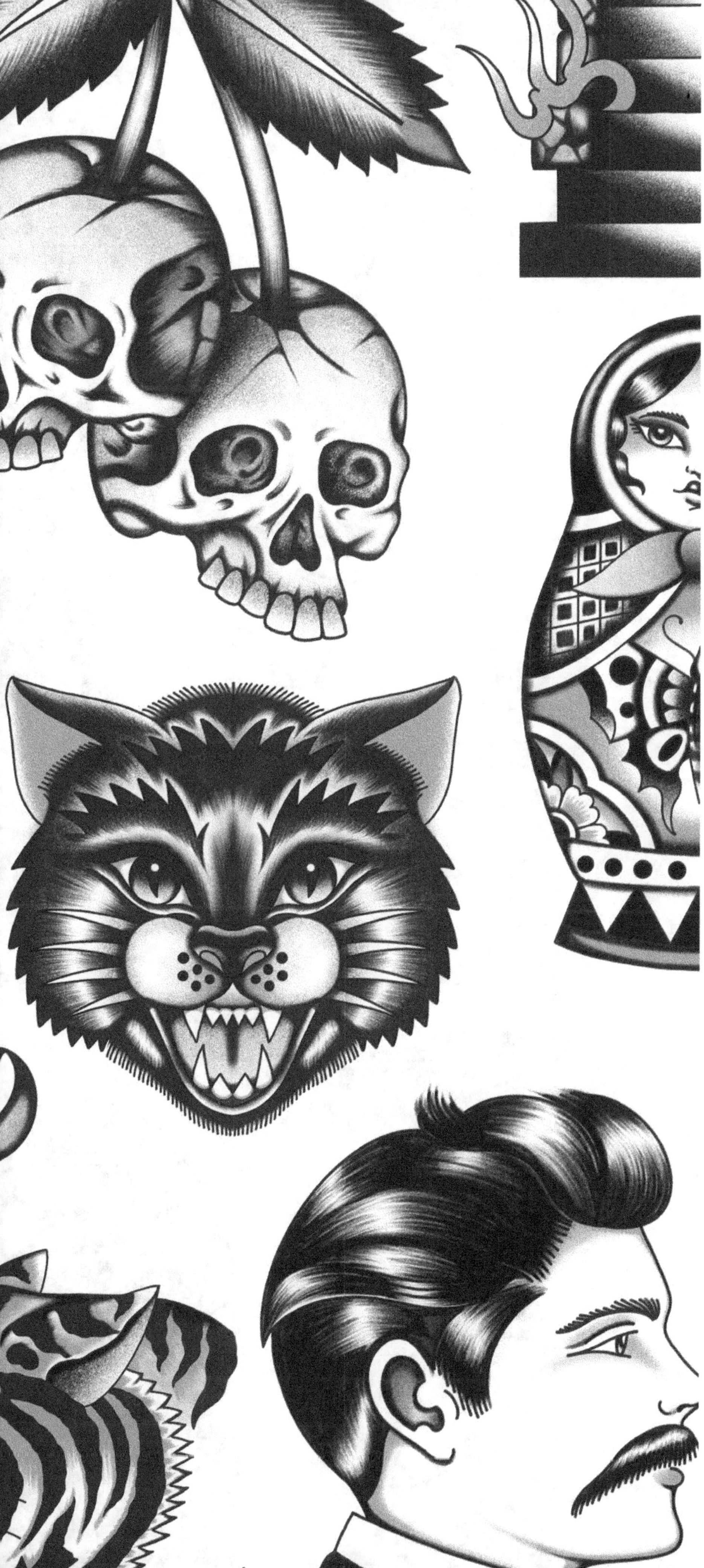

THE VAULT EDITIONS GUIDE TO
MASTERING
THE ART OF
DRAWING

HOW TO DRAW
TATTOO FLASH

A HELPFUL MANUAL FOR
ARTISTS AND DESIGNERS

STEP BY STEP

HAND DRAWN
UNIQUE 40 DESIGNS
BEST QUALITY

EDITIONS
Vault

VAULT EDITIONS

INTRODUCTION

Tattoos have long transcended simple body art, evolving into a powerful form of storytelling and self-expression through iconic symbols etched into the skin. For those drawn to the bold and timeless world of traditional tattoo flash, whether you're an aspiring artist or an enthusiast of this classic style, *How to Draw Tattoo Flash* is your gateway to mastering this captivating craft. This book is designed for both beginners and those looking to sharpen their skills, offering a structured learning process that guides you through creating stunning flash art from the ground up.

In this comprehensive guide, you'll explore the world of traditional tattoo flash, diving deep into the art's rich heritage. Discover the symbolism and enduring appeal of classic designs such as skulls, hearts and daggers, wolves, void doors, tigers, snakes and daggers, coffins, roses, flat flowers and more. Our step-by-step approach ensures you learn how to draw these iconic designs and gain insight into the cultural and historical significance behind each design.

Whether you aspire to become a tattoo artist, design your own tattoos, or simply appreciate the timeless artistry of traditional tattoo flash, *How to Draw Tattoo Flash* will be your trusted companion. Let your creative journey begin as you unlock the skills to produce bold, meaningful designs that celebrate the rich tradition of tattoo art. Unleash your inner artist and transform your imagination into a striking, lasting tattoo flash design that stands the test of time.

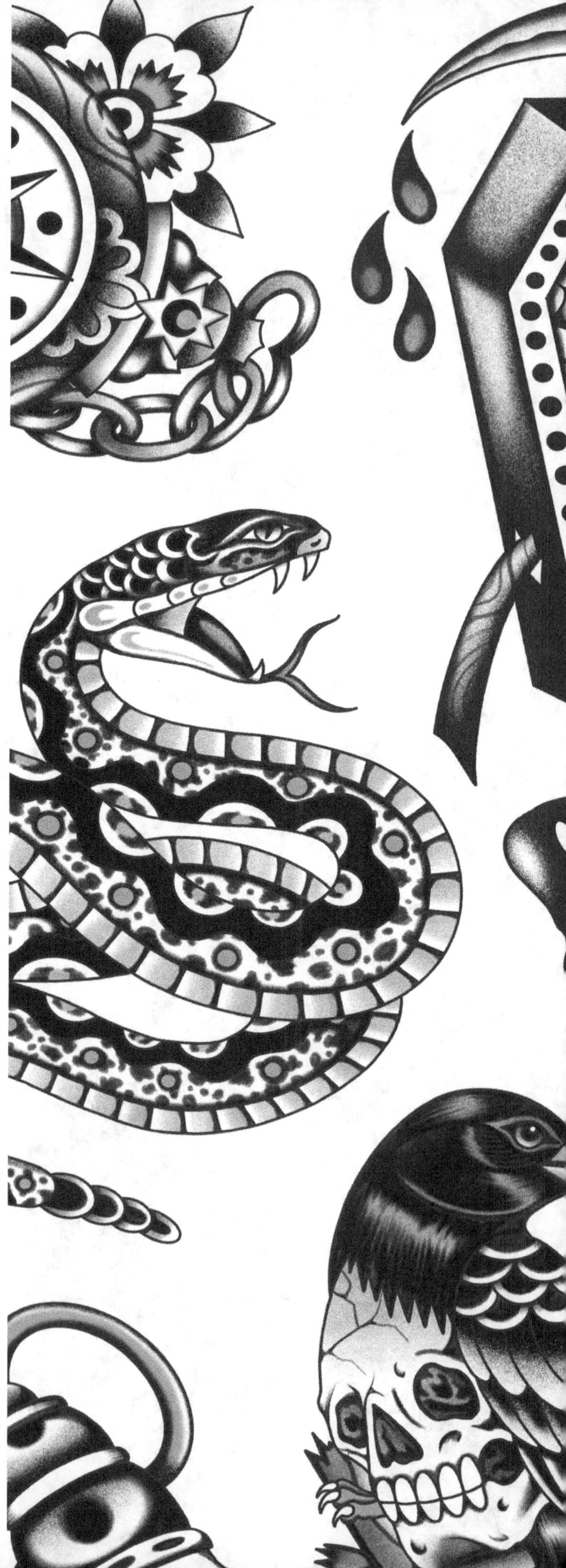

04

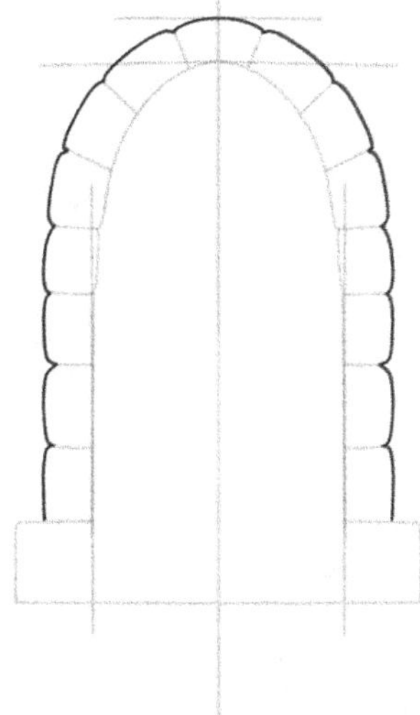

05

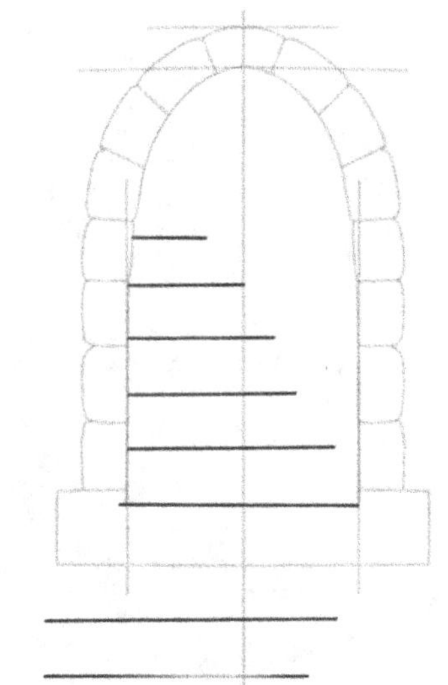

06

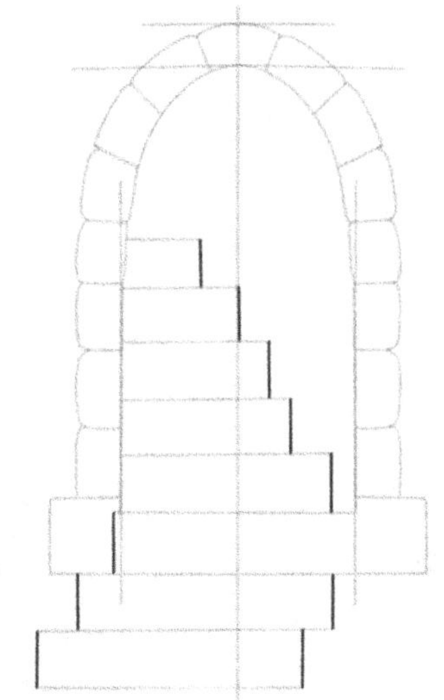

07

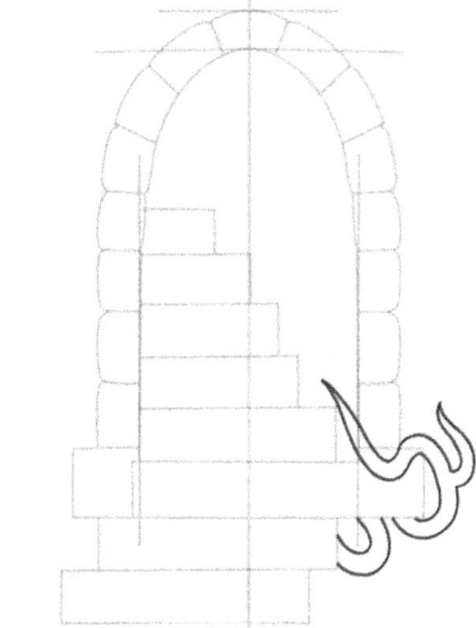

08

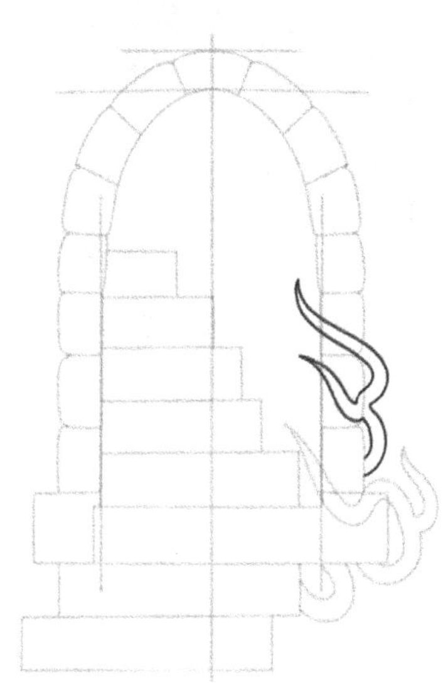

09

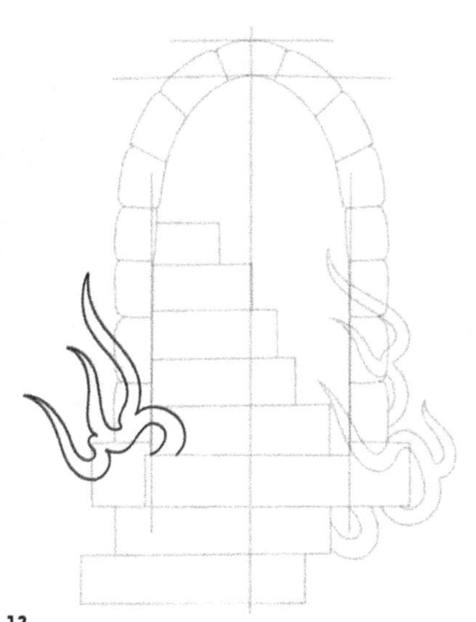

10

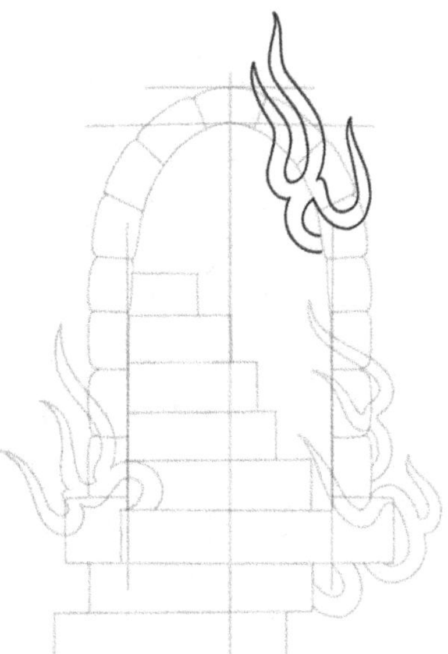

11

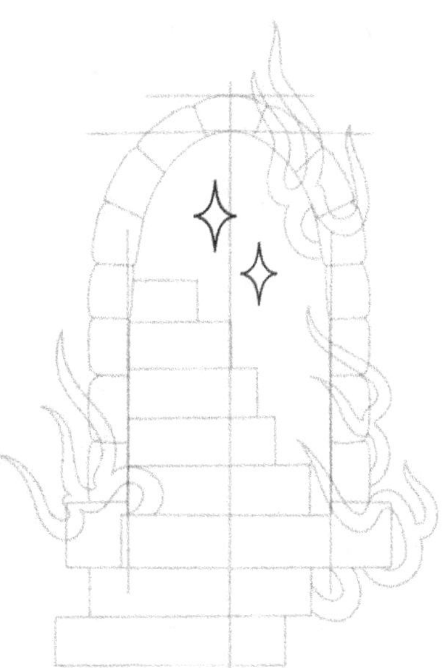

12

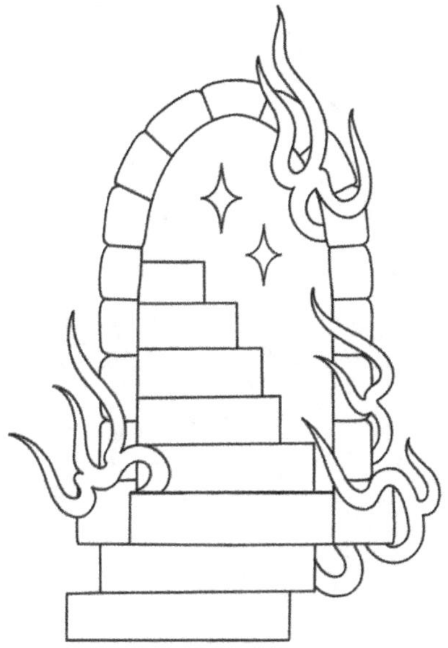

HOW TO DRAW TATTOO FLASH

FAN

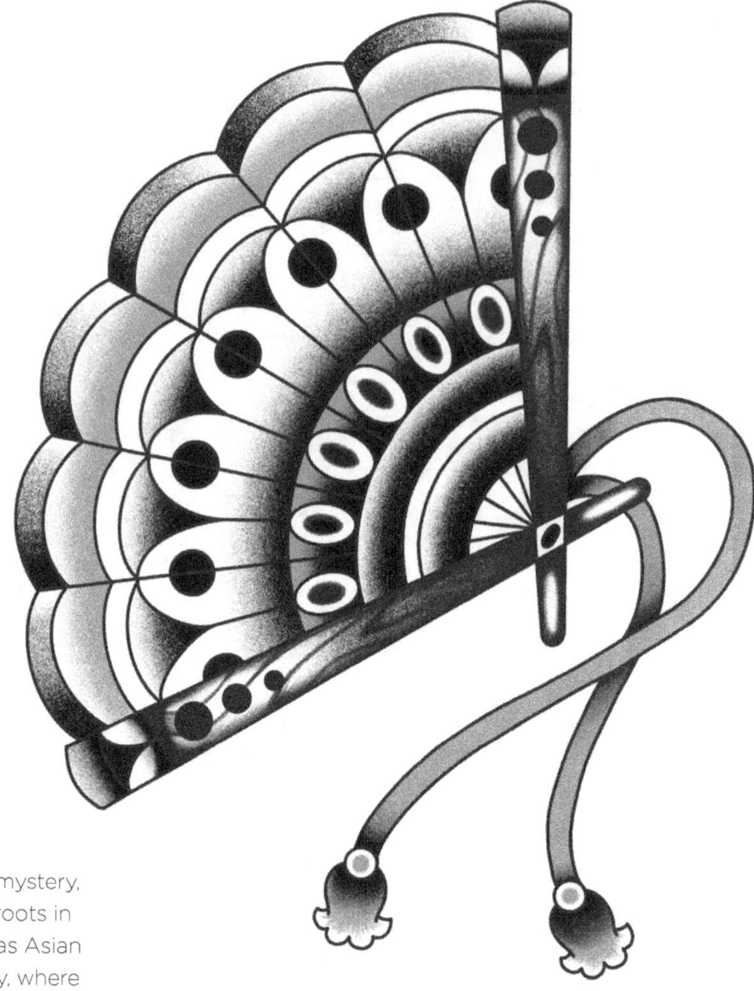

A fan tattoo often symbolises mystery, elegance, and discretion, with roots in various cultural contexts such as Asian traditions, and Victorian society, where it was a symbol of hidden emotions and secret communication.

01

02

03

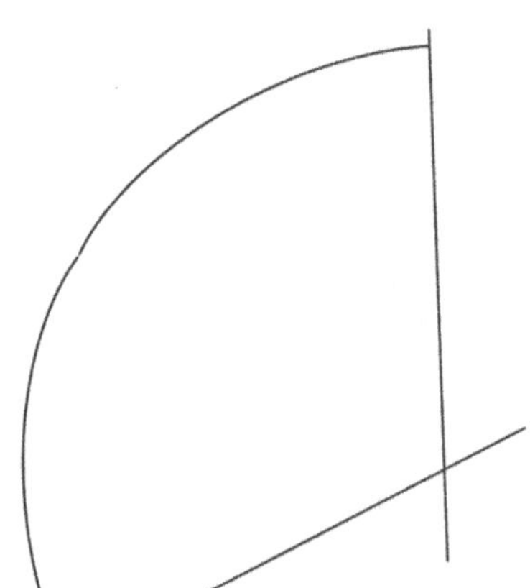

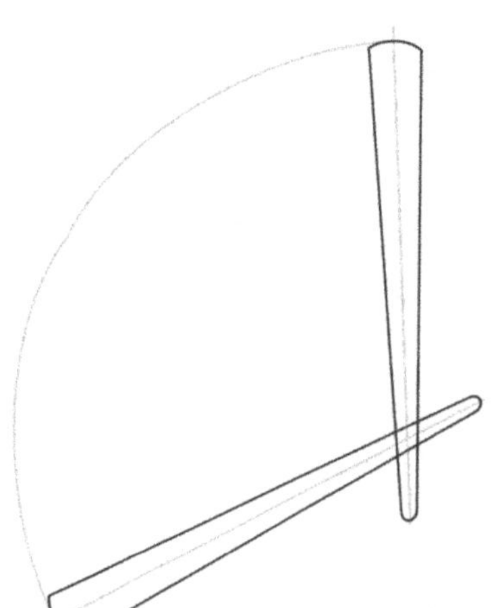

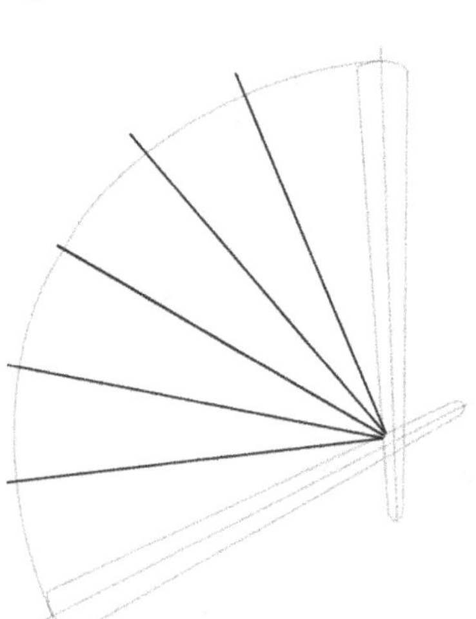

04

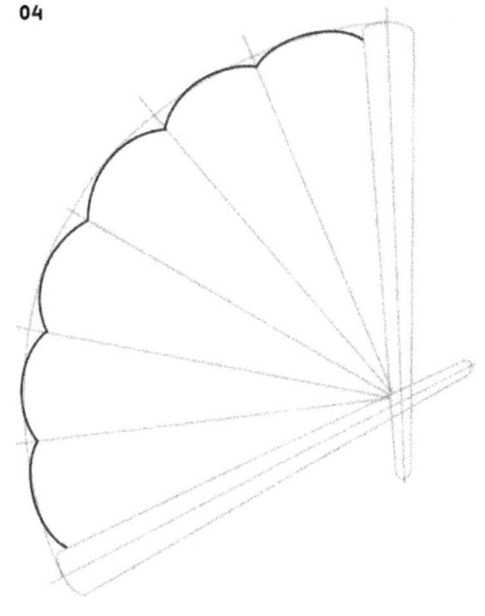

05

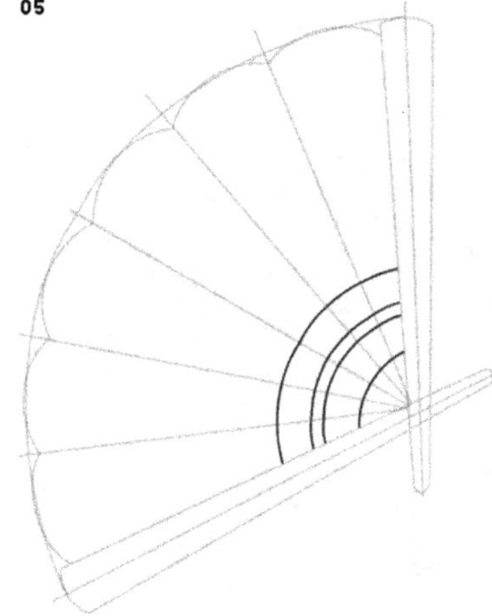

06

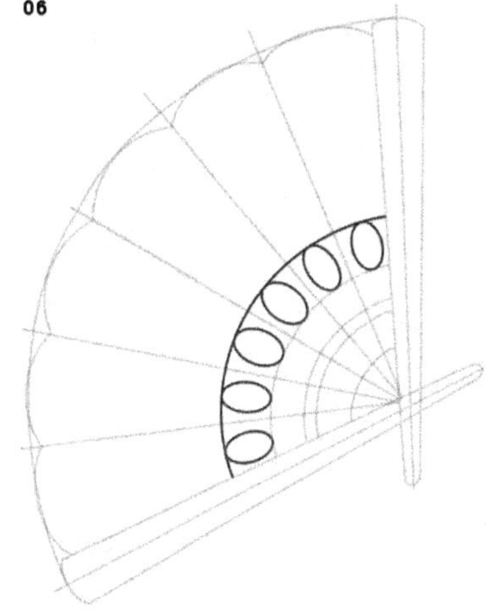

07

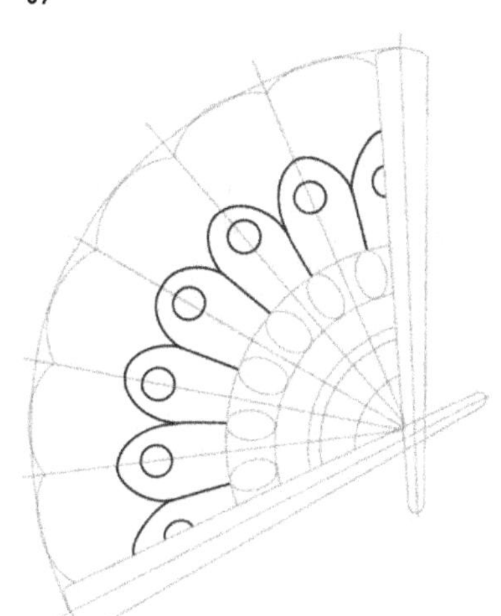

08

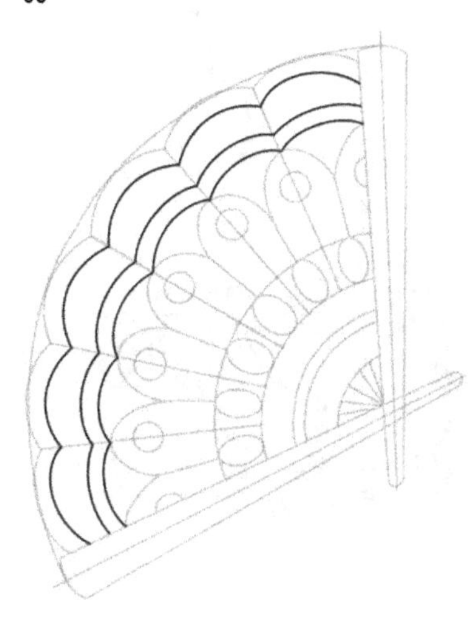

09

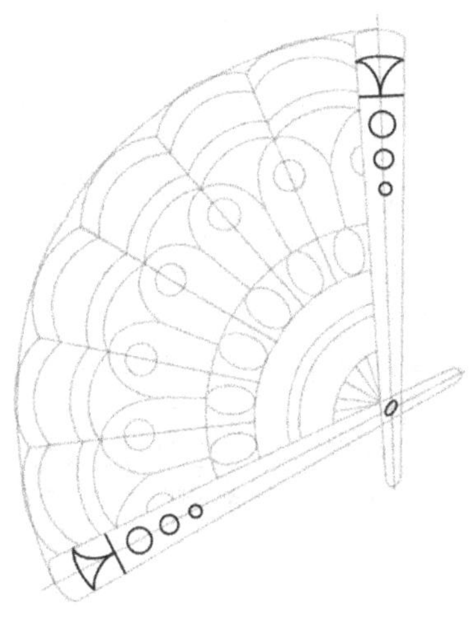

10

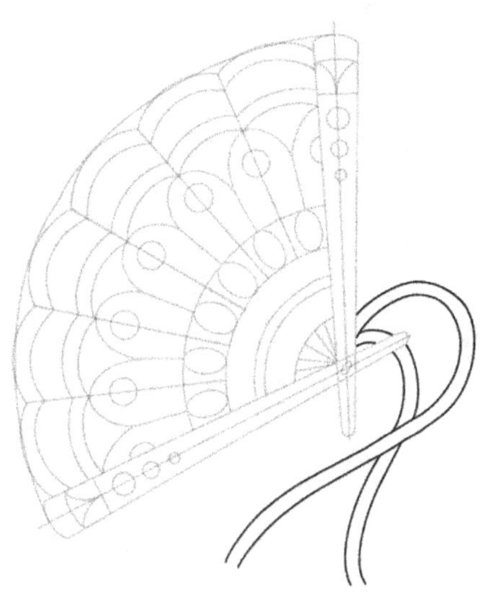

11

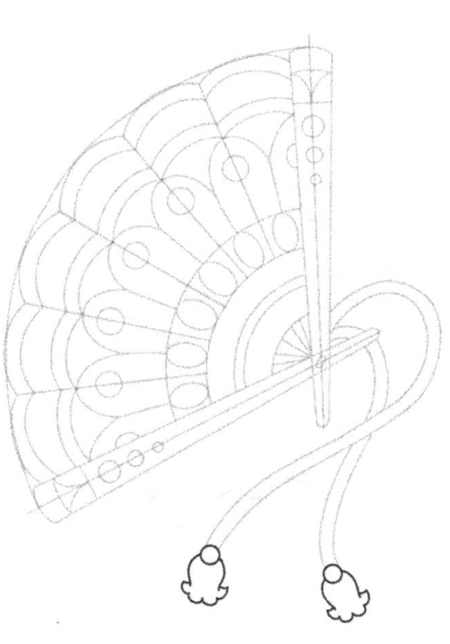

12

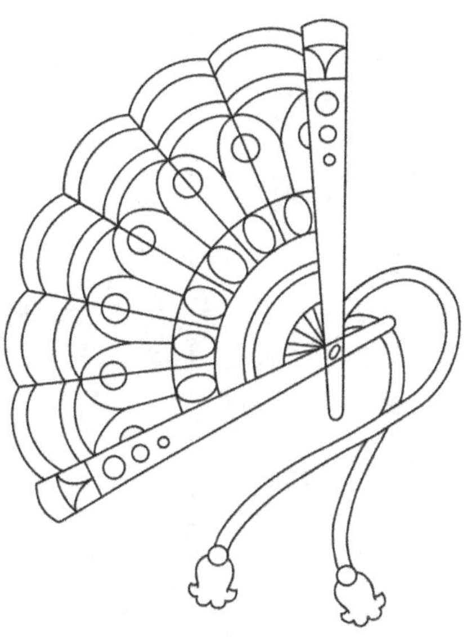

HOW TO DRAW TATTOO FLASH

CANDLE

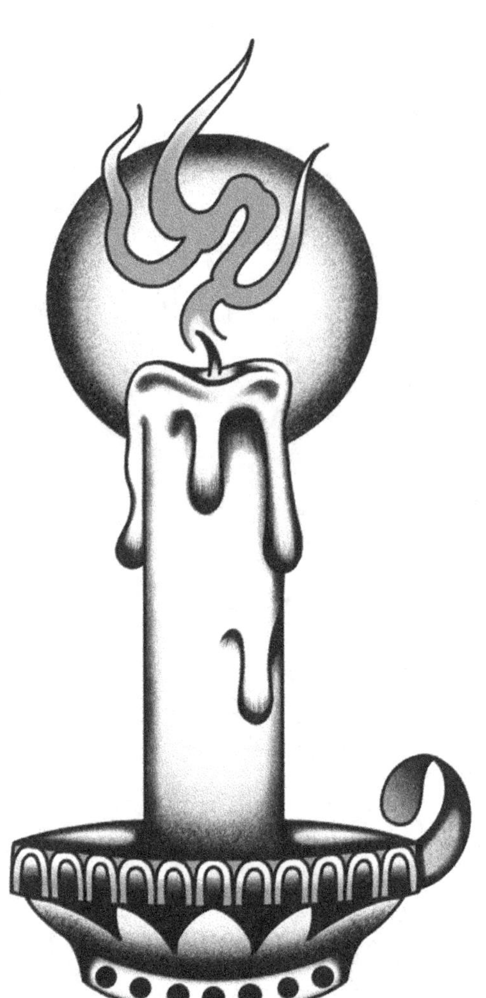

A lit candle represents hope, guidance, and memory. It can signify holding onto faith in dark times or paying tribute to a loved one who has passed away.

01

02

03

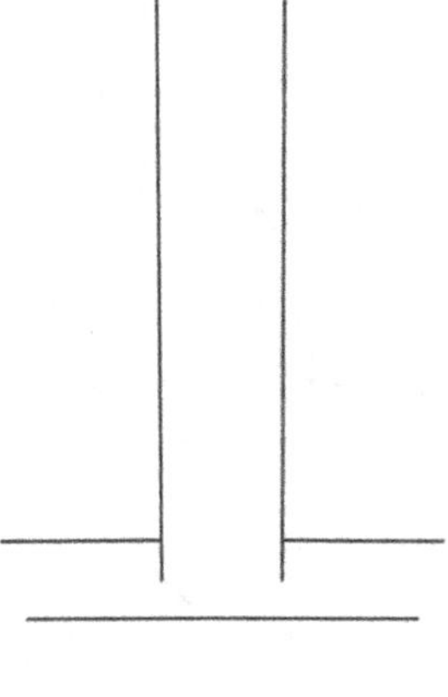

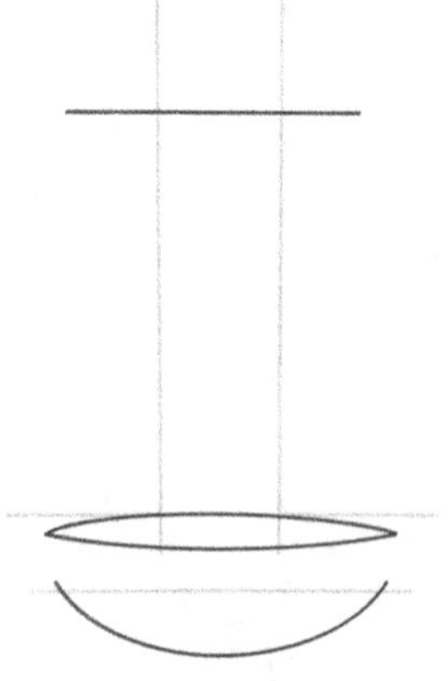

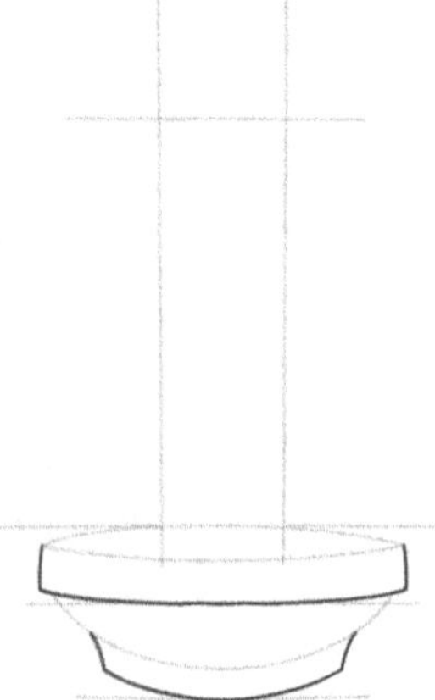

04

05

06

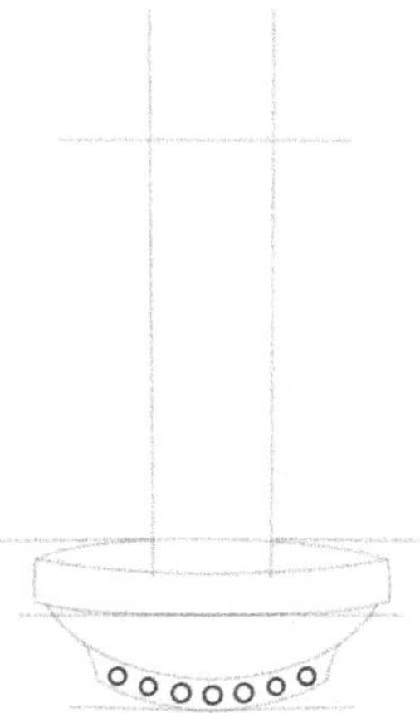

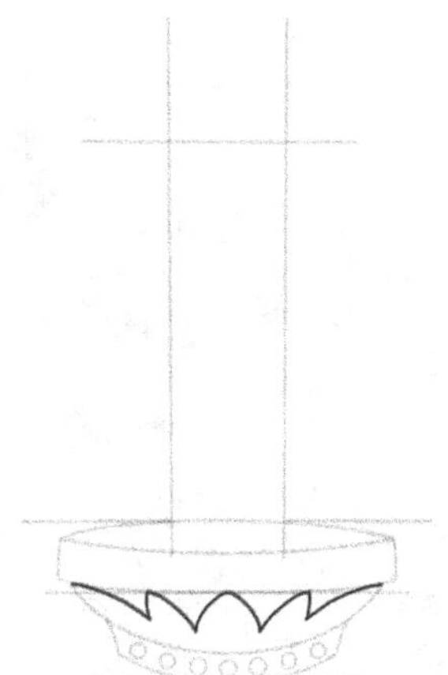

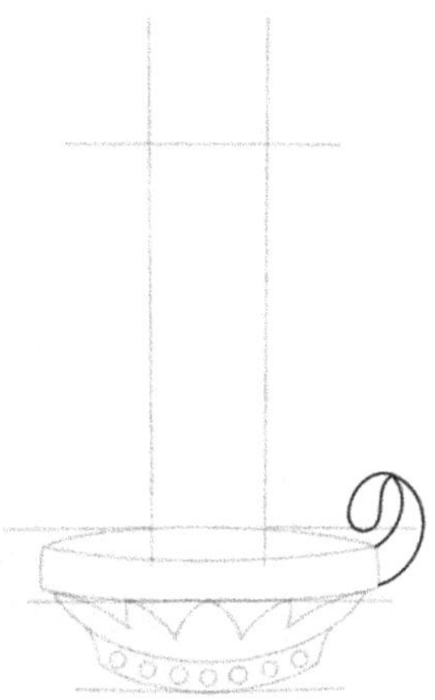

07

08

09

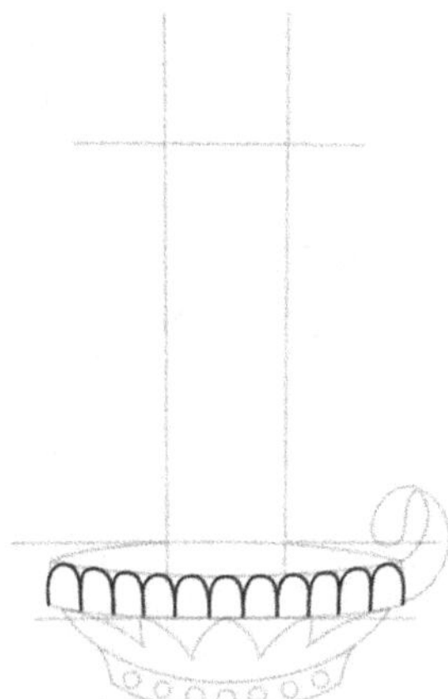

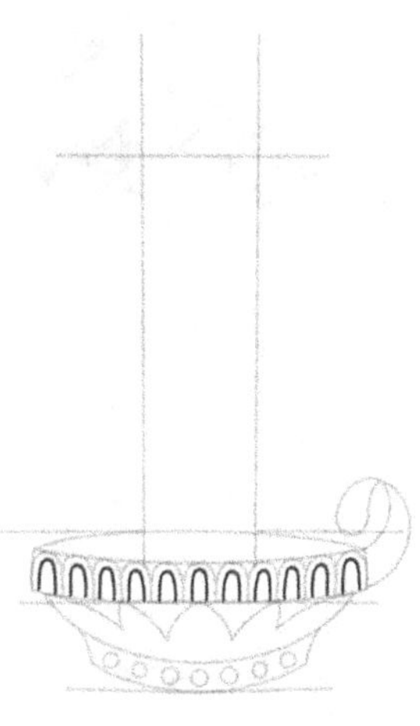

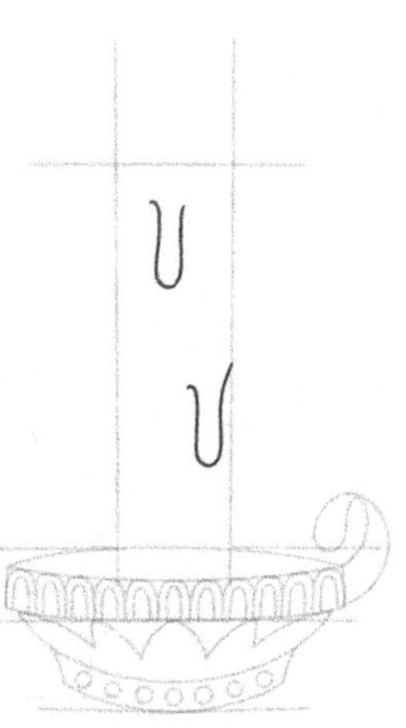

10

11

12

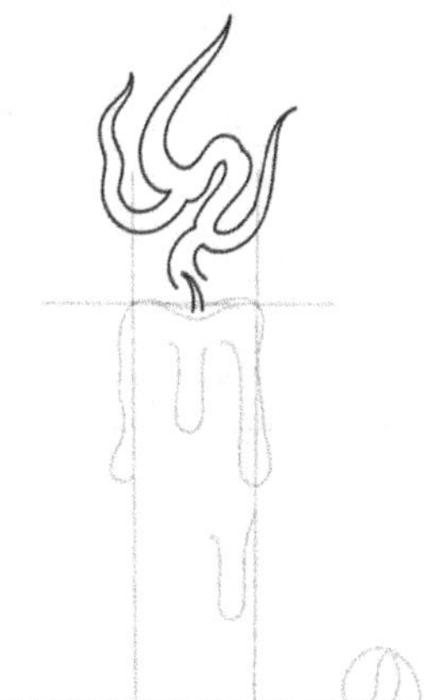

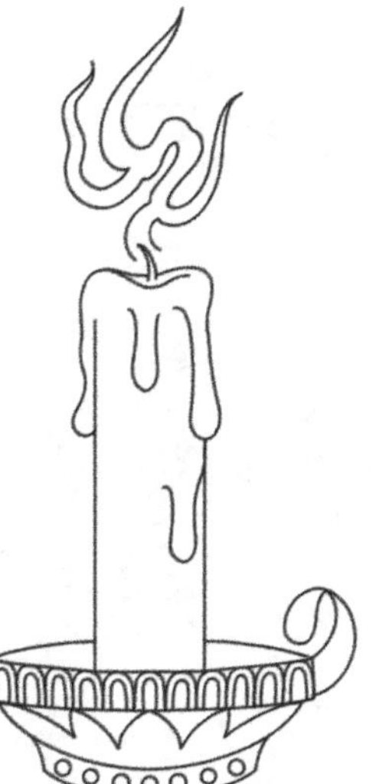

HOW TO DRAW TATTOO FLASH

DOG OF WAR

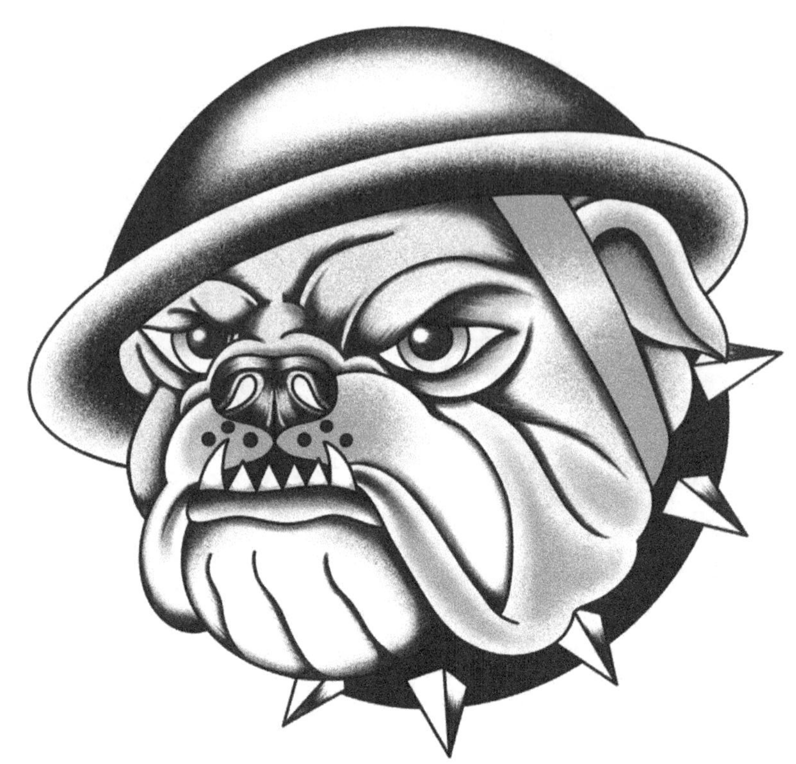

The dog of war tattoo symbolises unleashed aggression, loyalty in battle, and the destructive chaos of warfare, often representing the warrior spirit and readiness for combat.

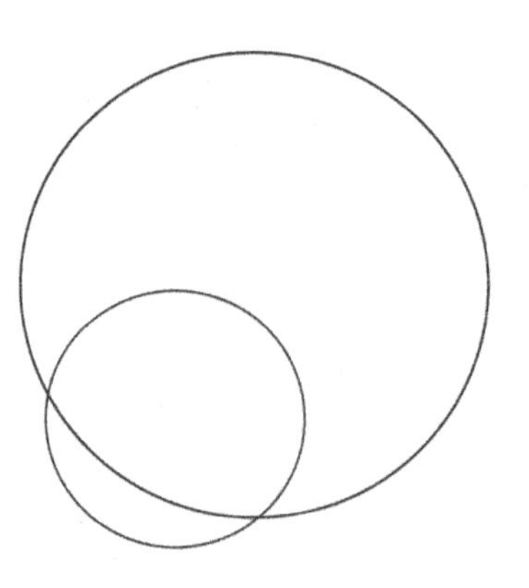

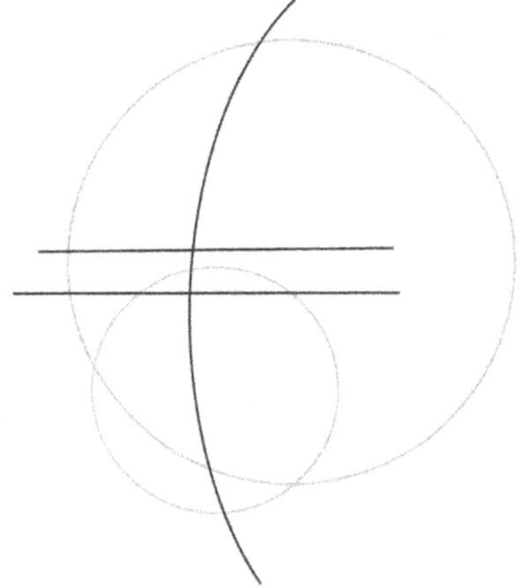

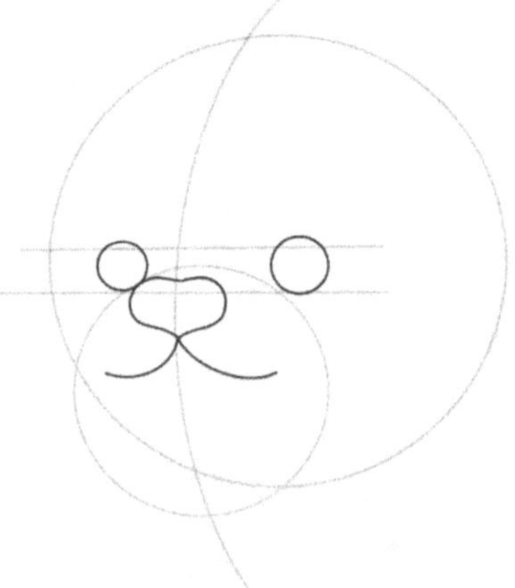

04

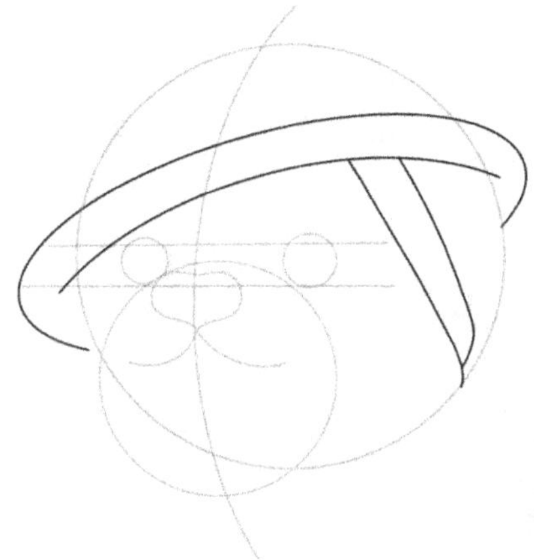

05

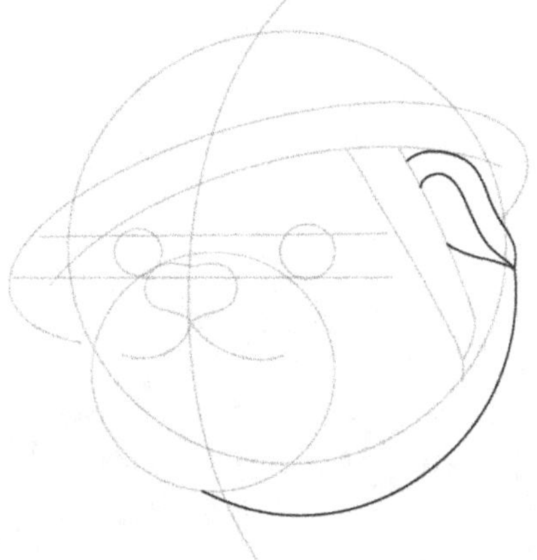

06

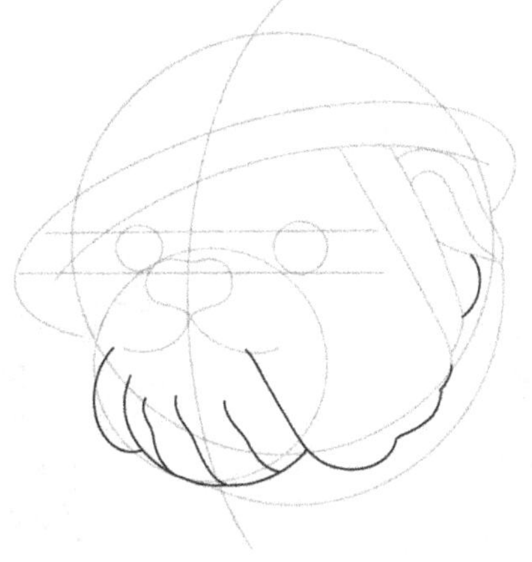

07

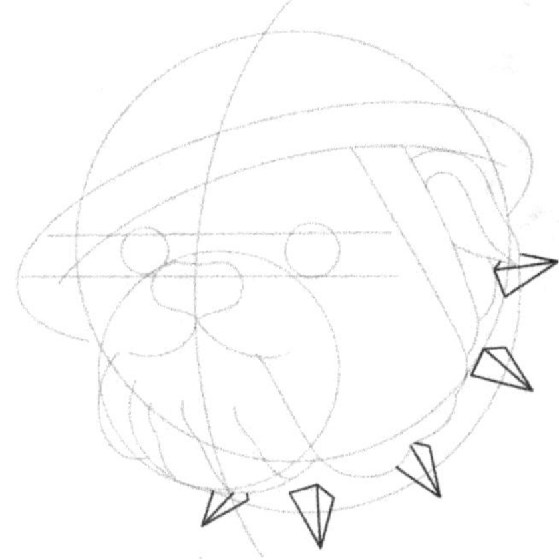

08

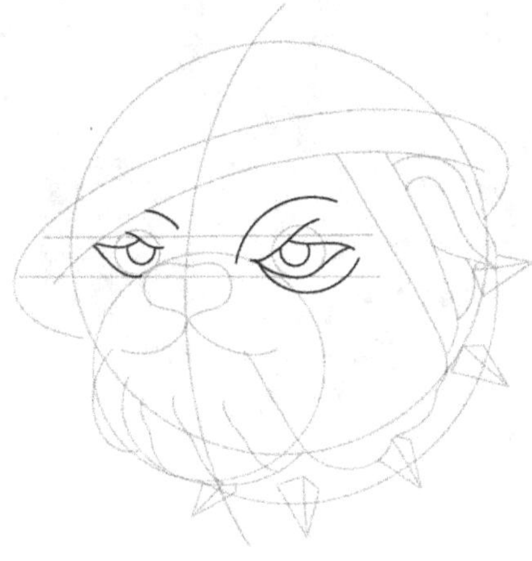

09

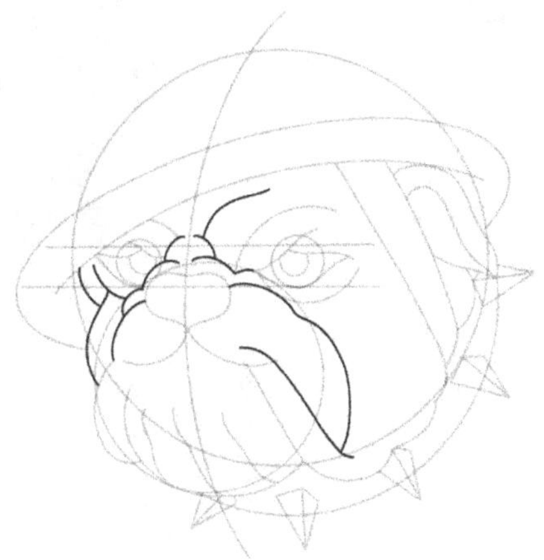

10

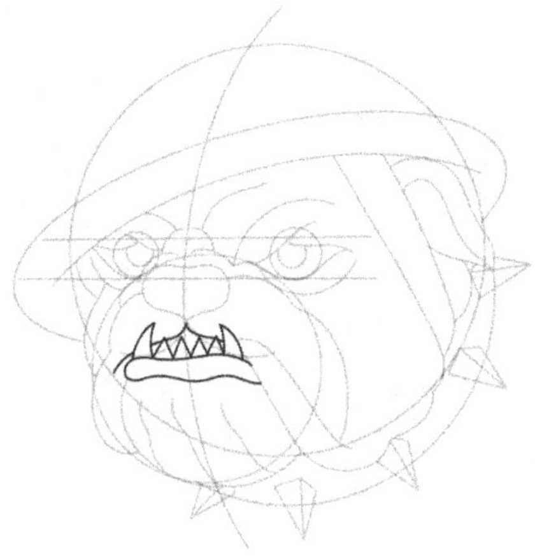

11

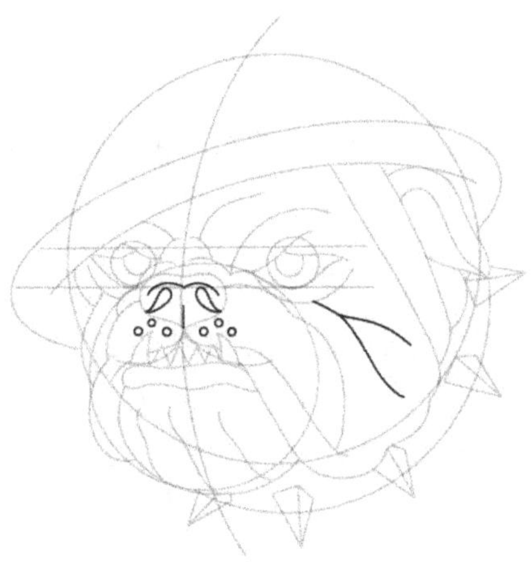

12

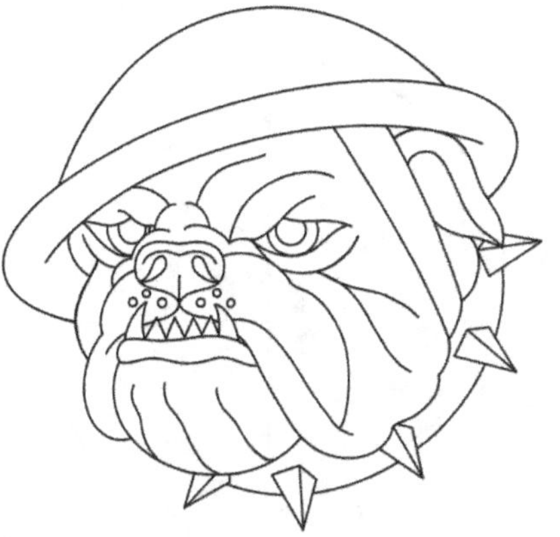

HOW TO DRAW TATTOO FLASH

BLACK CAT

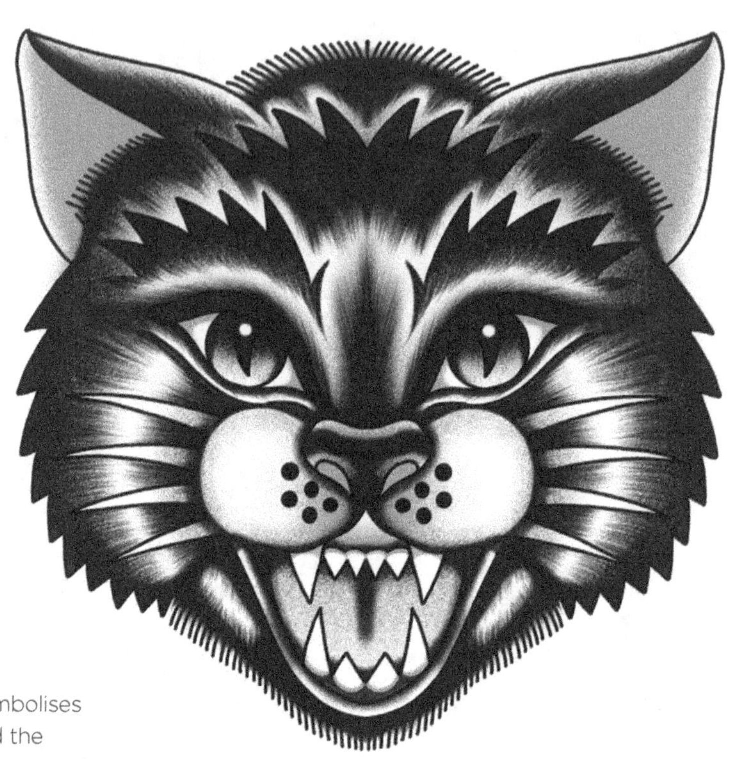

A black cat tattoo often symbolises mystery, independence, and the supernatural, with associations ranging from good luck and protection to themes of magic and rebellion, depending on cultural context.

01

02

03

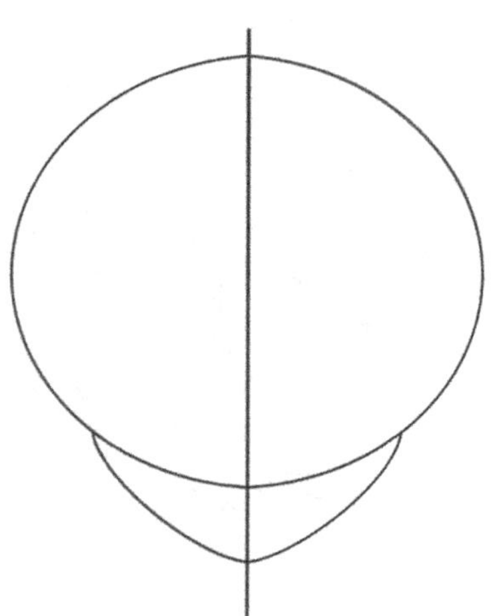

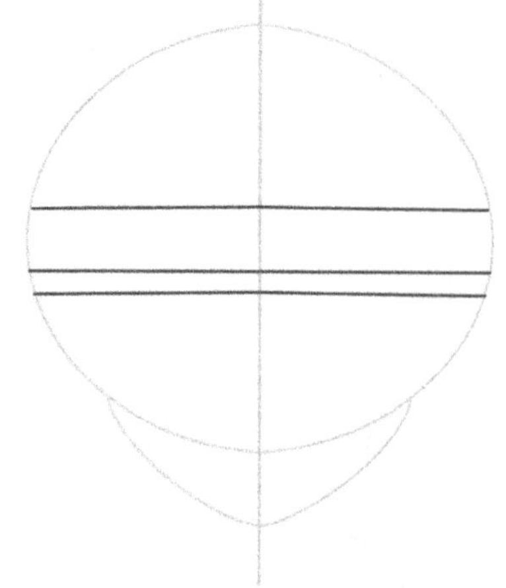

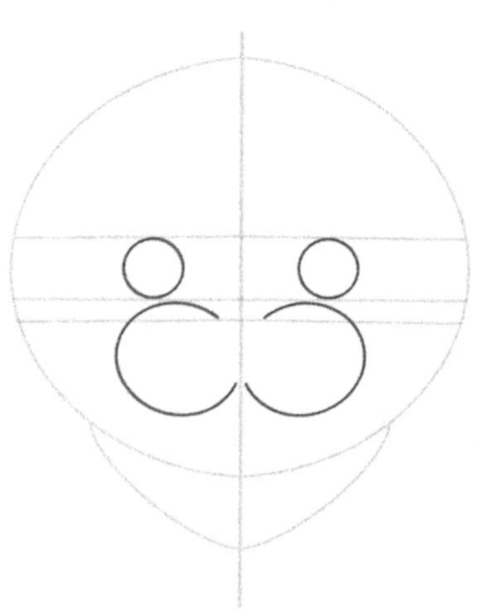

04
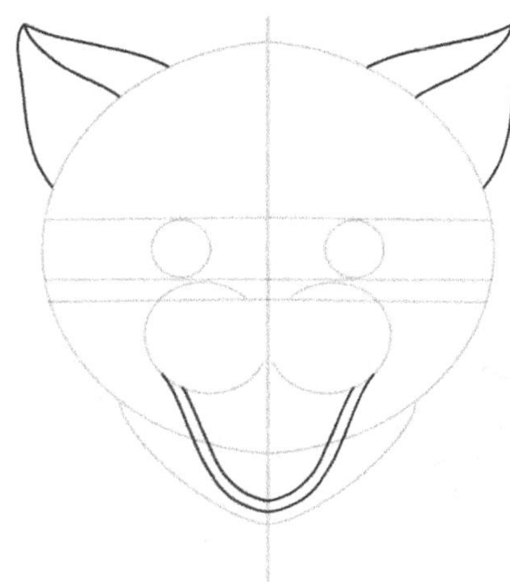

05
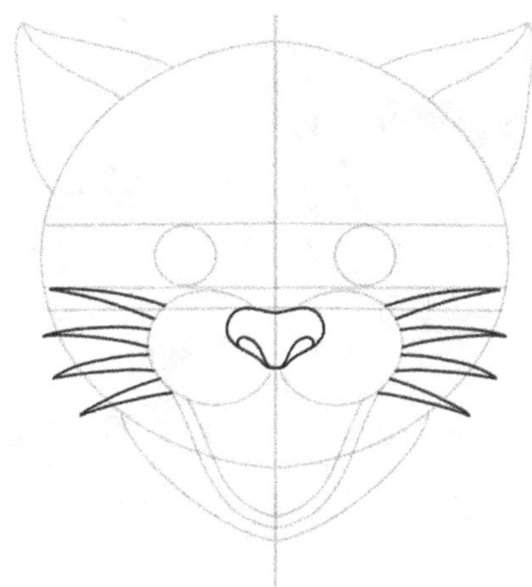

06
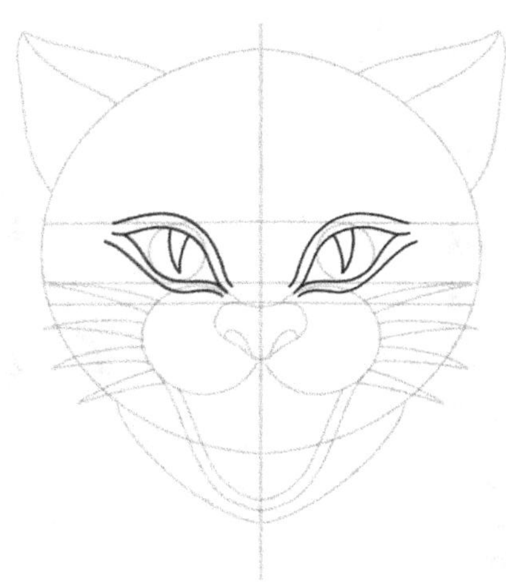

07
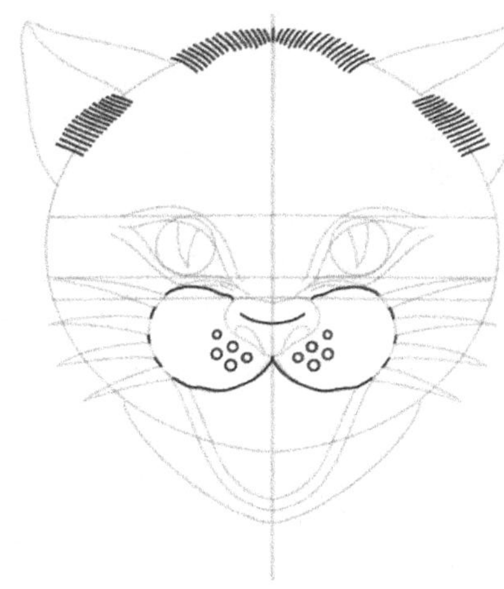

08
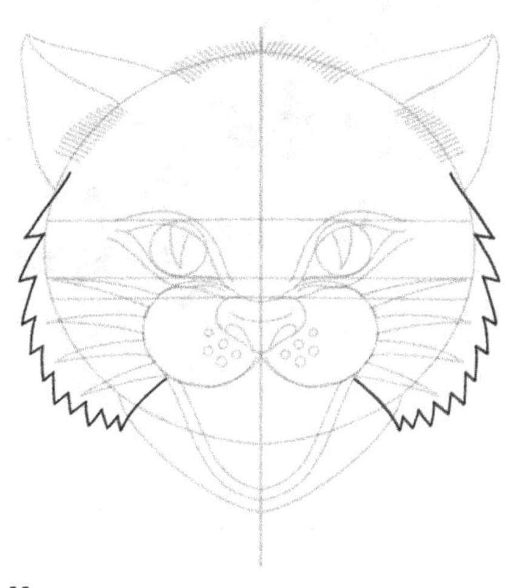

09
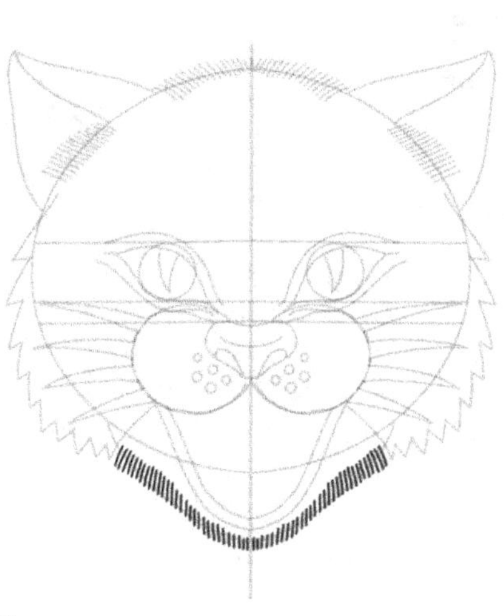

10
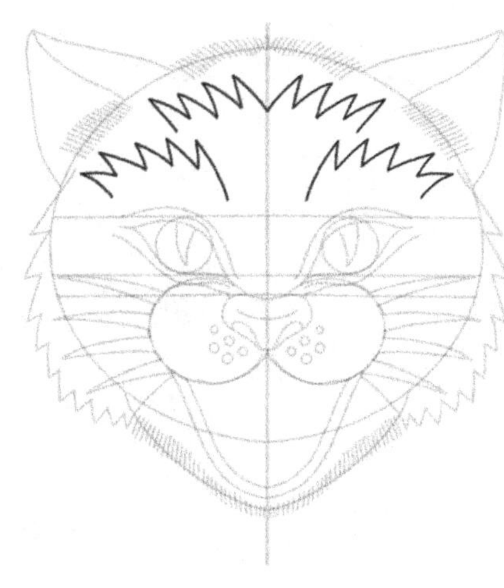

11
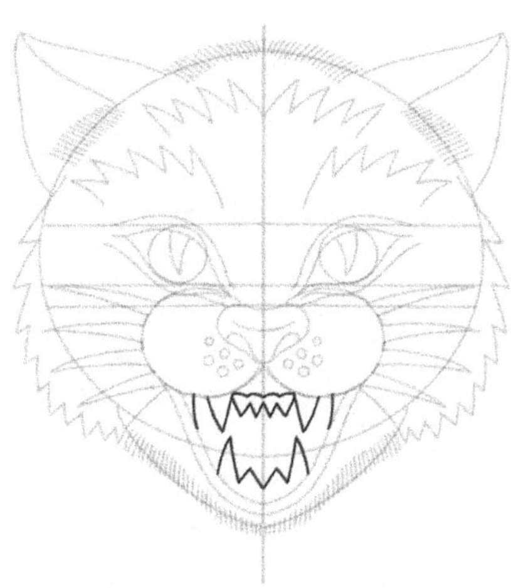

12
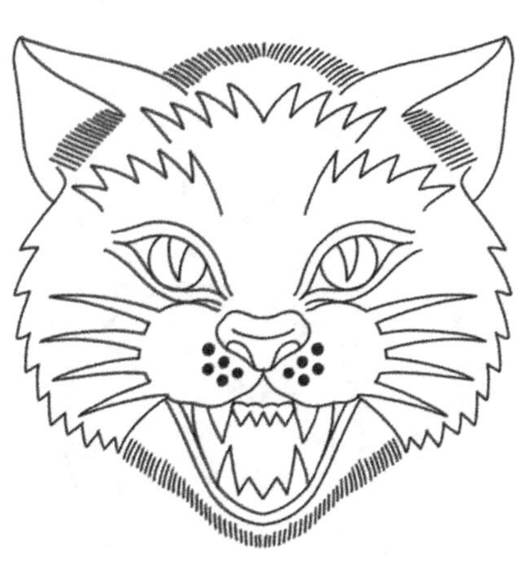

HOW TO DRAW TATTOO FLASH

HOW TO DRAW TATTOO FLASH

CHERRY SKULLS

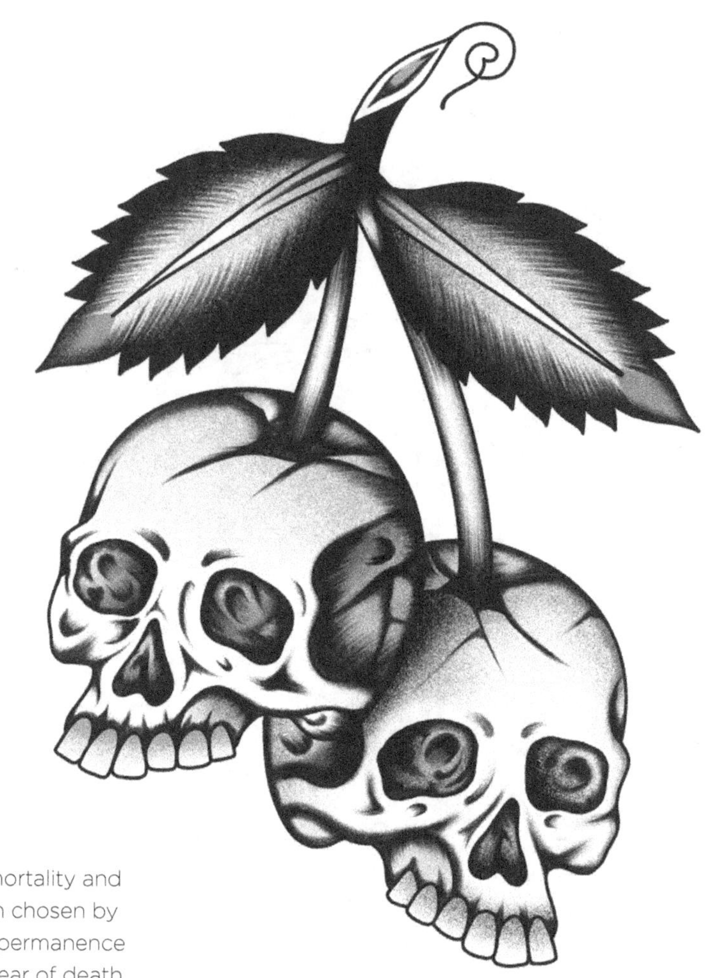

A skull tattoo symbolises mortality and the fragility of life. It is often chosen by those who embrace the impermanence of life so they live without fear of death.

01

02

03

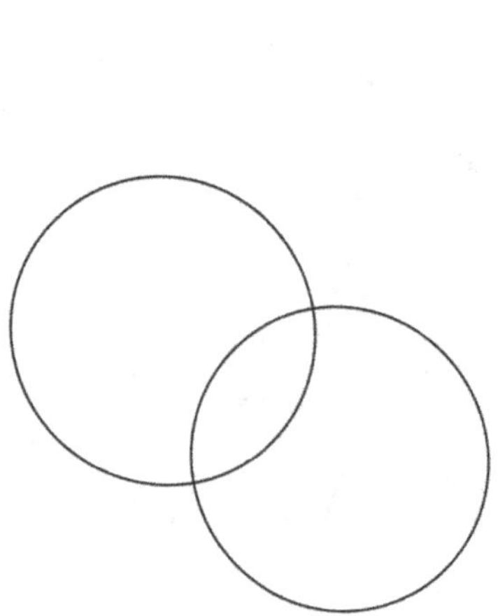

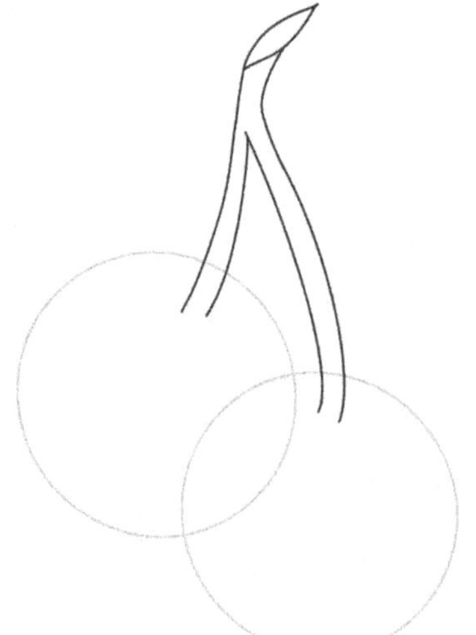

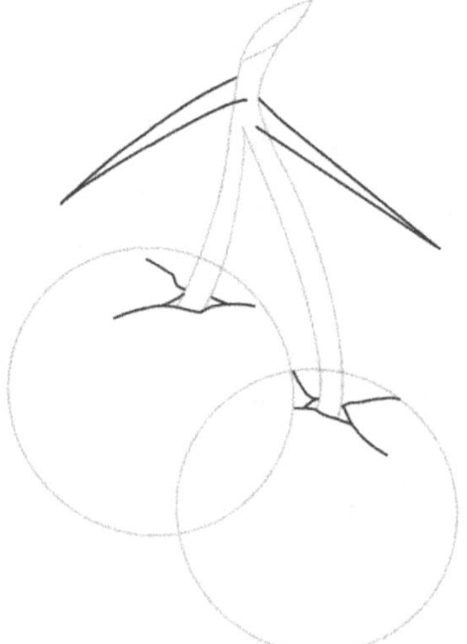

04

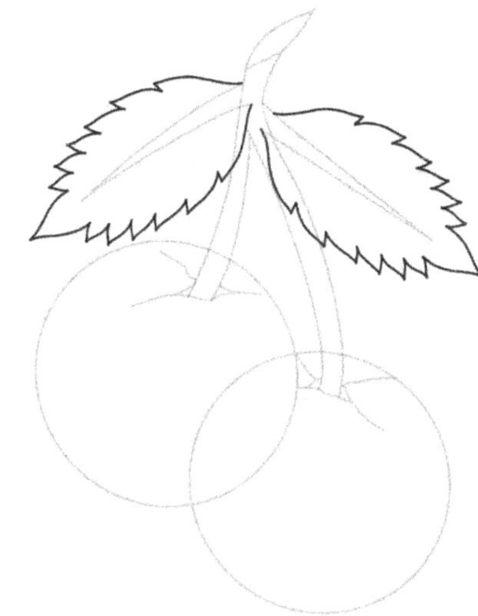

05

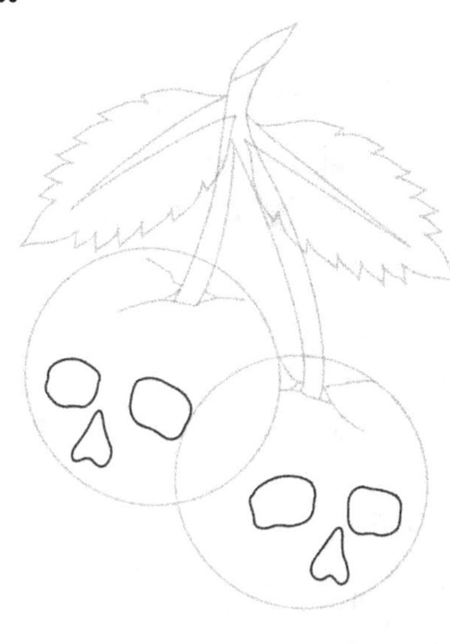

06

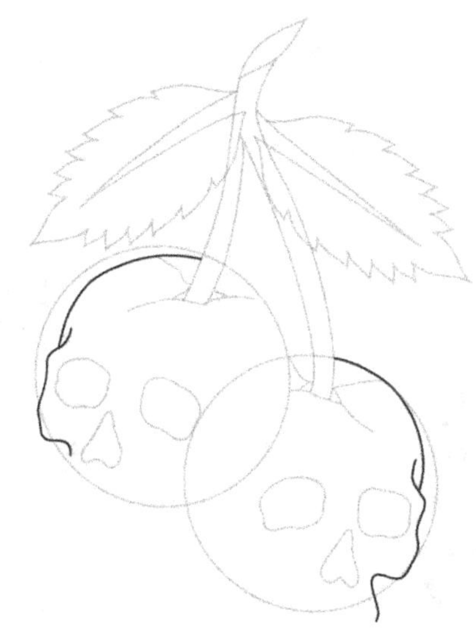

07

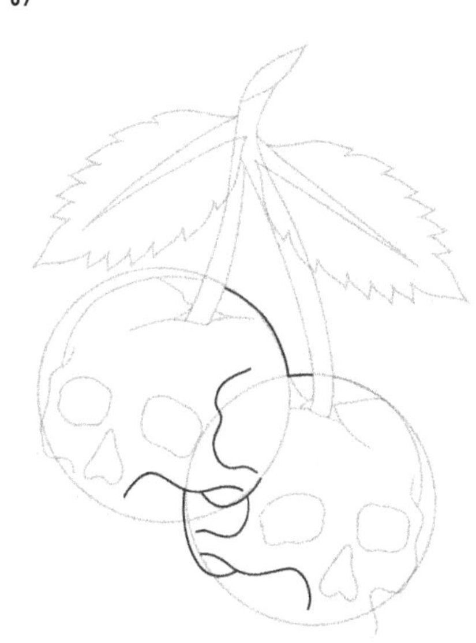

08

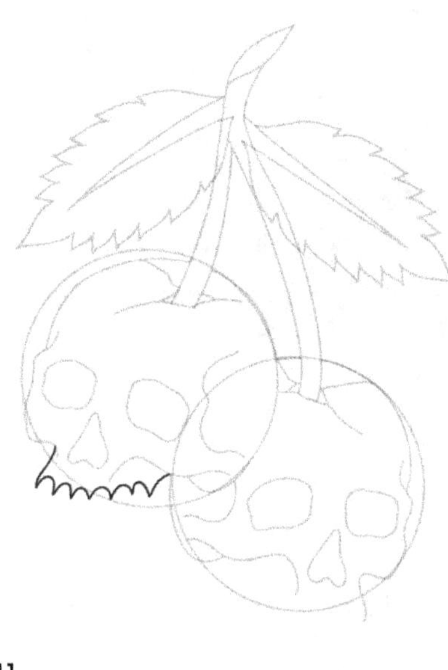

09

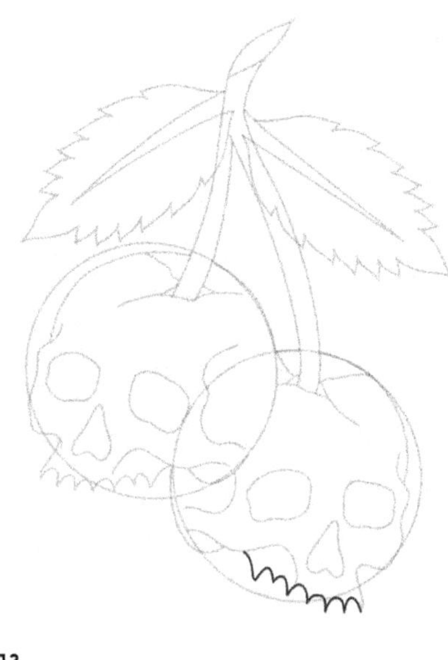

10

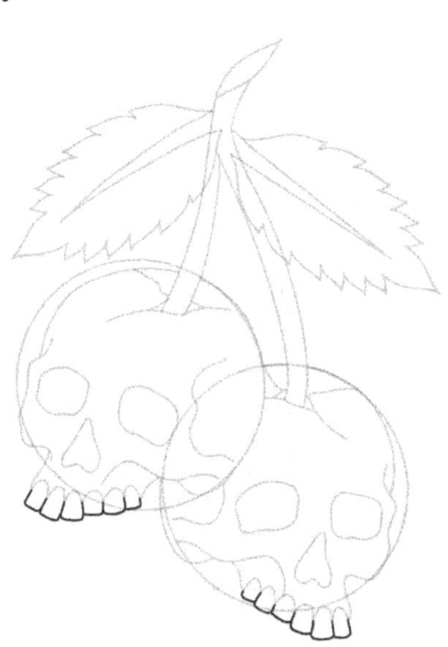

11

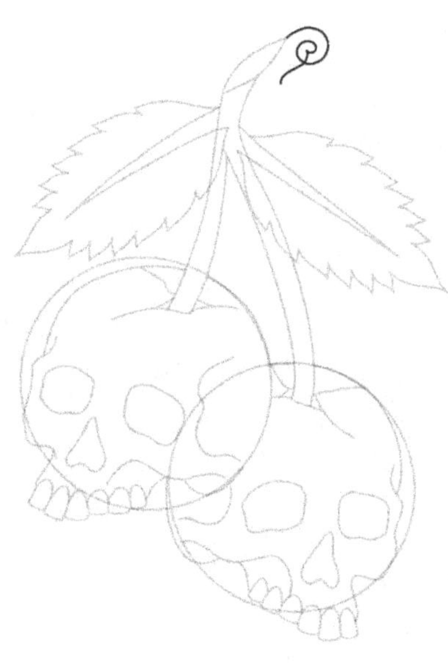

12

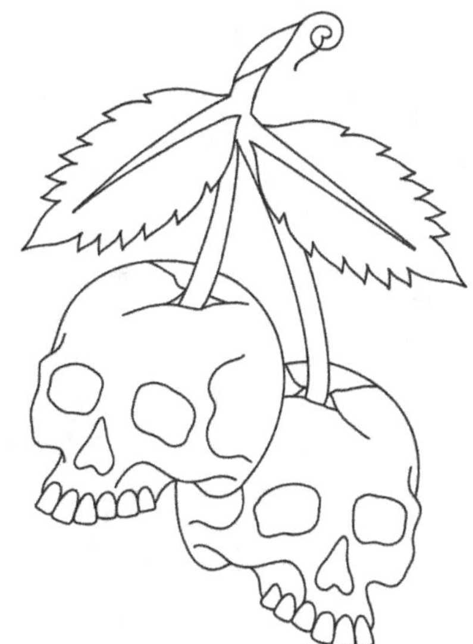

HOW TO DRAW TATTOO FLASH

HOW TO DRAW TATTOO FLASH

COFFIN

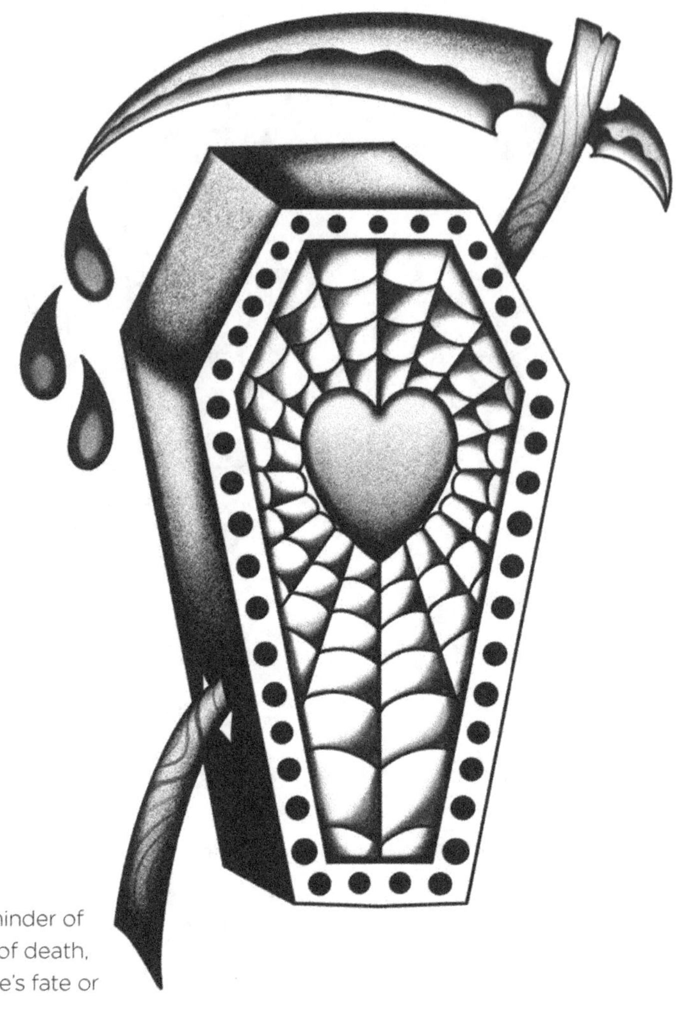

The coffin can represent a reminder of mortality and the inevitability of death, symbolising acceptance of one's fate or the closing of a chapter in life.

01

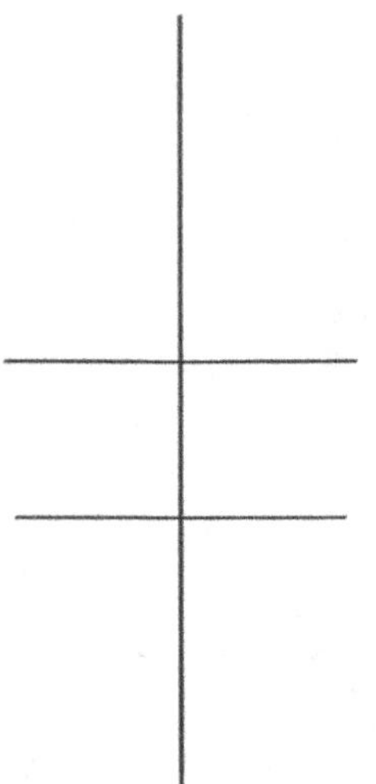

02

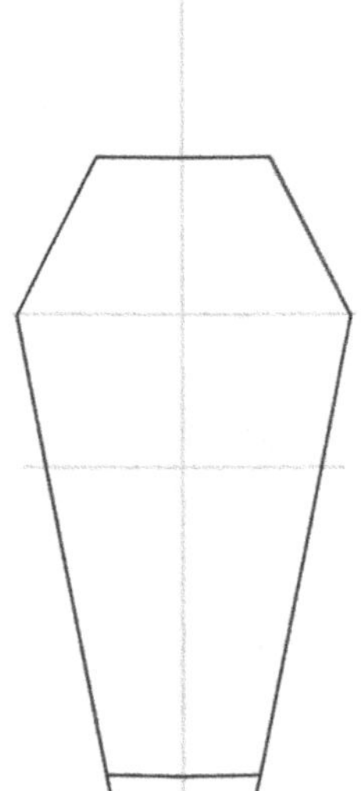

03

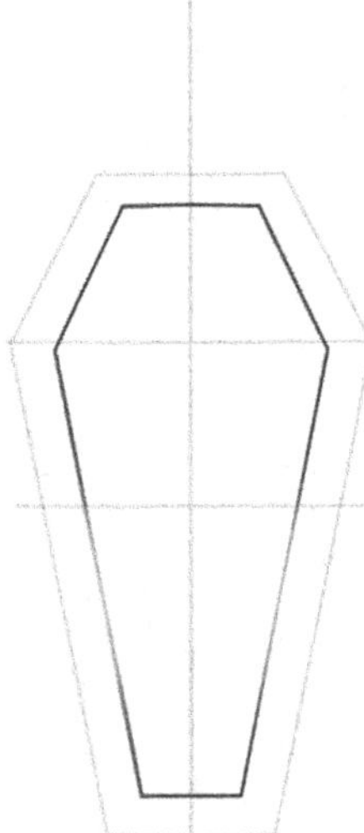

04

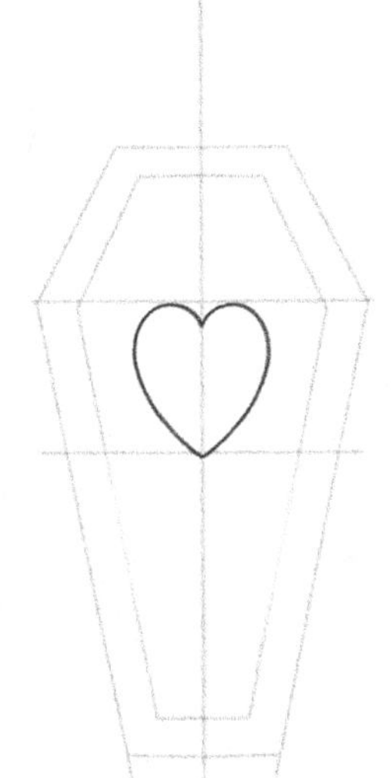

05

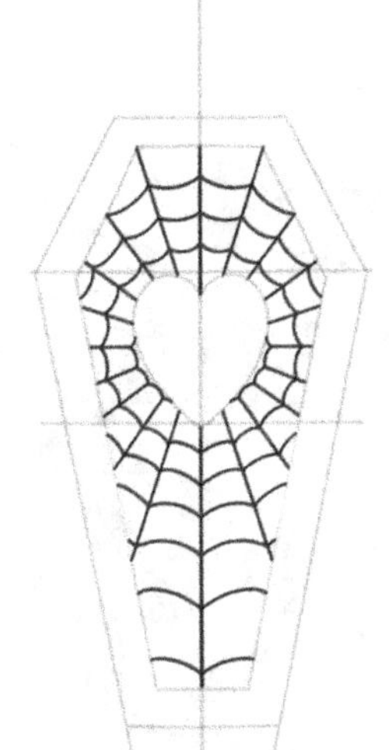

06

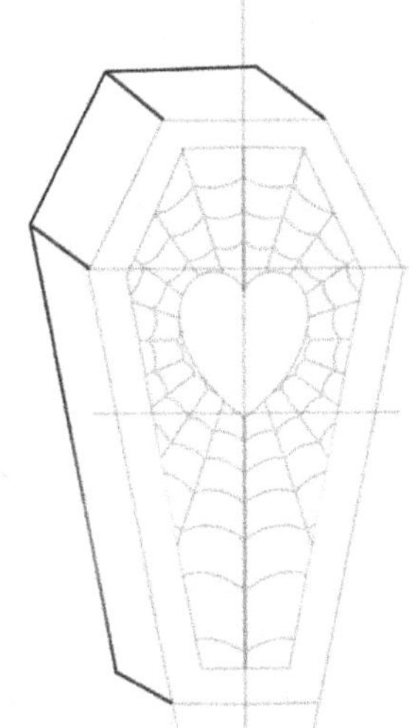

07

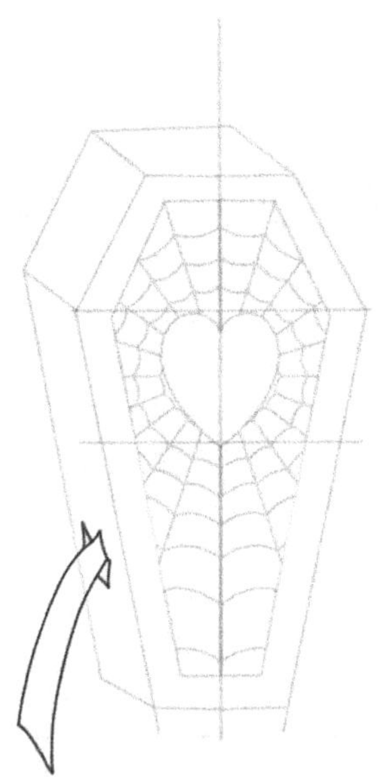

08

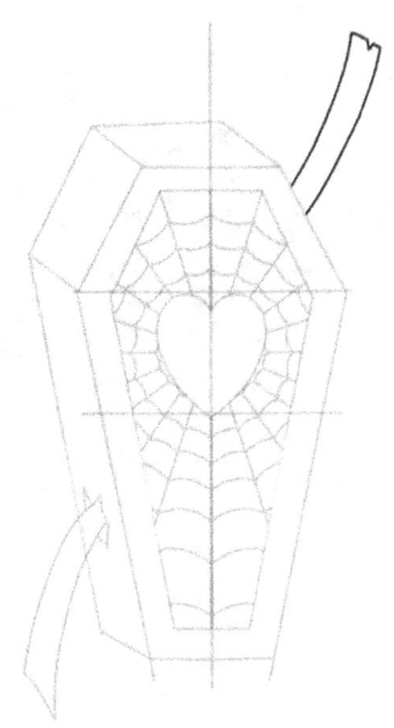

09

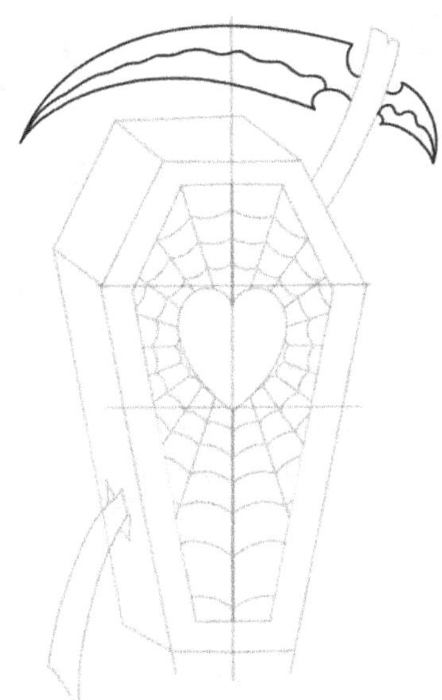

10

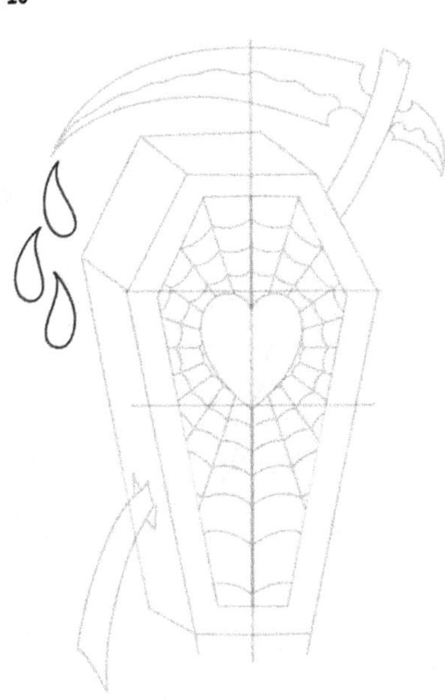

11

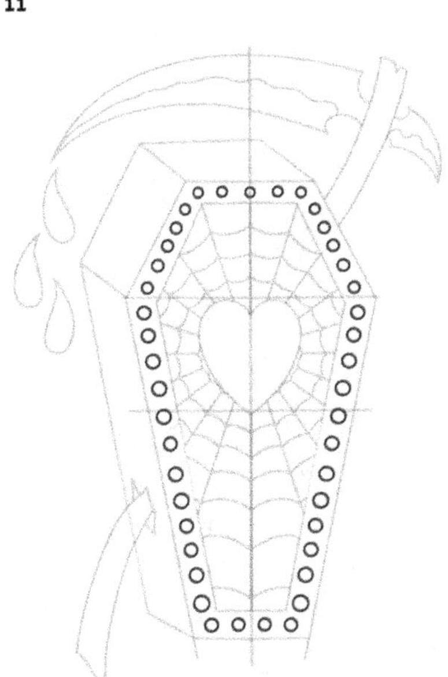

12

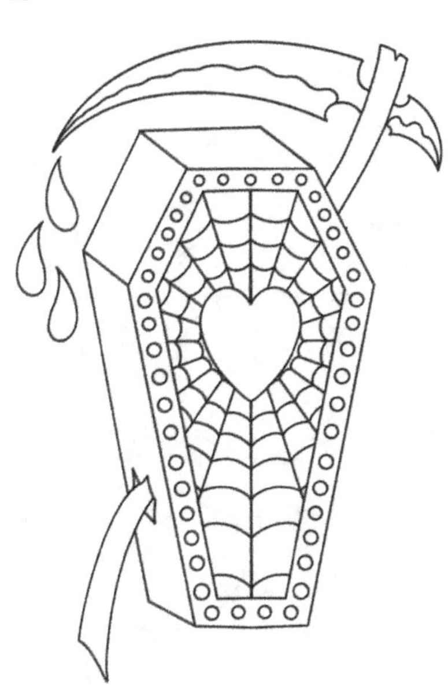

HOW TO DRAW TATTOO FLASH

COMPASS

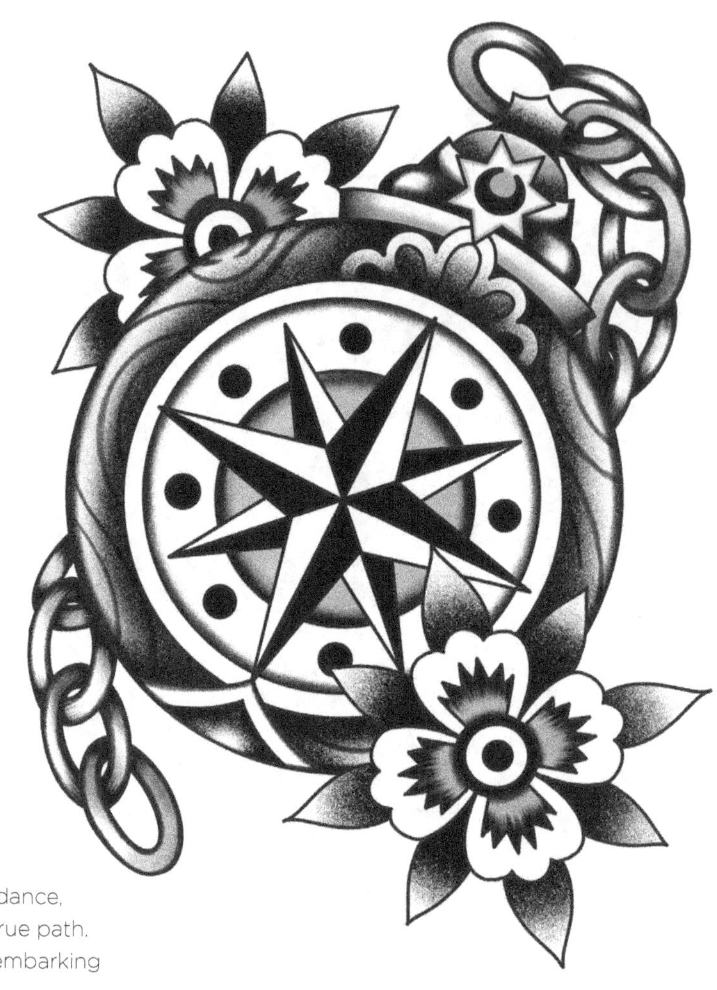

The compass represents guidance, direction, and finding one's true path. It's often chosen by people embarking on a new journey.

01

02

03

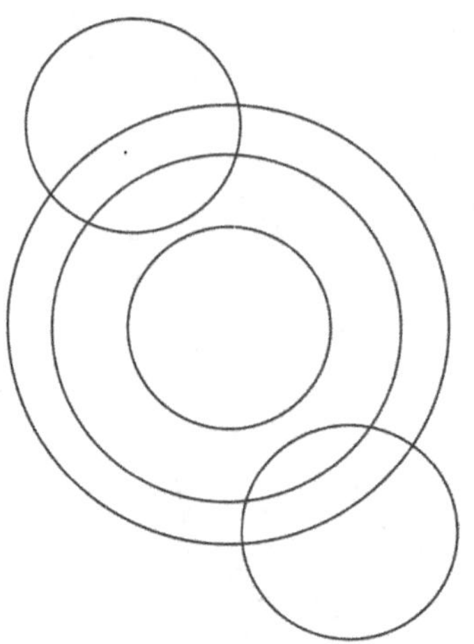

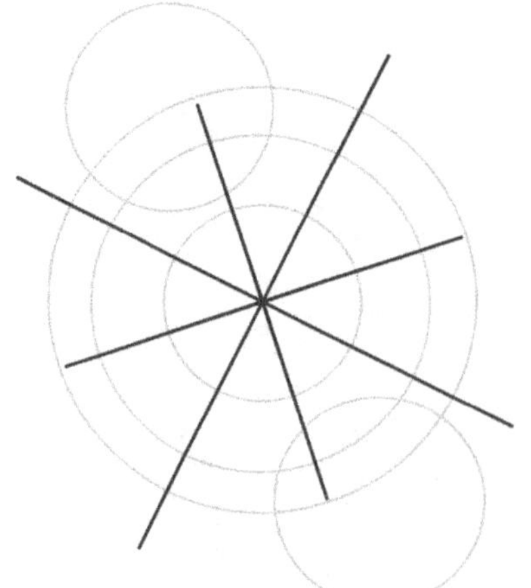

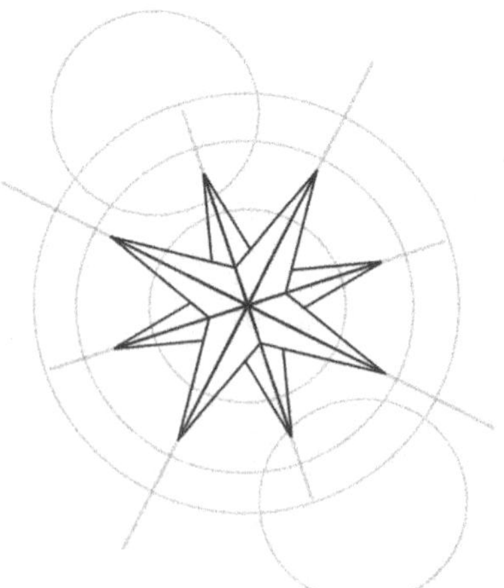

04

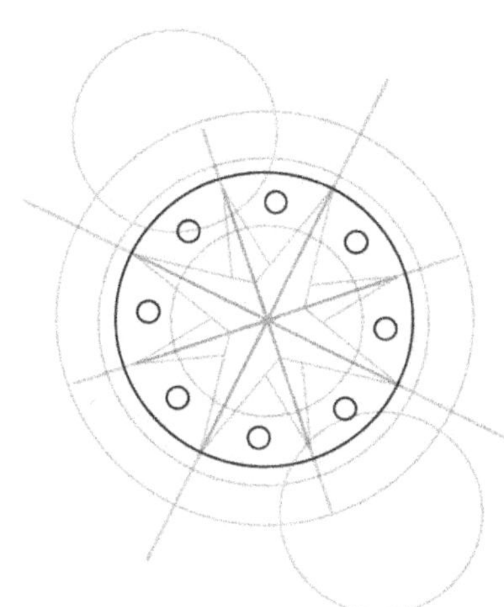

05

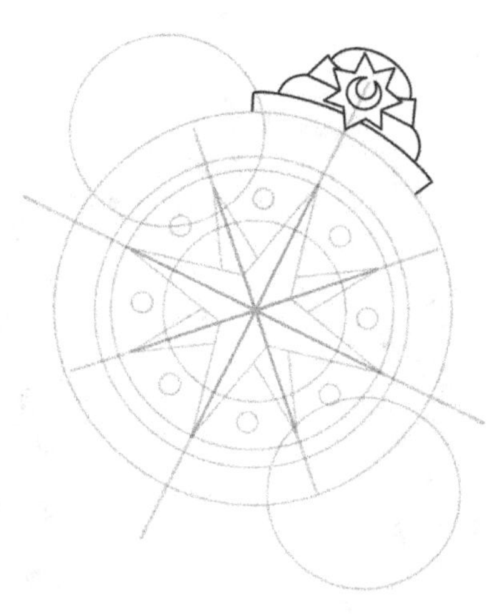

06

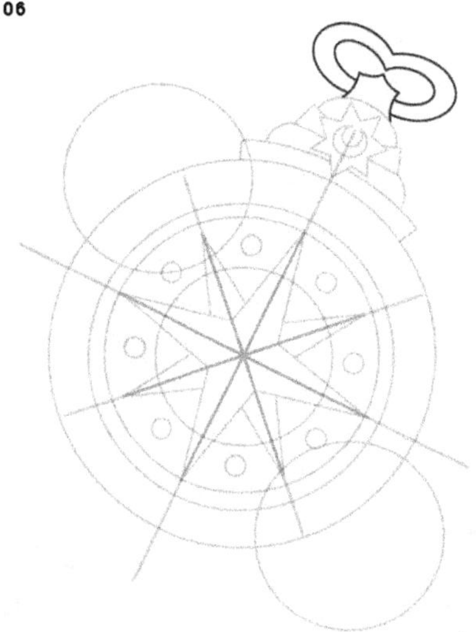

07

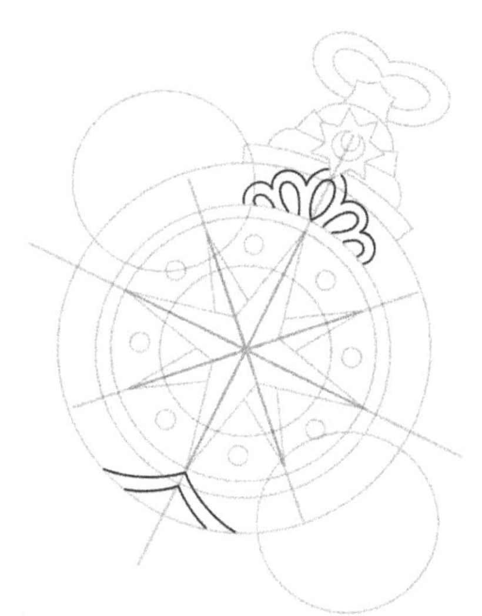

08

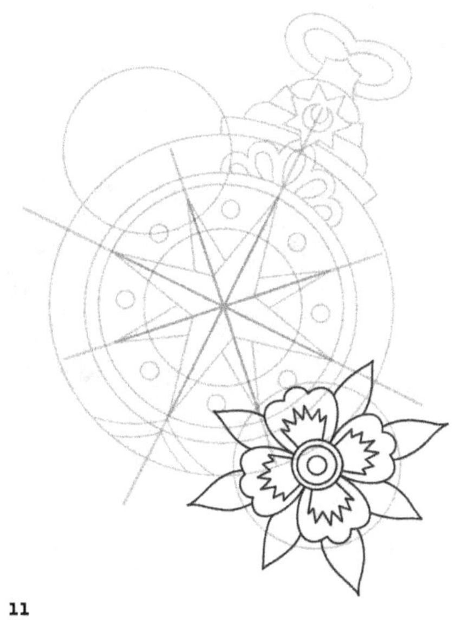

09

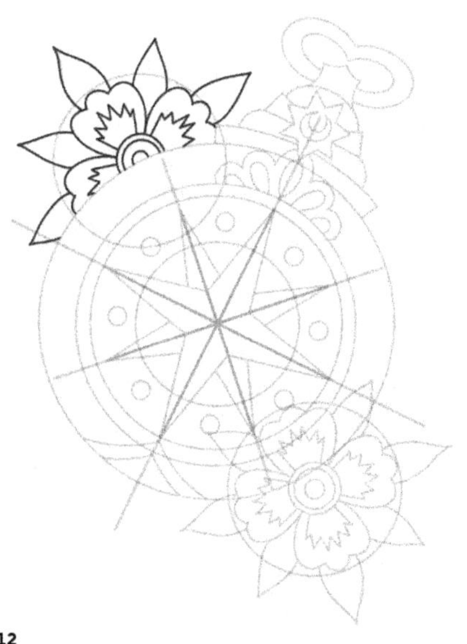

10

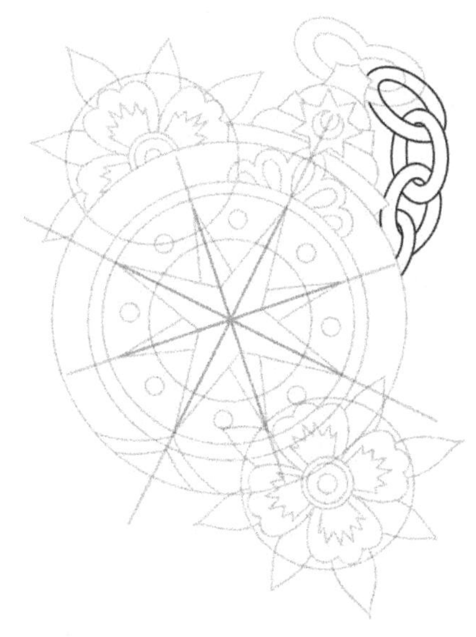

11

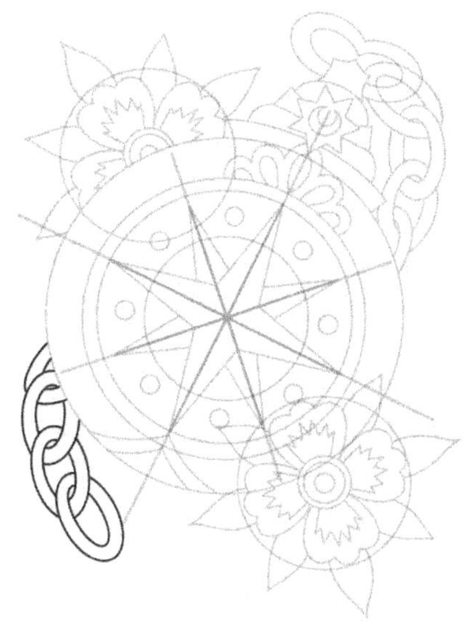

12

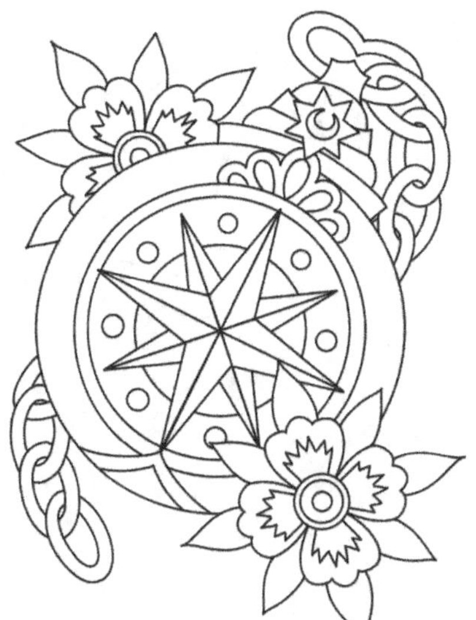

HOW TO DRAW TATTOO FLASH

HOW TO DRAW TATTOO FLASH

COWGIRL

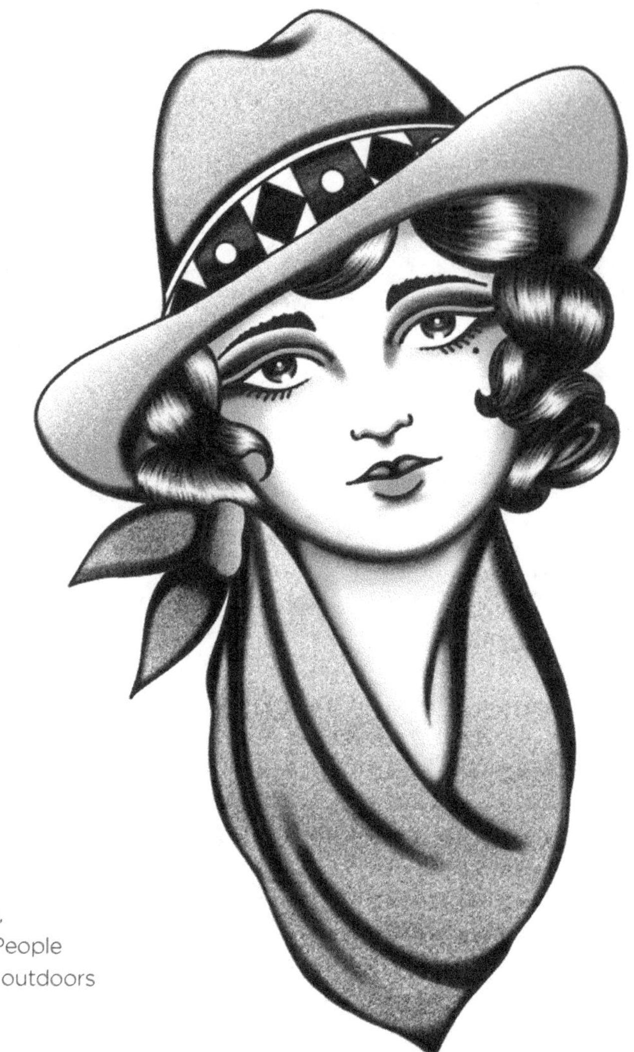

A cowgirl symbolises strength, independence, and freedom. People with a wild spirit who love the outdoors often choose this tattoo.

01

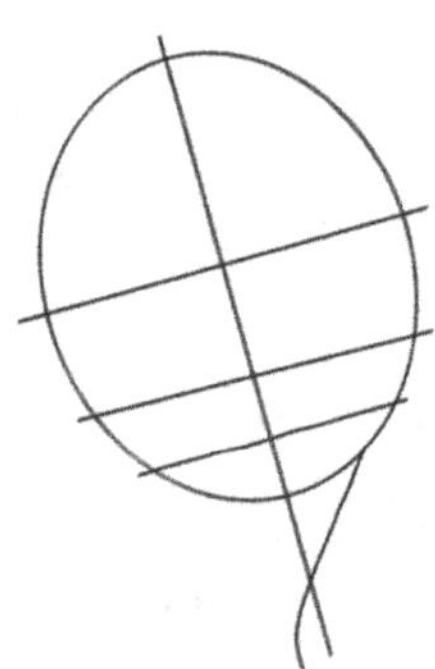

02

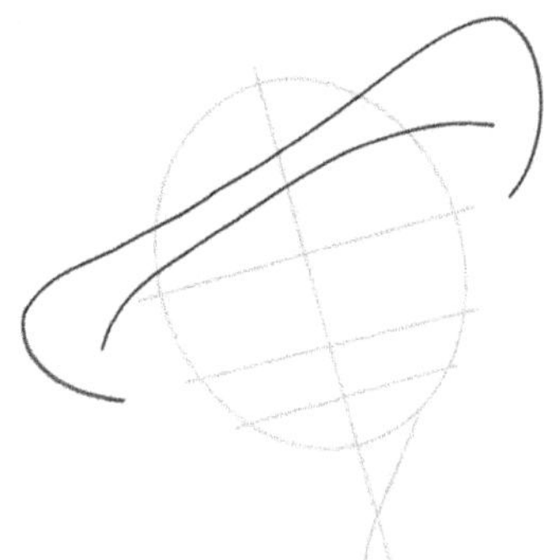

03

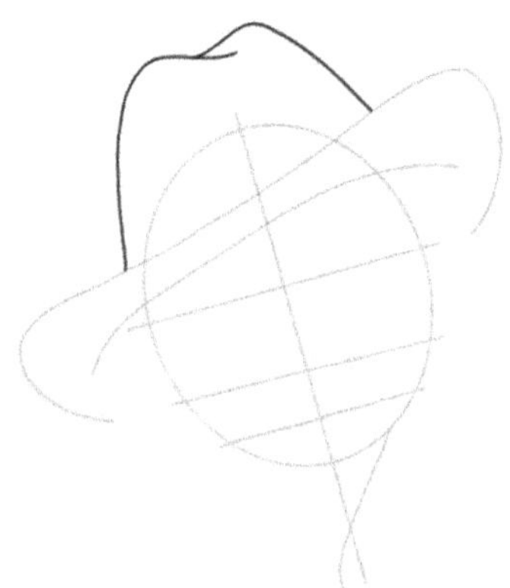

04

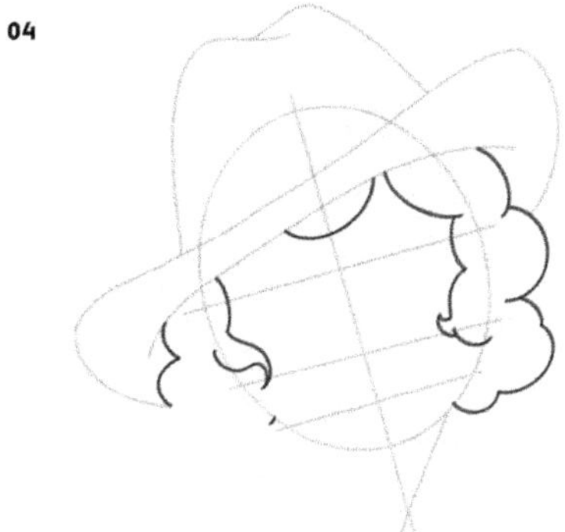

05

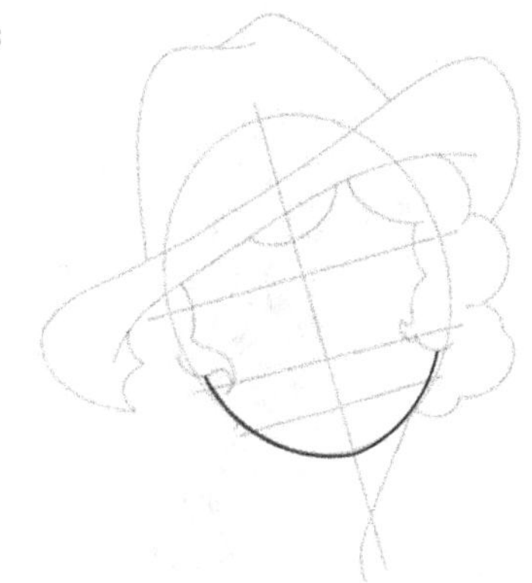

06

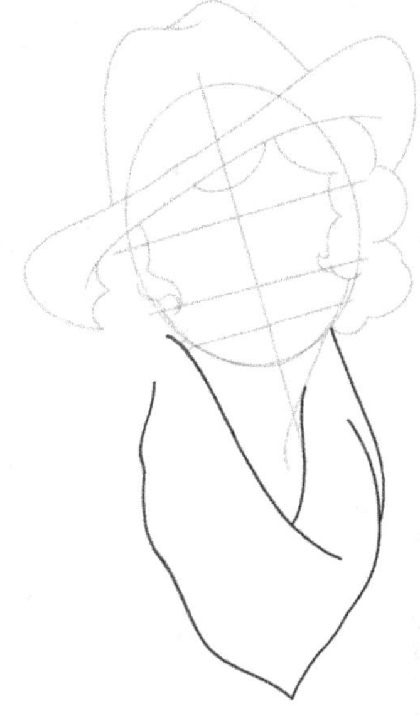

07

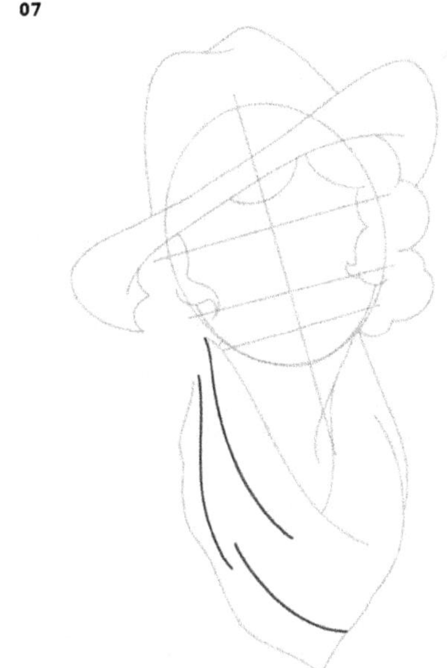

08

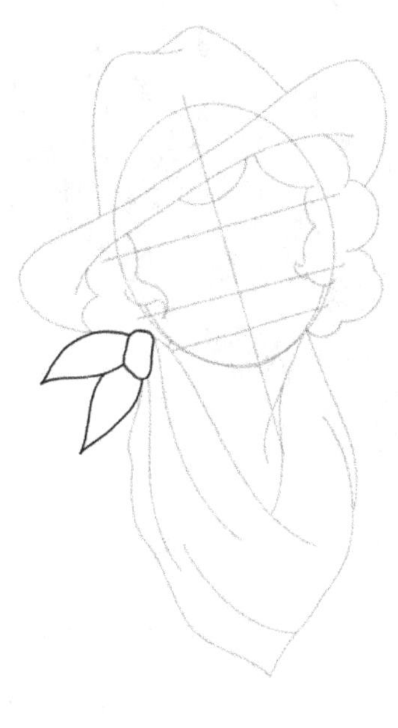

09

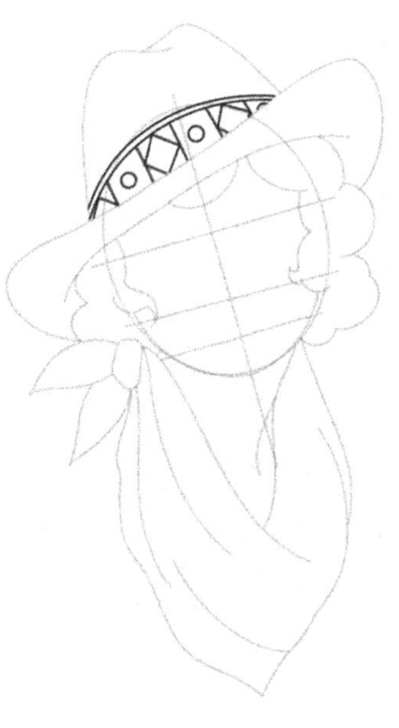

10

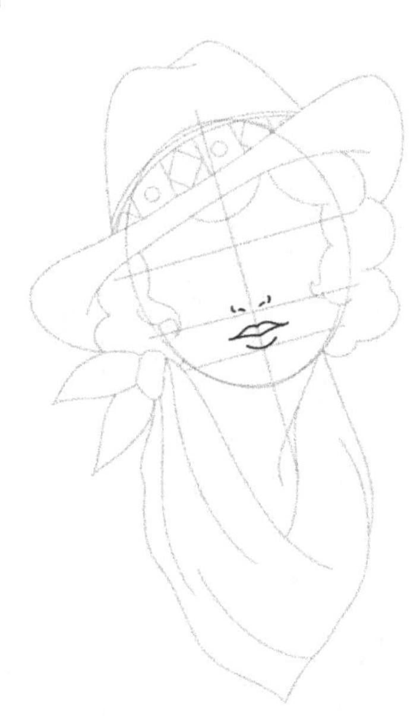

11

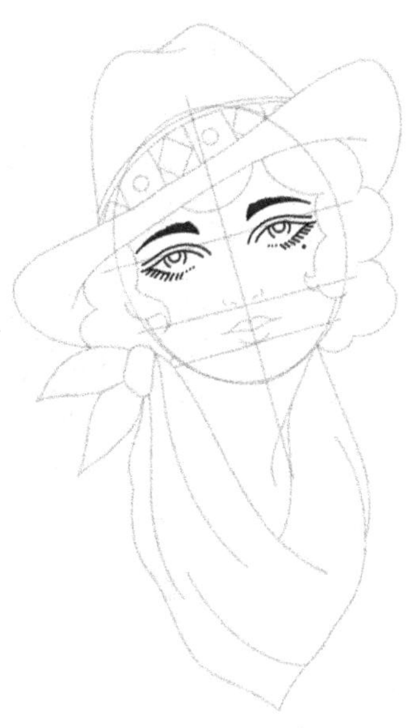

12

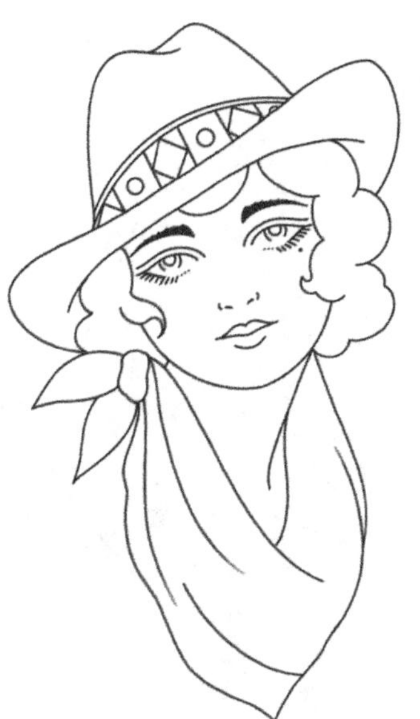

HOW TO DRAW TATTOO FLASH

HOW TO DRAW TATTOO FLASH

CUT-THROAT RAZOR

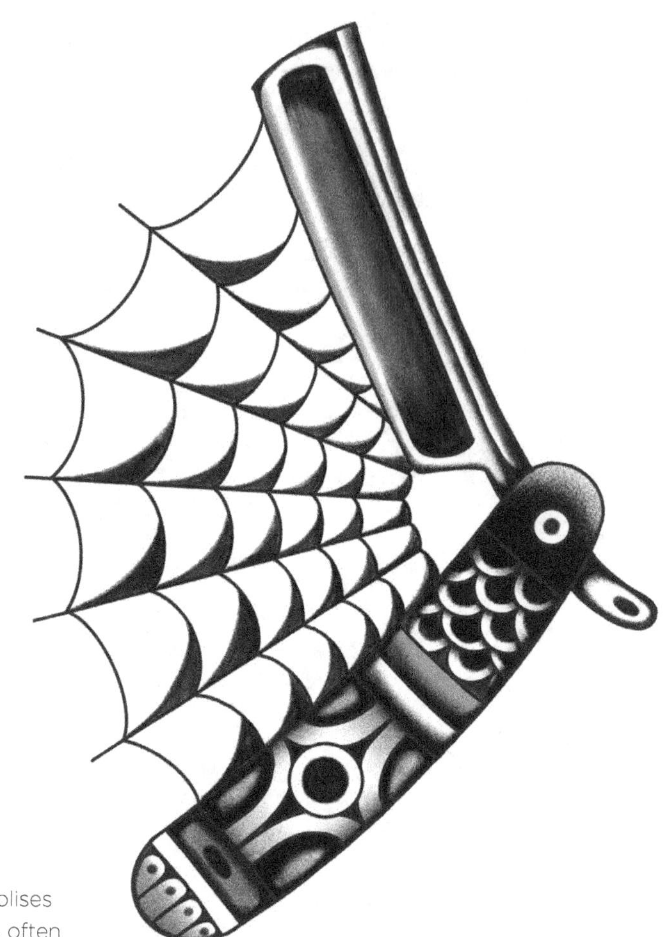

A cut-throat razor tattoo symbolises precision, danger, and rebellion, often representing a nod to traditional craftsmanship or a rough, independent lifestyle, while also conveying themes of risk and personal strength.

01

02

03

04

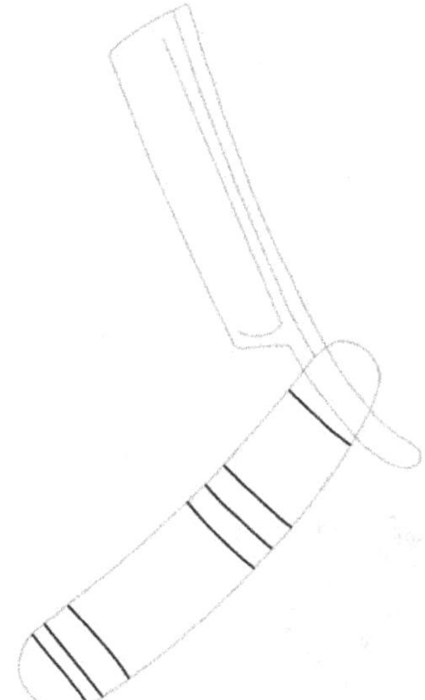

05

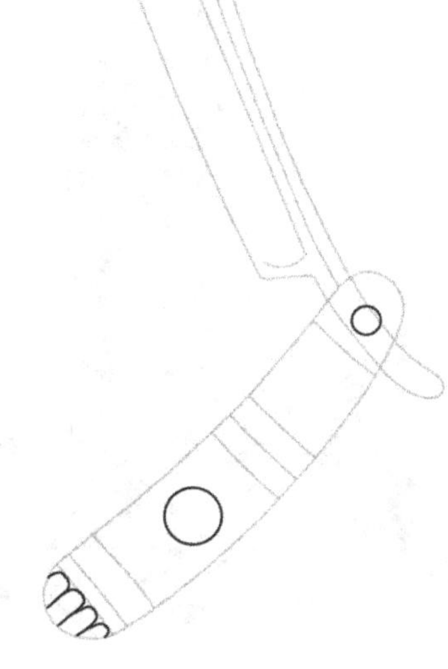

06

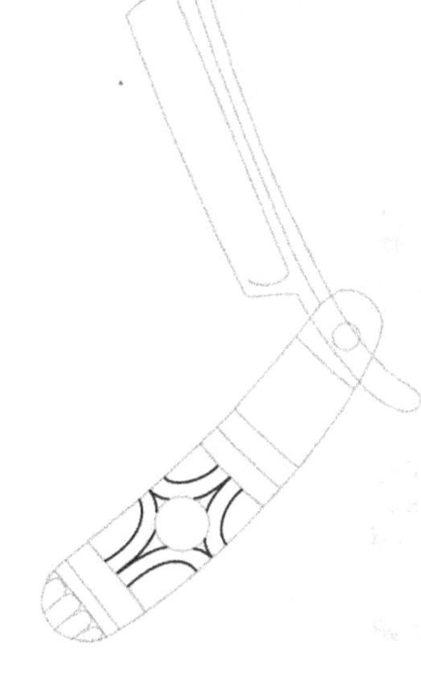

07

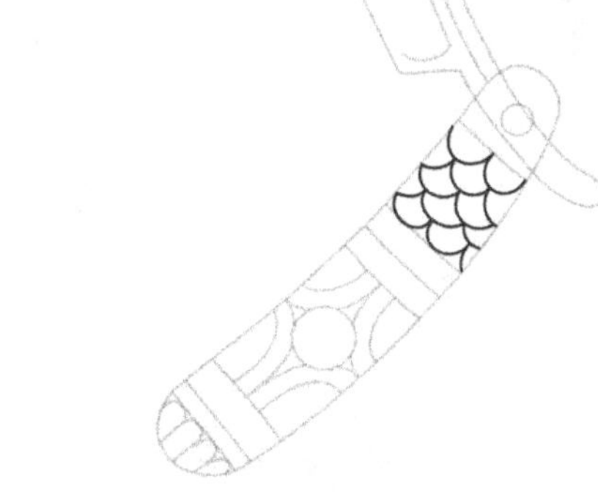

08

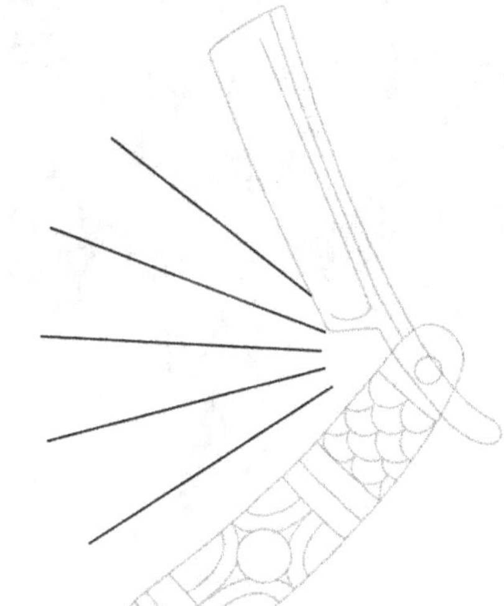

09

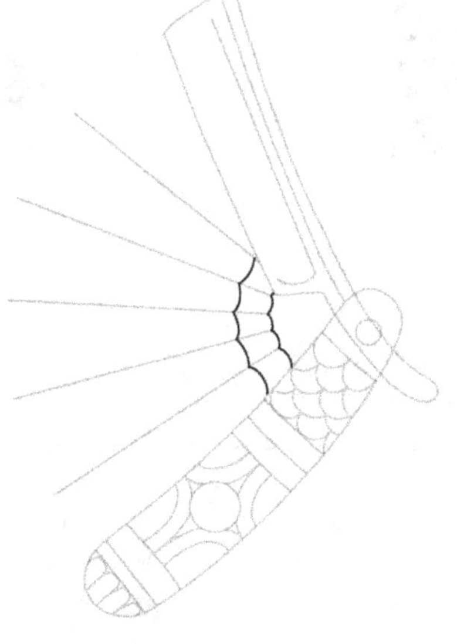

10

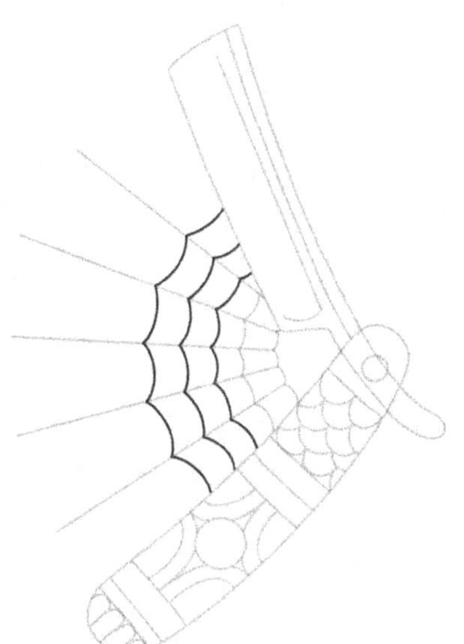

11

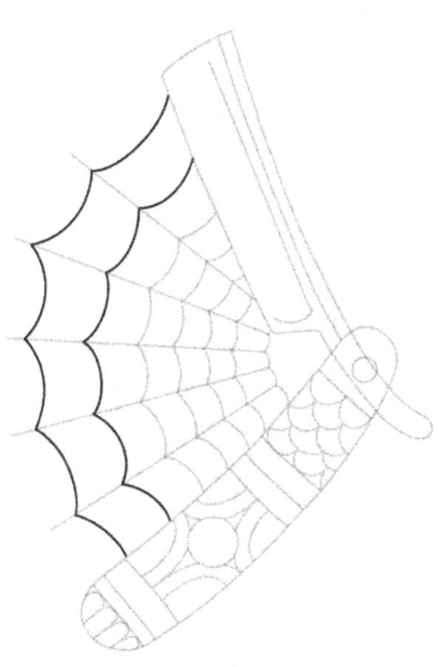

12

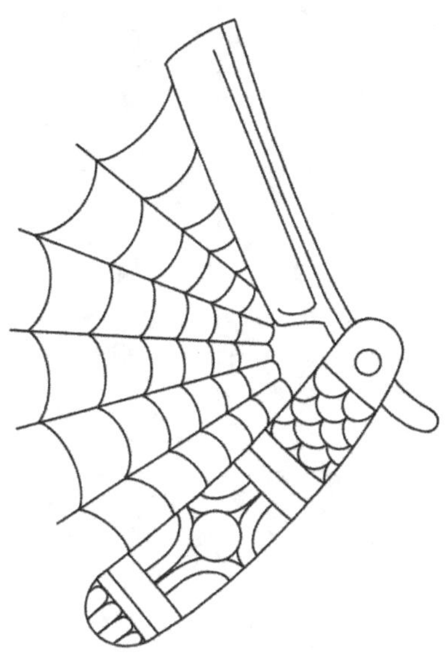

HOW TO DRAW TATTOO FLASH

ROSE & DAGGER

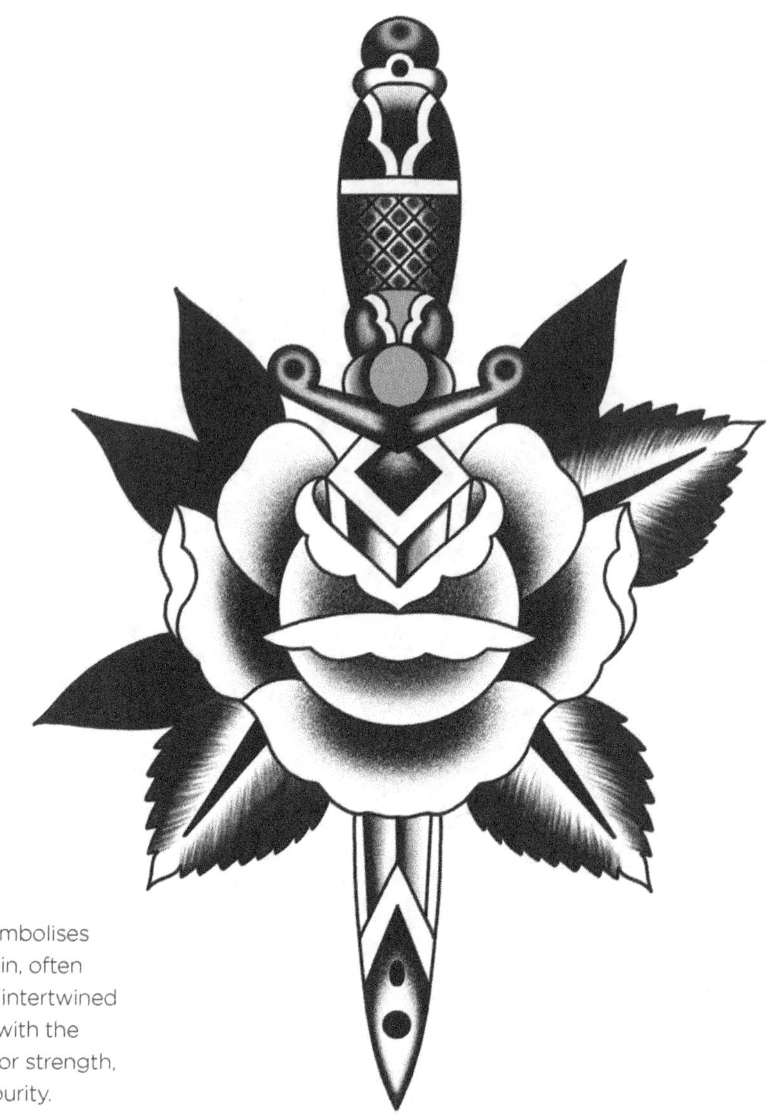

A rose and dagger tattoo symbolises the duality of beauty and pain, often representing themes of love intertwined with heartbreak or betrayal, with the dagger standing for danger or strength, and the rose for passion or purity.

01

02

03

04

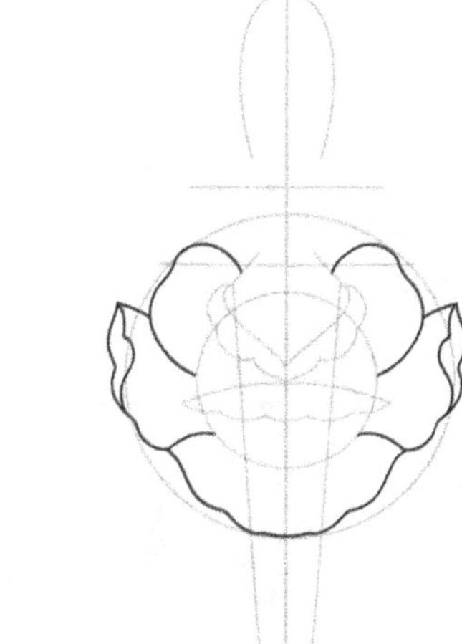

05

06

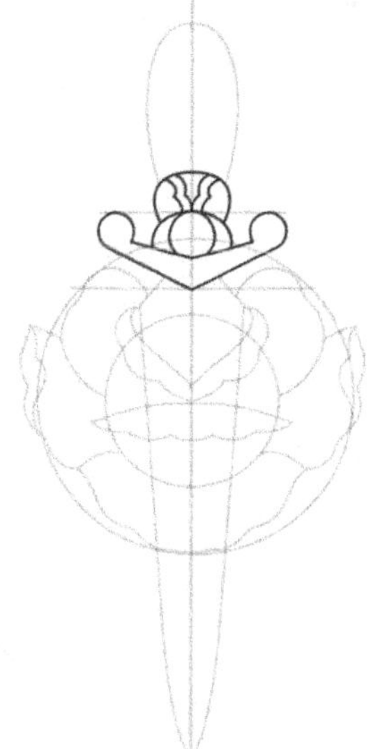

07

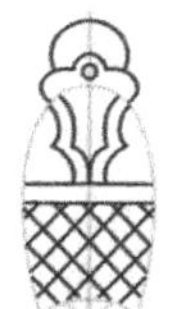

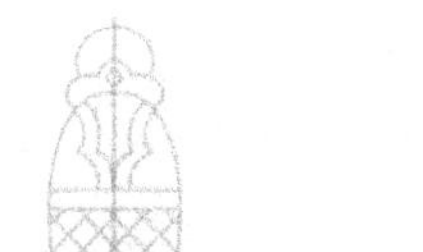

08

09

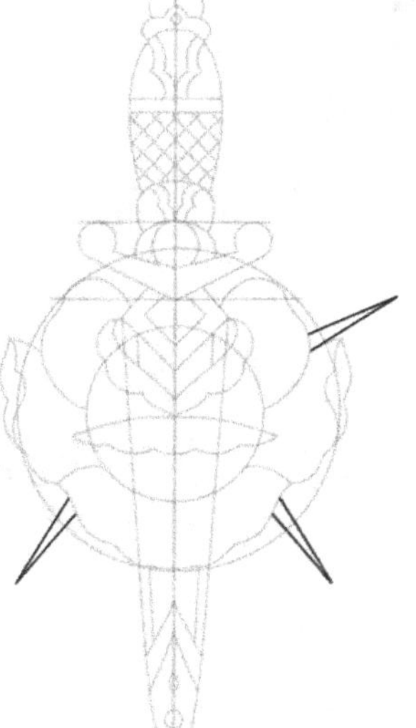

10

11

12

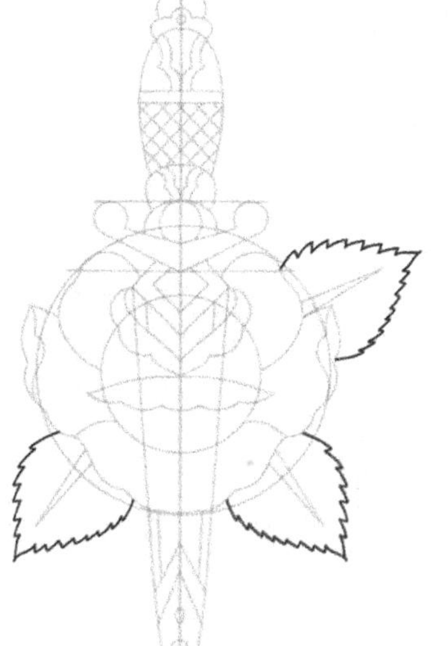
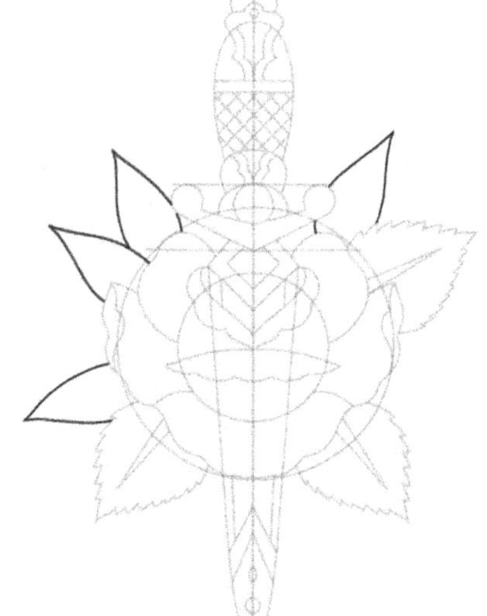
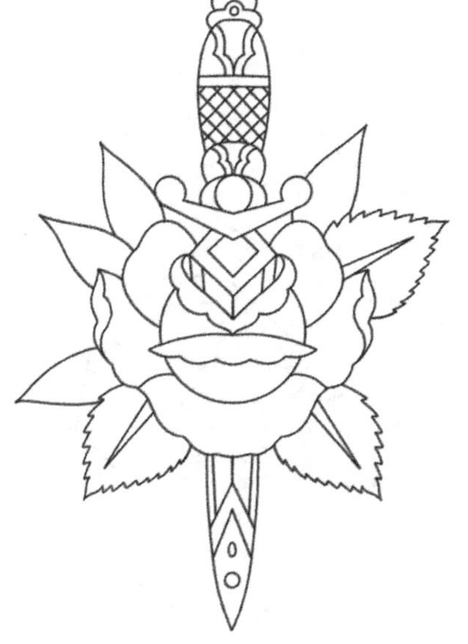

HOW TO DRAW TATTOO FLASH

FLAMING DICE

HOW TO DRAW TATTOO FLASH

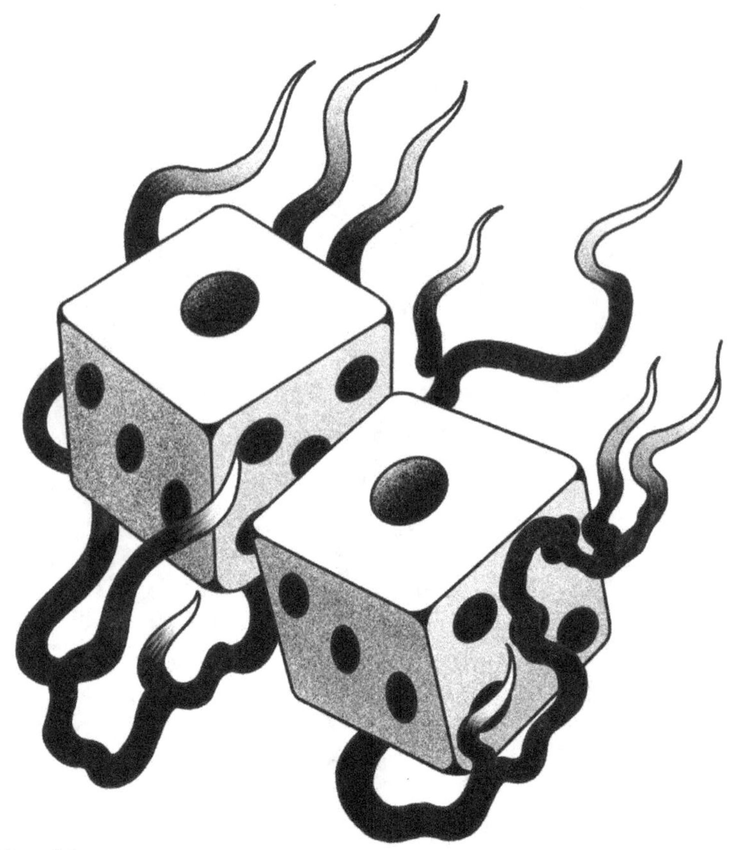

The flaming dice symbolise taking risks and embracing fate, often associated with luck and the thrill of living life on the edge.

01

02

03

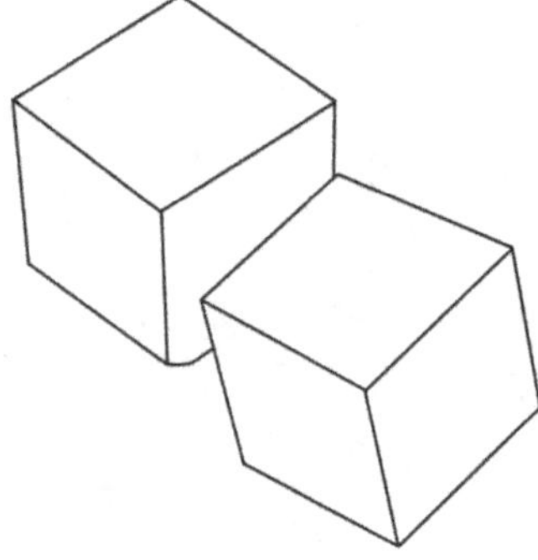

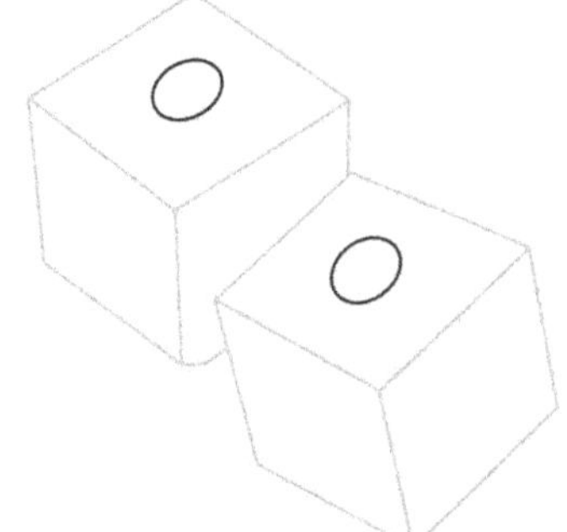

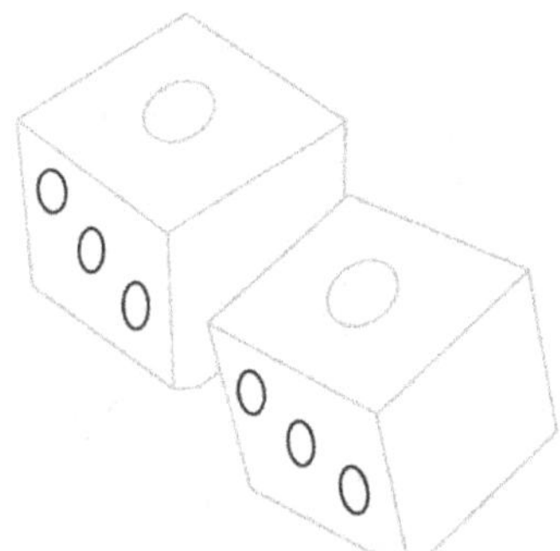

04

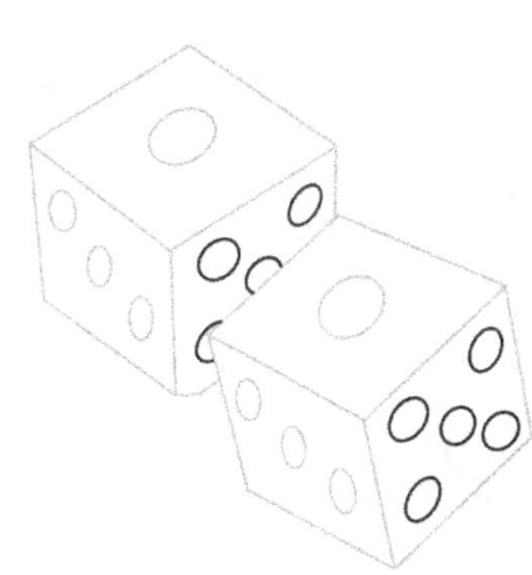

05

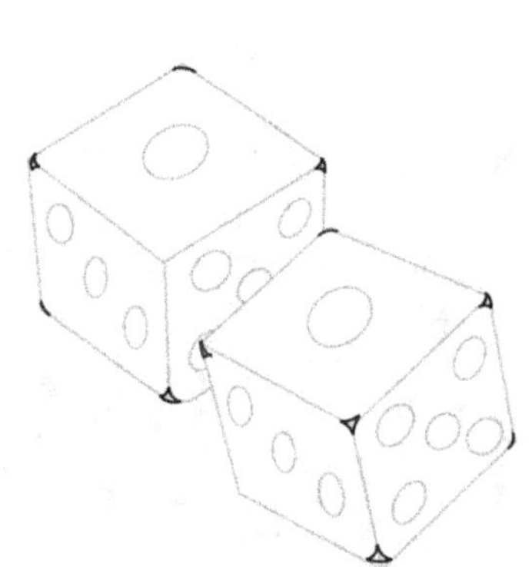

06

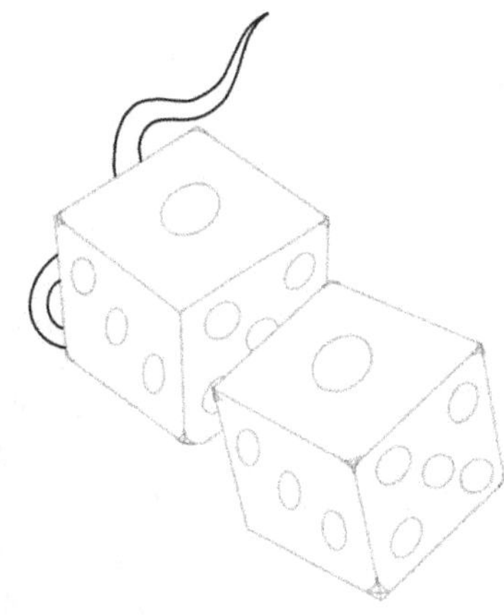

07

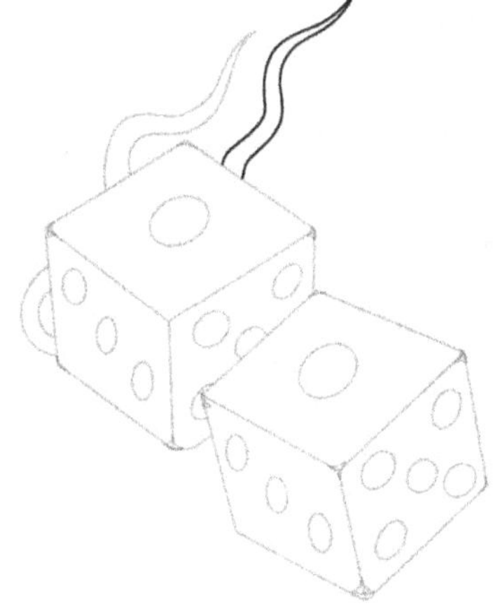

08

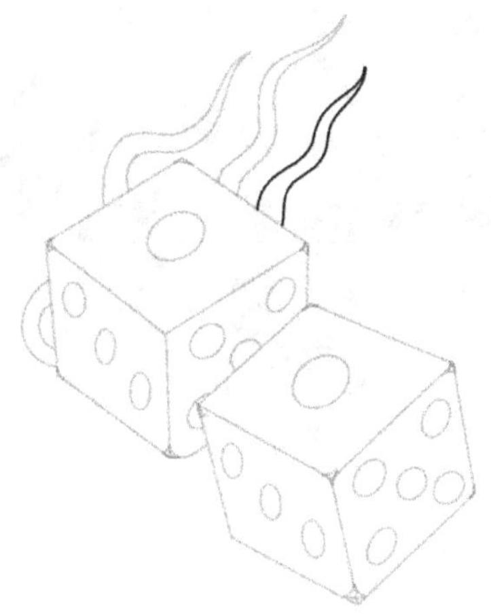

09

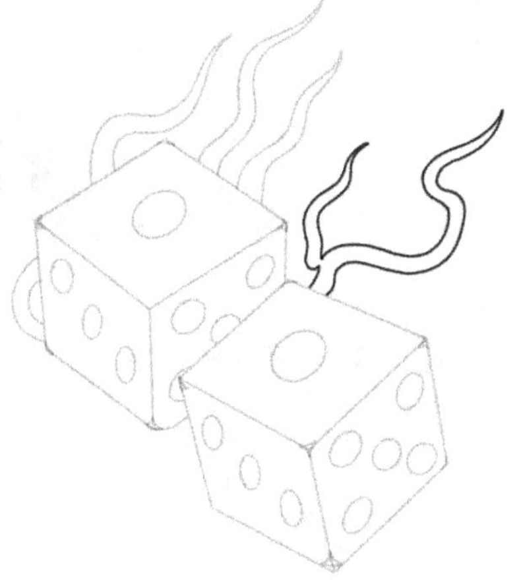

10

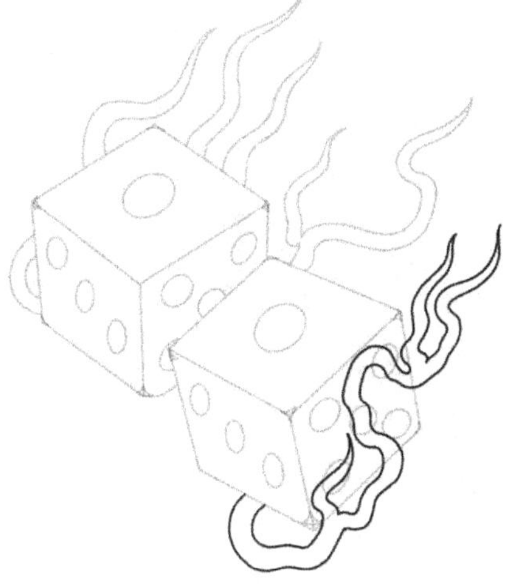

11

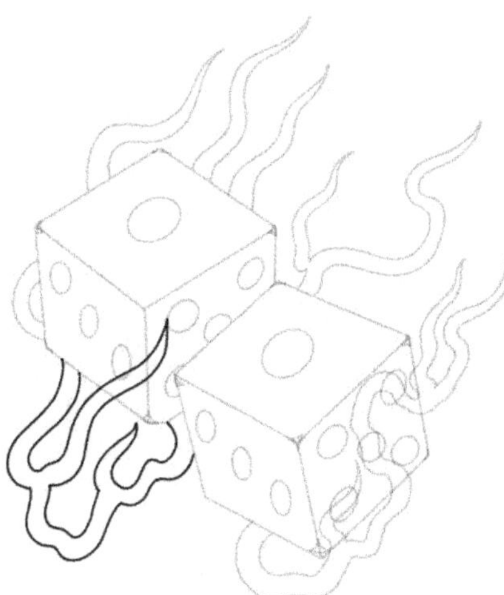

12

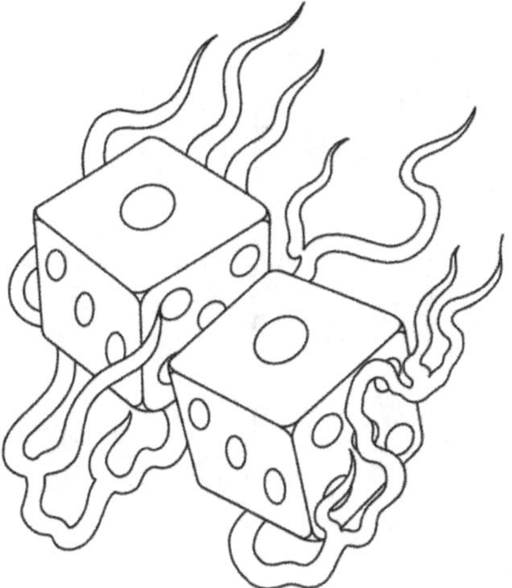

HOW TO DRAW TATTOO FLASH

FLAT FLOWER

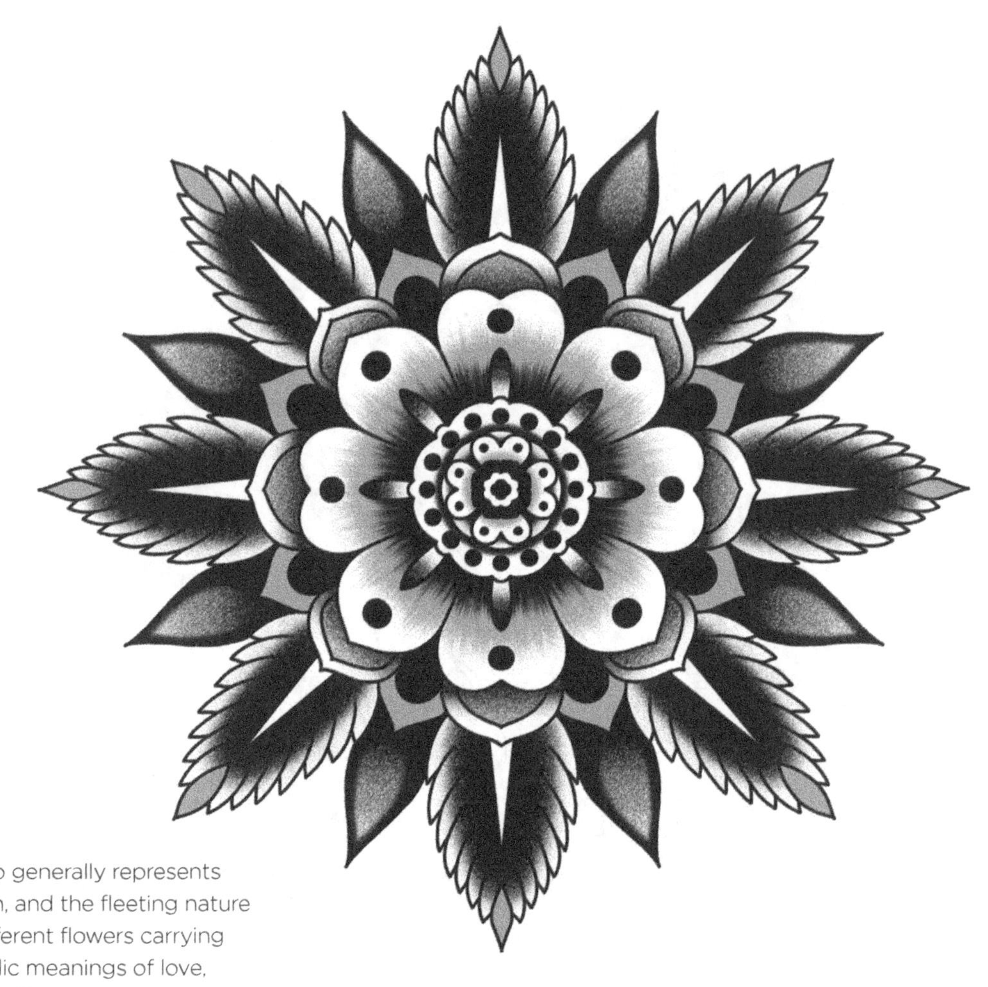

A flower tattoo generally represents beauty, growth, and the fleeting nature of life, with different flowers carrying unique symbolic meanings of love, renewal, and resilience.

01 **02** **03**

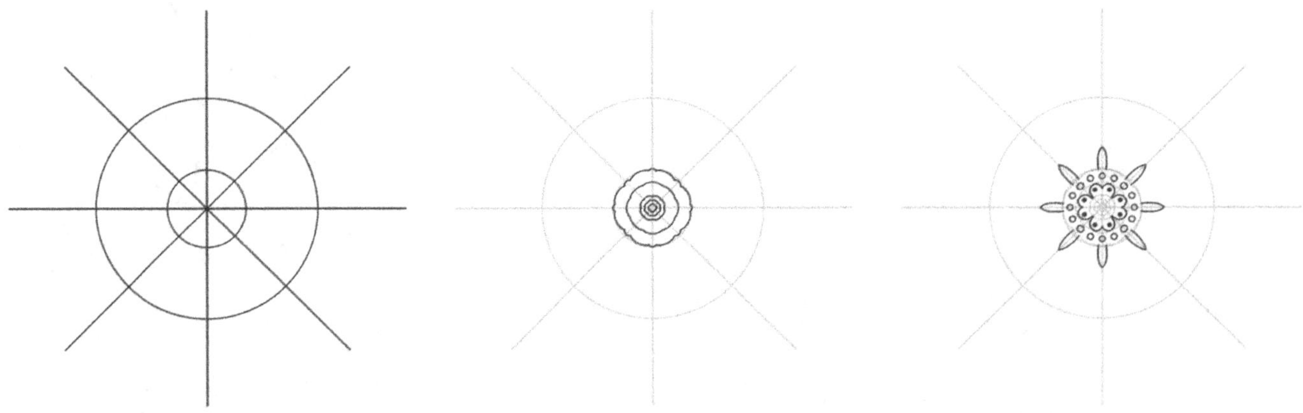

04

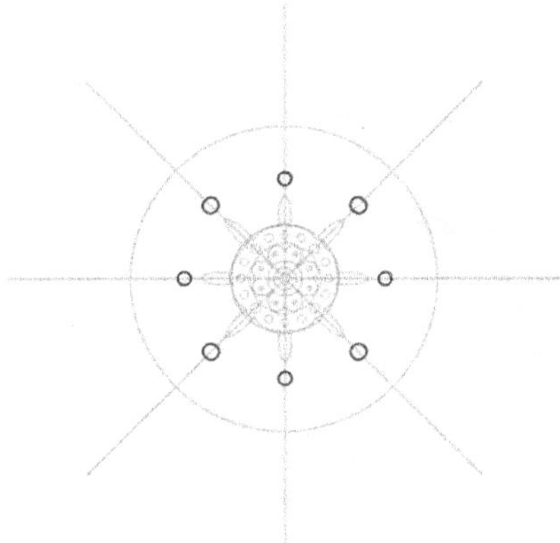

05

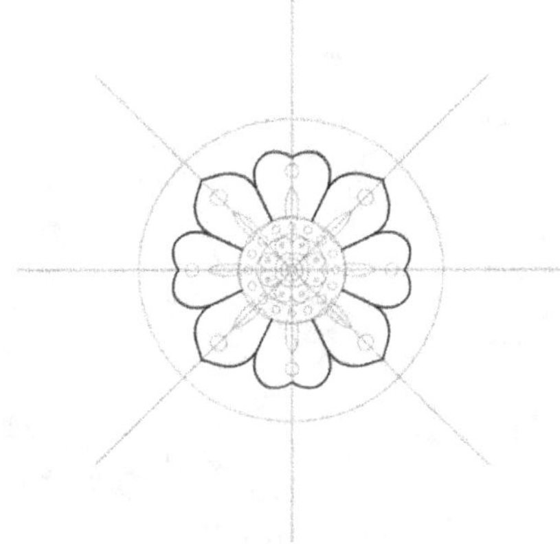

06

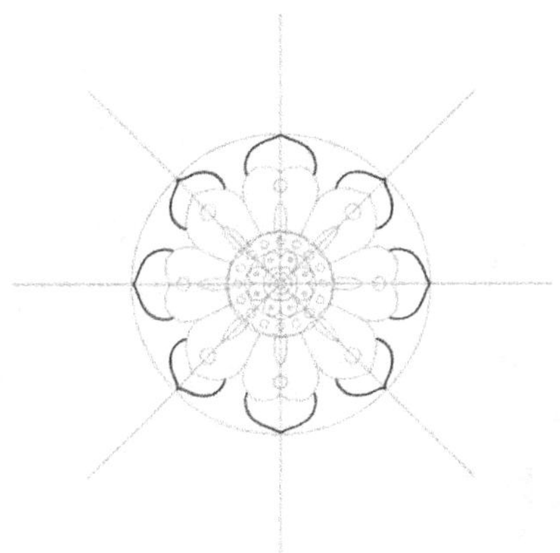

07

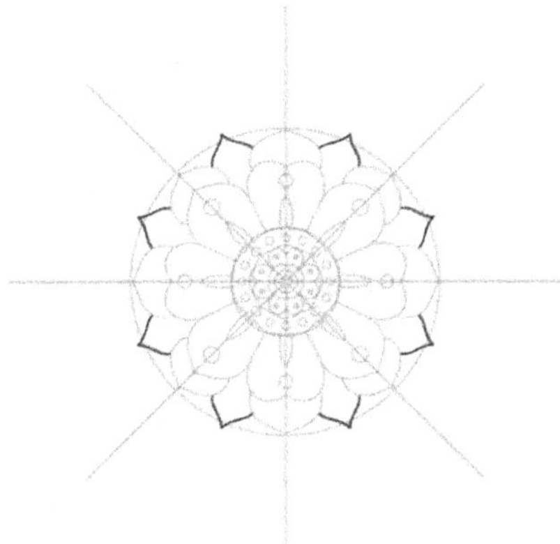

08

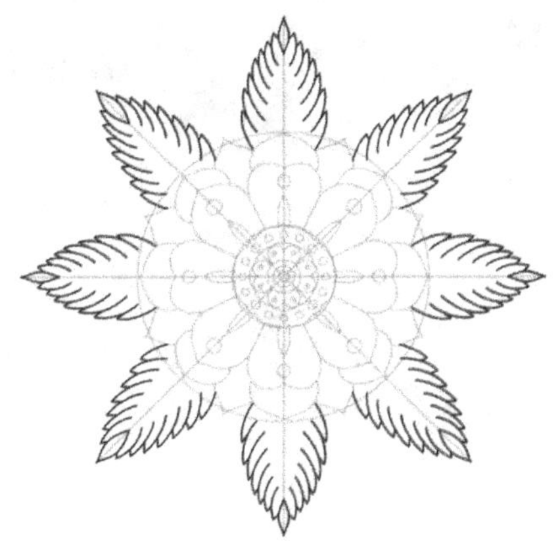

09

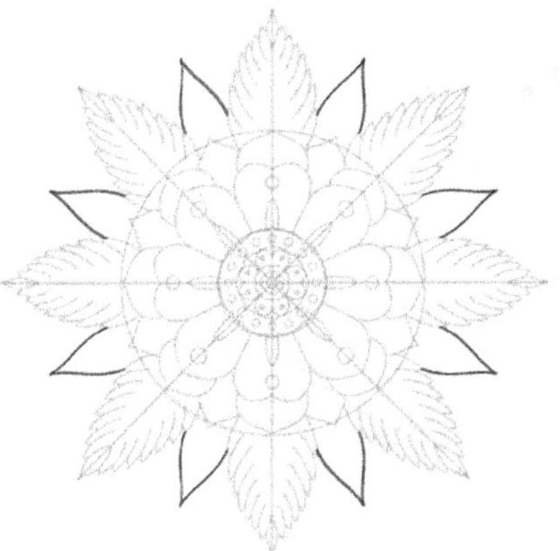

10

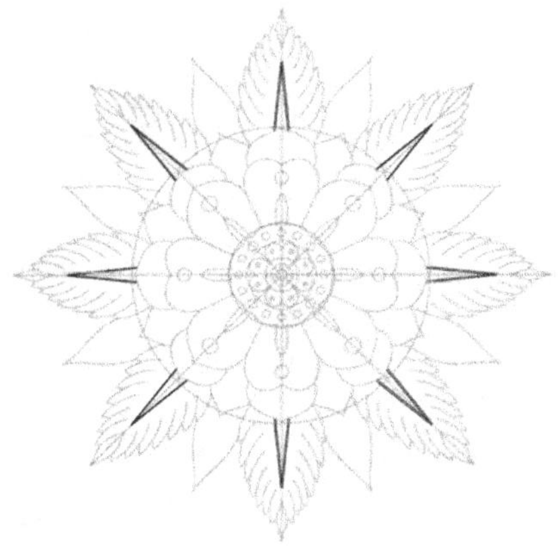

11

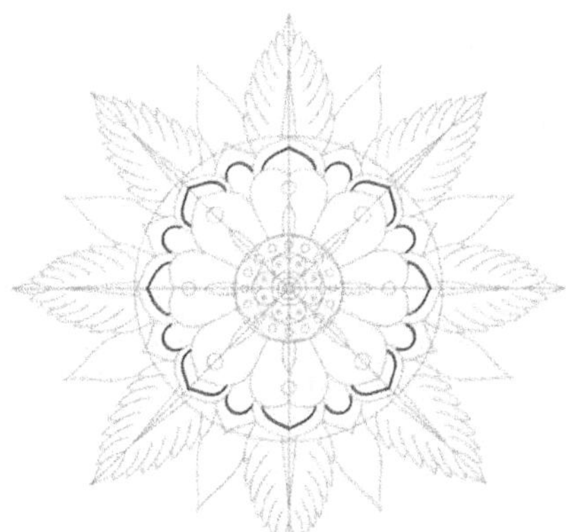

12

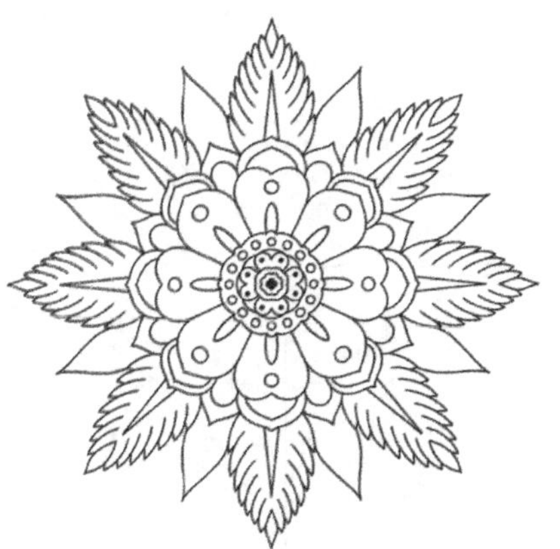

HOW TO DRAW TATTOO FLASH

FLAT FLOWER 2

HOW TO DRAW TATTOO FLASH

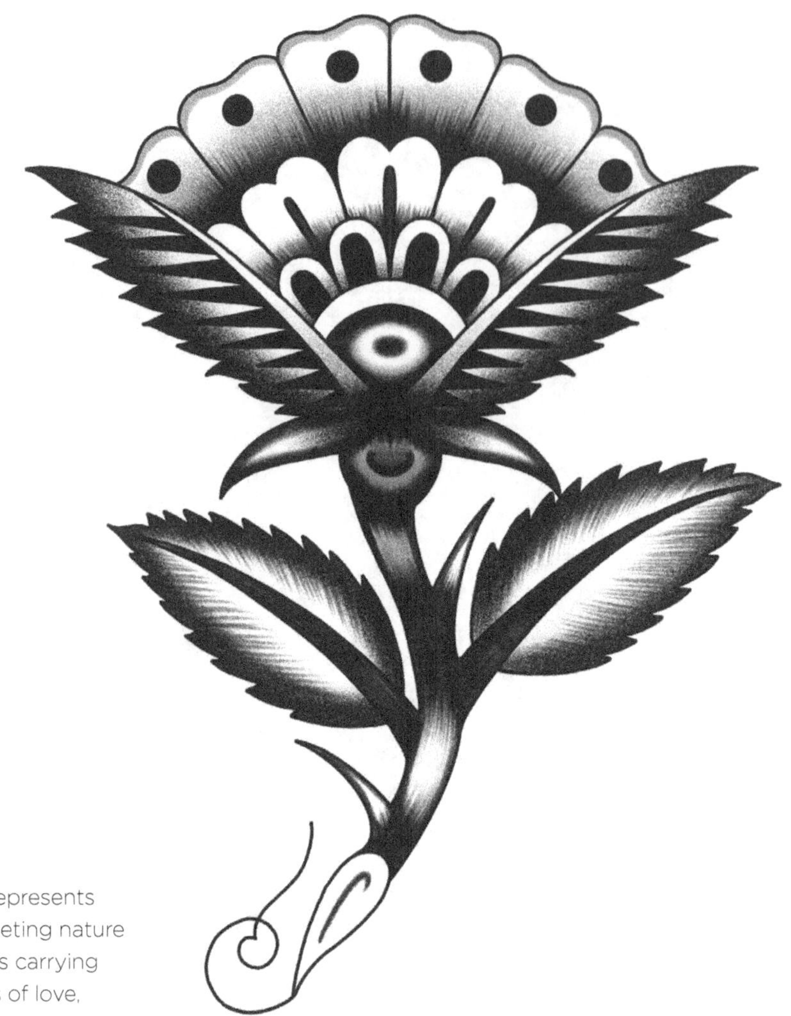

A flower tattoo generally represents beauty, growth, and the fleeting nature of life, with different flowers carrying unique symbolic meanings of love, renewal, and resilience.

01

02

03

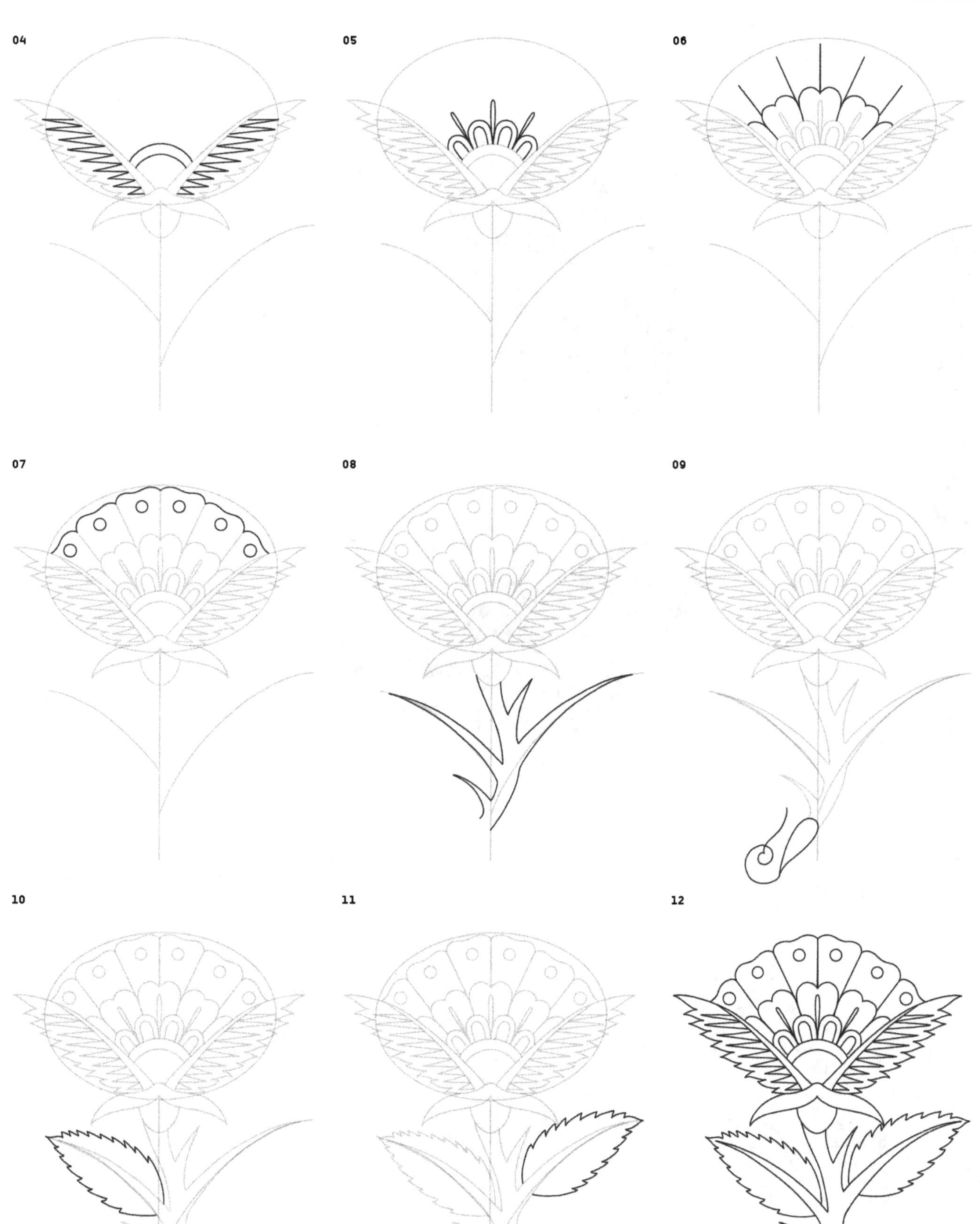

HOW TO DRAW TATTOO FLASH

HOW TO DRAW TATTOO FLASH

GENTLEMAN

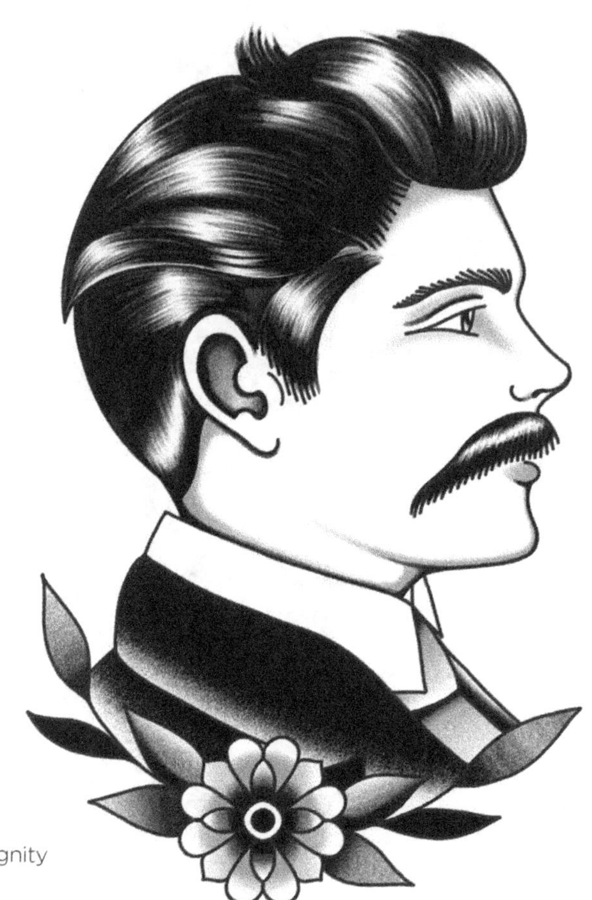

The image of a gentleman can represent elegance, tradition, dignity and class.

01

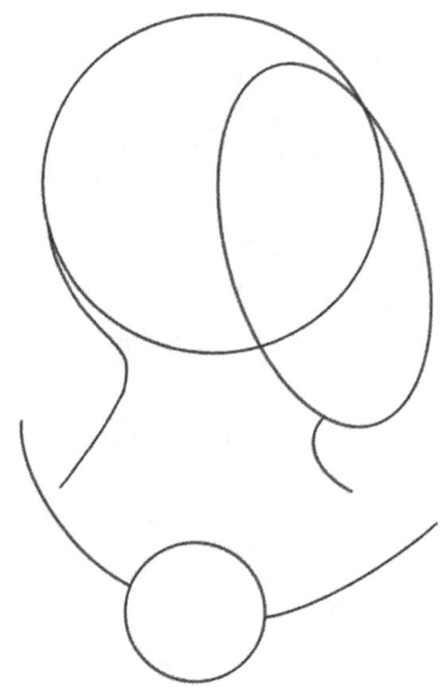

02

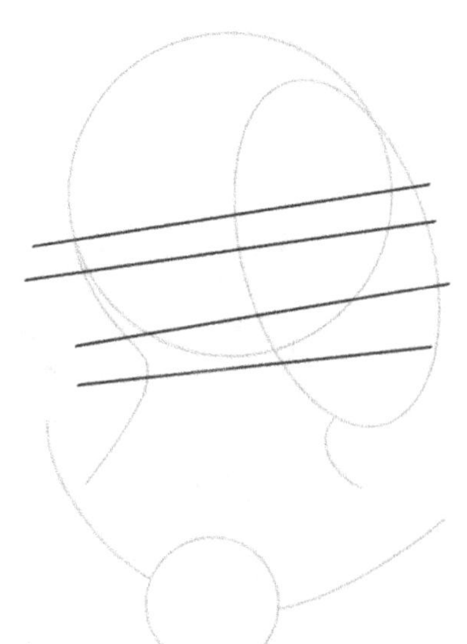

03

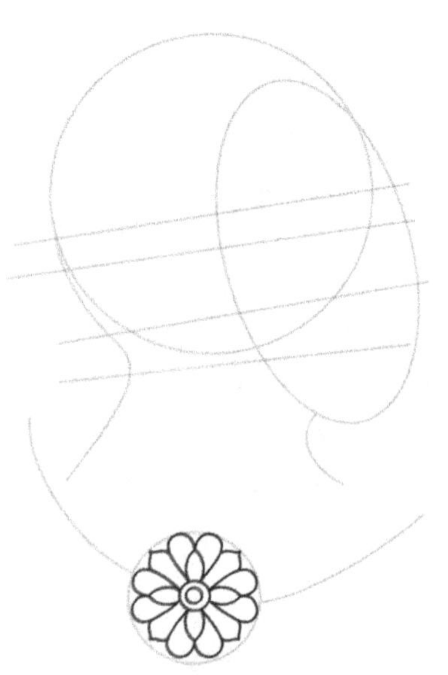

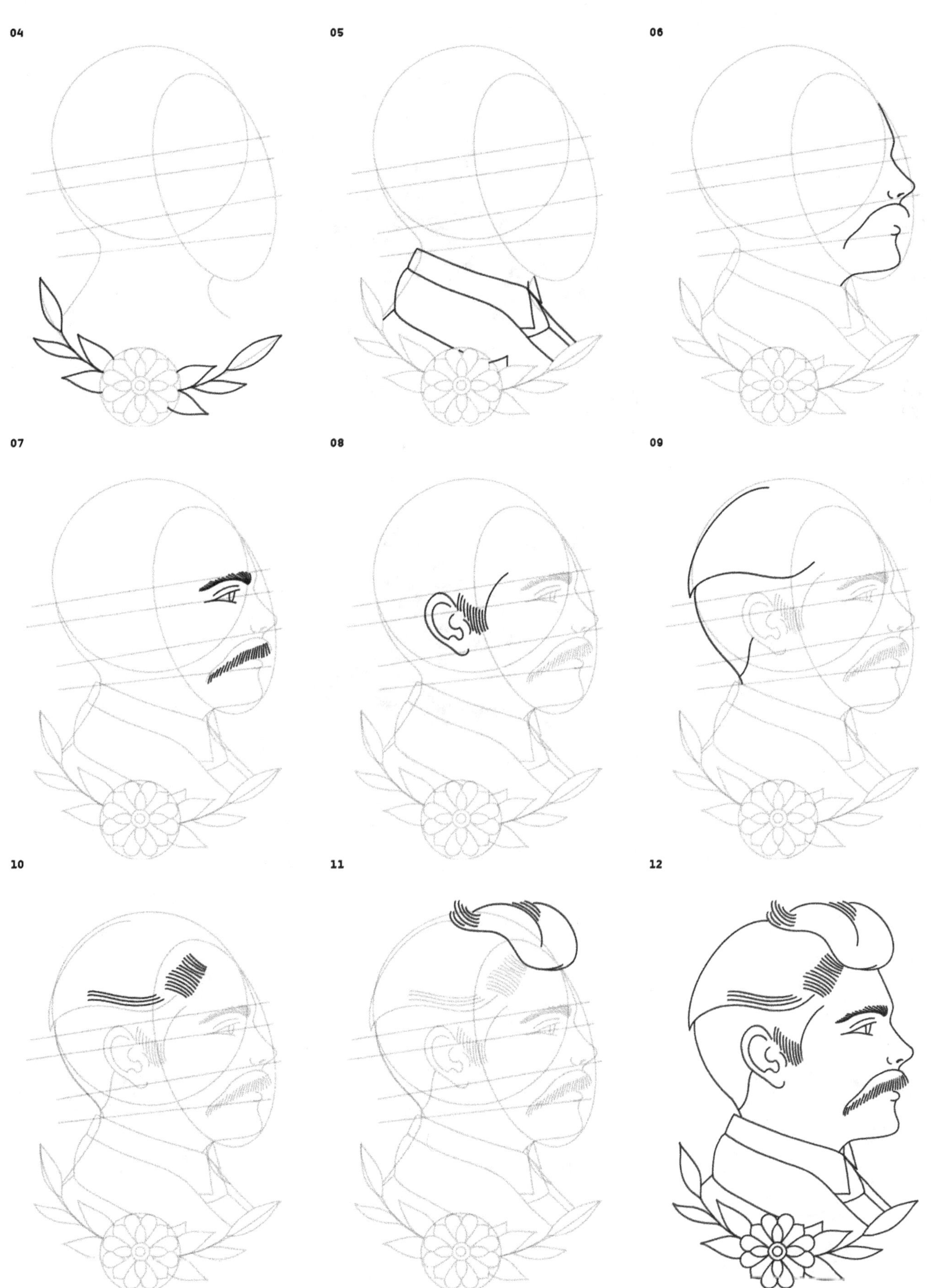
04
05
06
07
08
09
10
11
12

HOW TO DRAW TATTOO FLASH

HAND & ACE

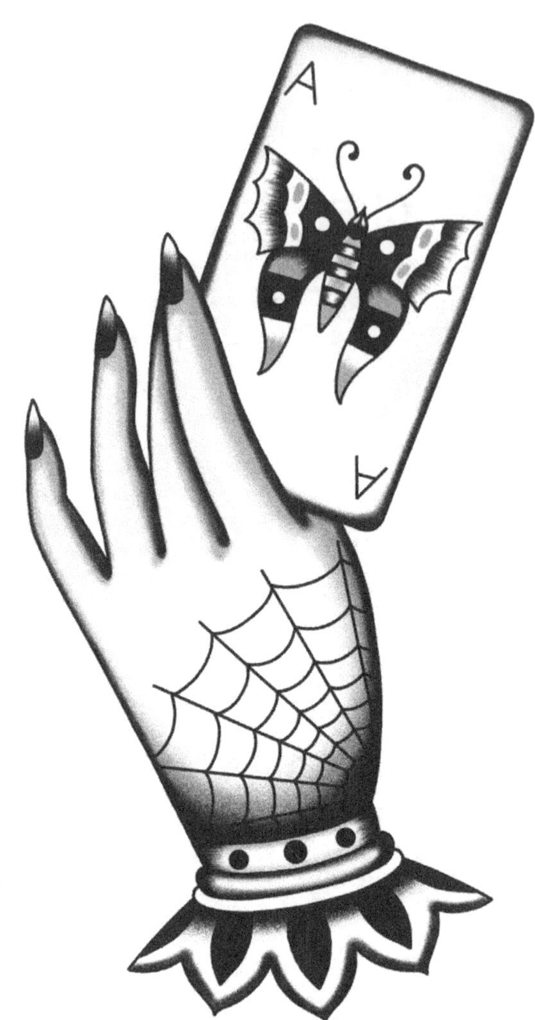

A hand holding an ace card symbolises confidence, luck, and a winning mindset. It's a mark of someone who plays their cards wisely in life.

01

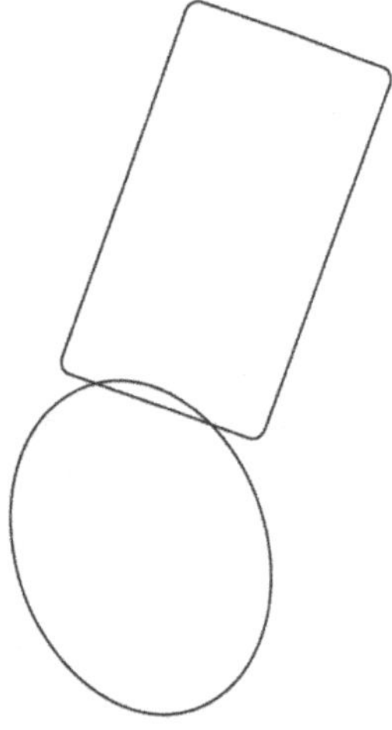

02

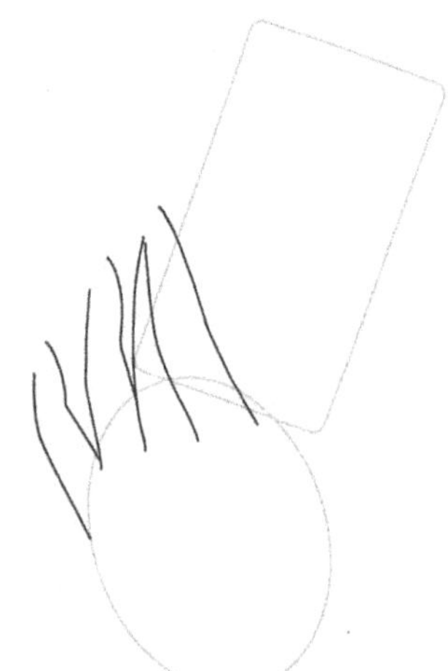

03

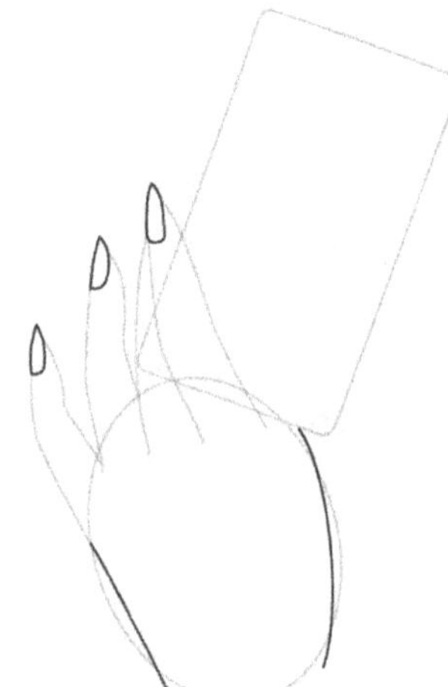

04

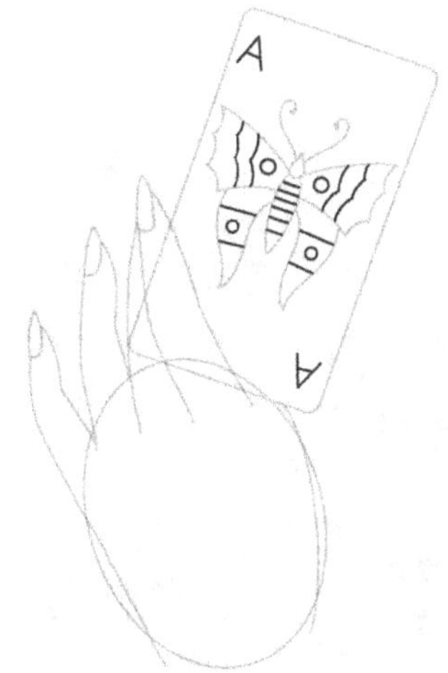

05

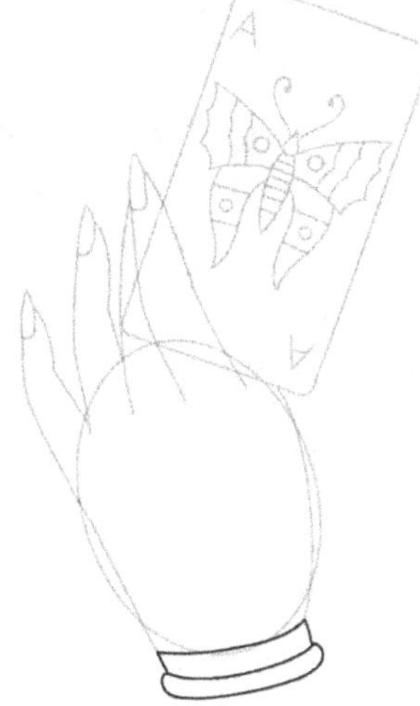

06

07

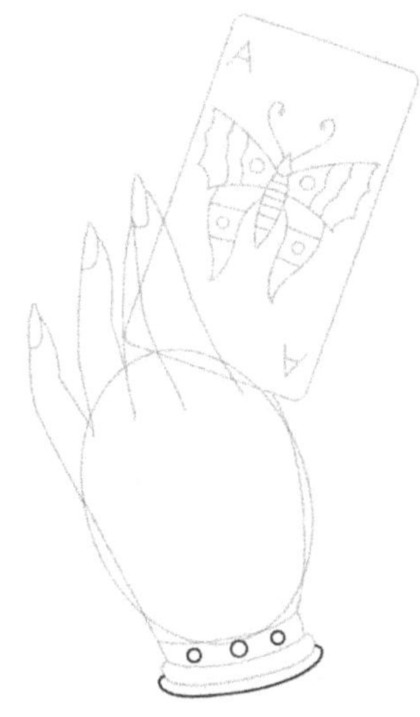

08

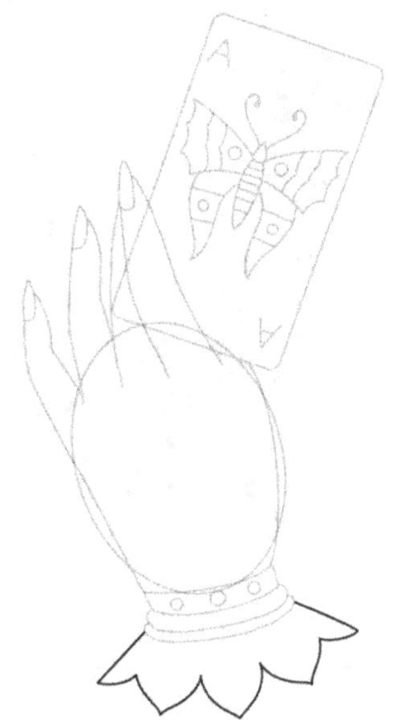

09

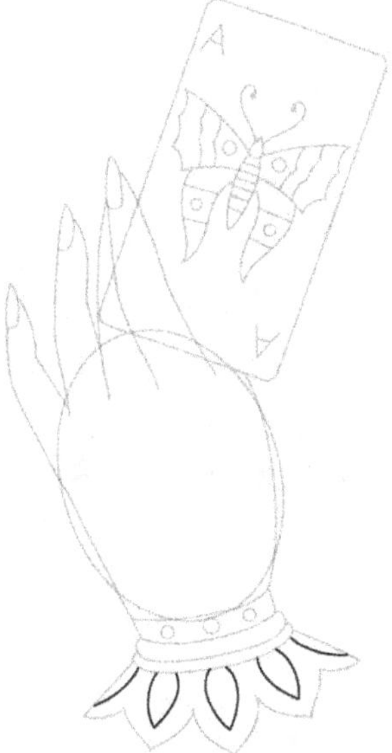

10

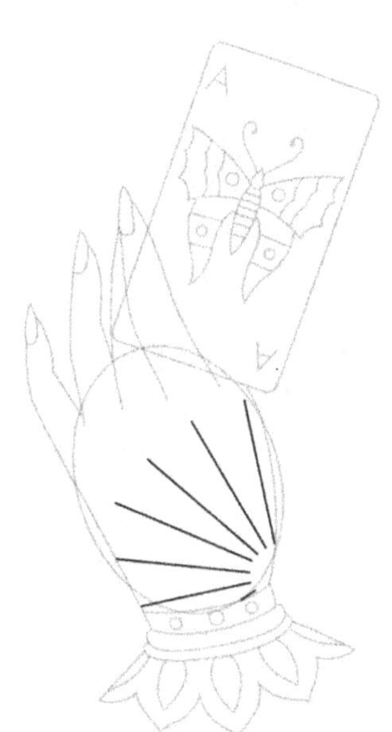

11

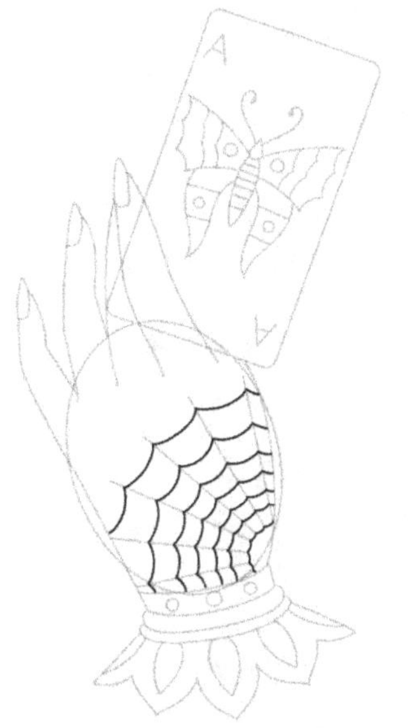

12

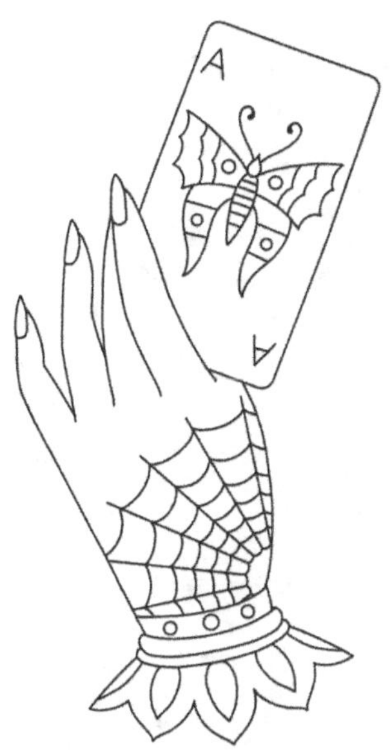

HAND & ROSE

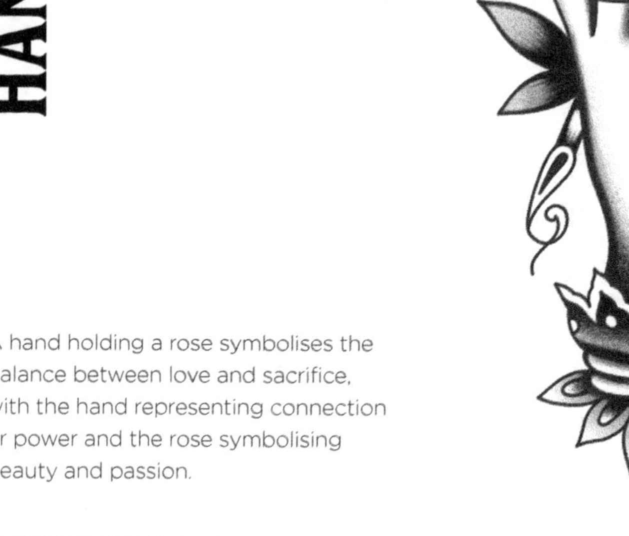

A hand holding a rose symbolises the balance between love and sacrifice, with the hand representing connection or power and the rose symbolising beauty and passion.

01

02

03

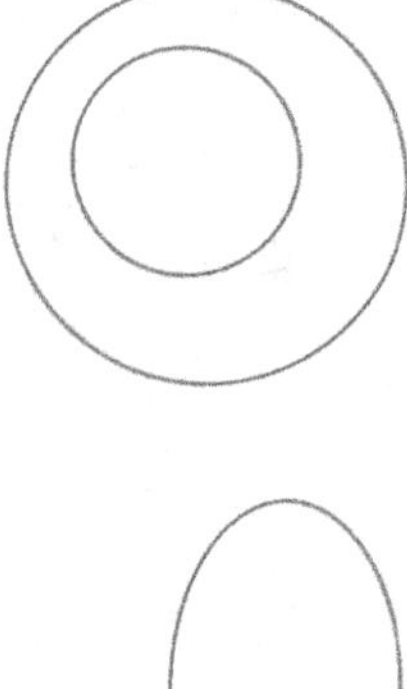

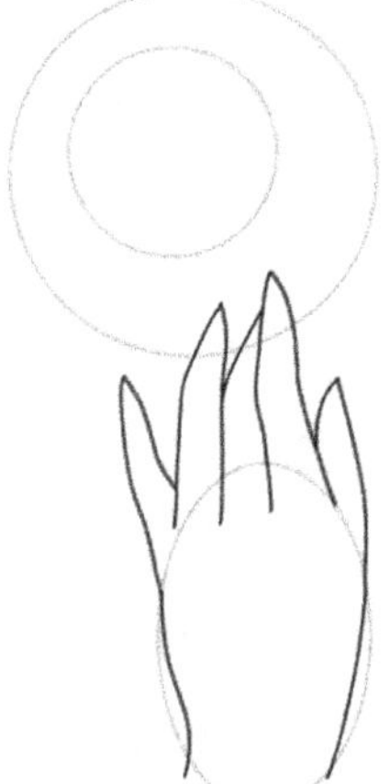

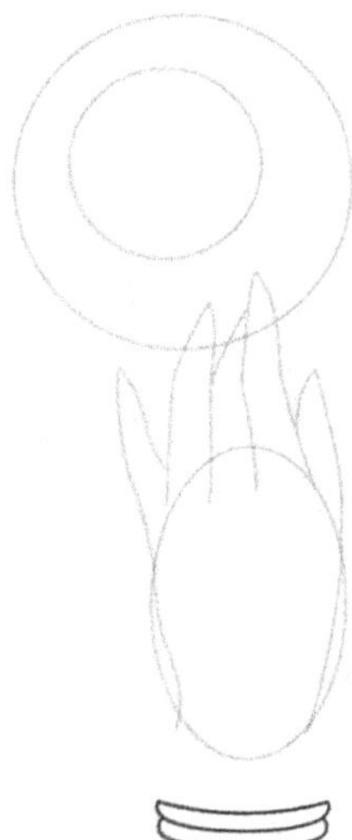

04

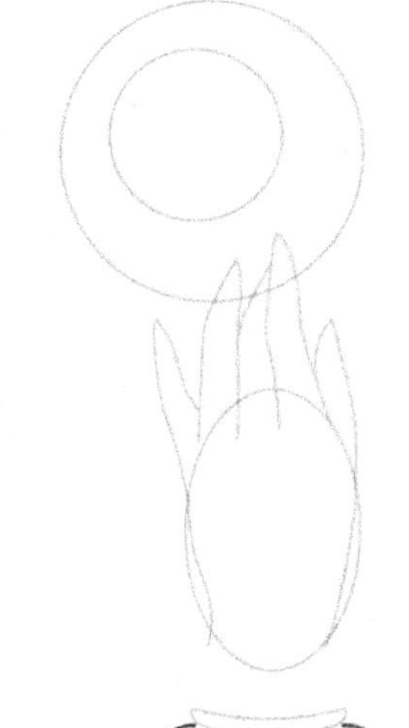

05

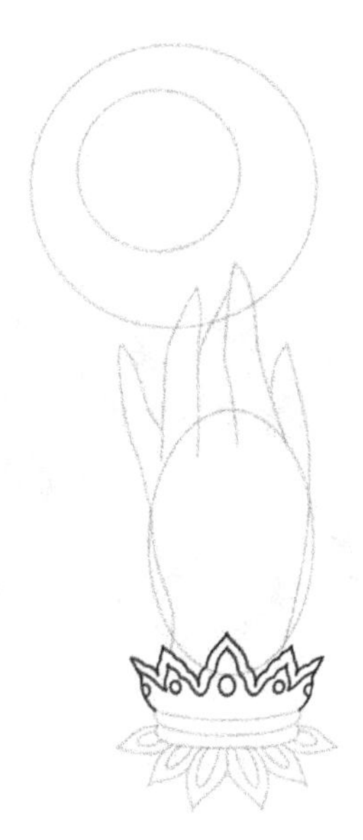

06

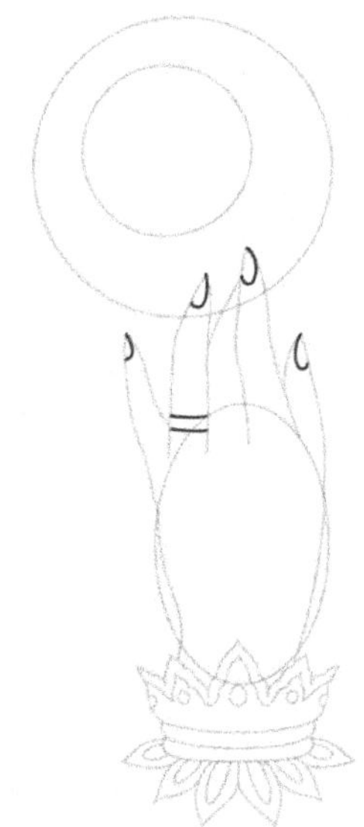

07

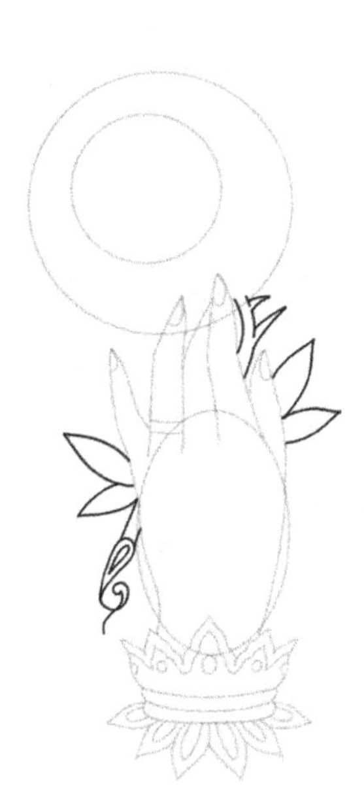

08

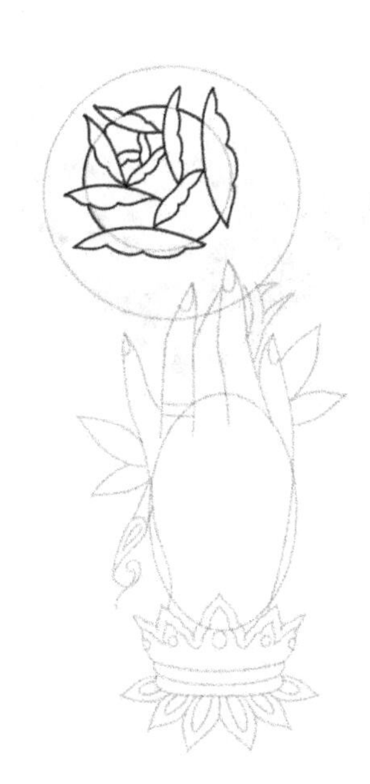

09

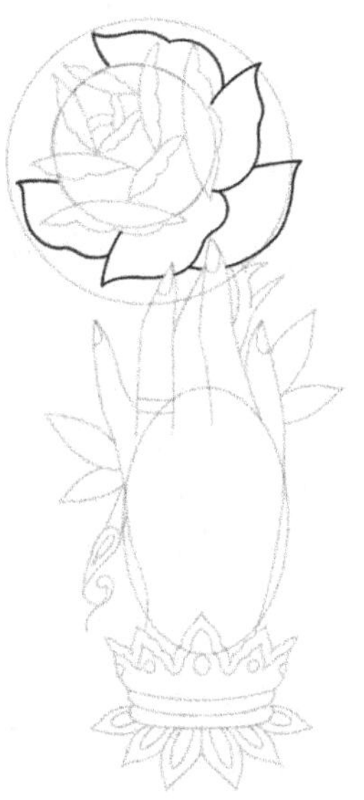

10

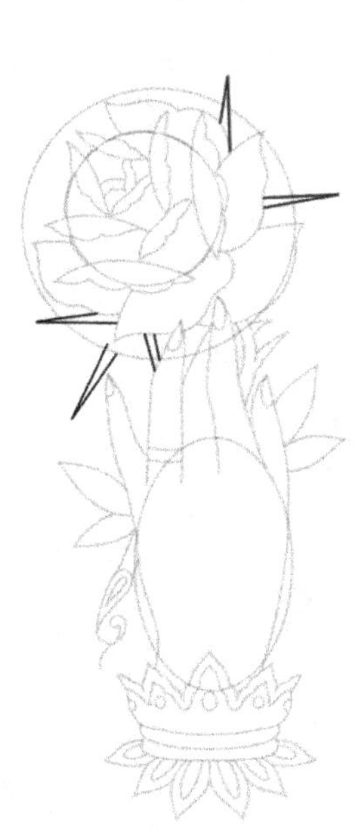

11

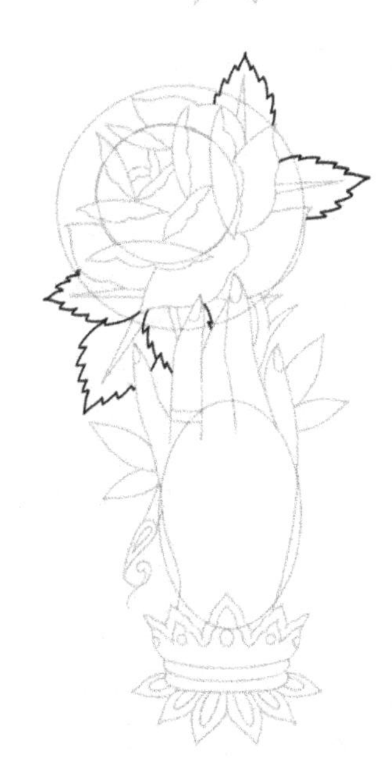

12

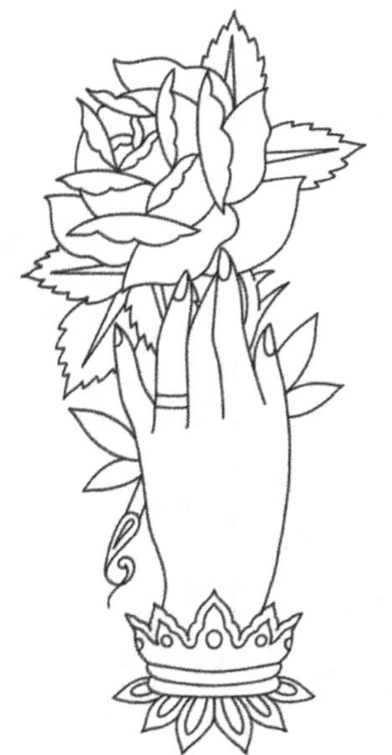

HOW TO DRAW TATTOO FLASH

HOW TO DRAW TATTOO FLASH

HEART & ARROW

A heart with an arrow signifies love, passion, and vulnerability. It's a symbol of the thrill and pain of falling in love.

01   **02**   **03**

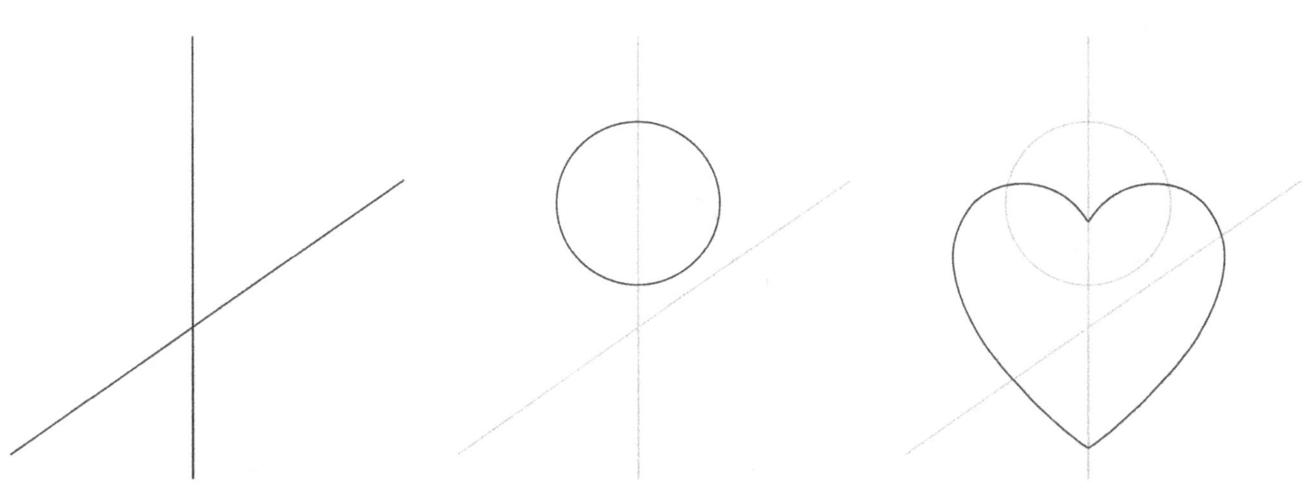

04

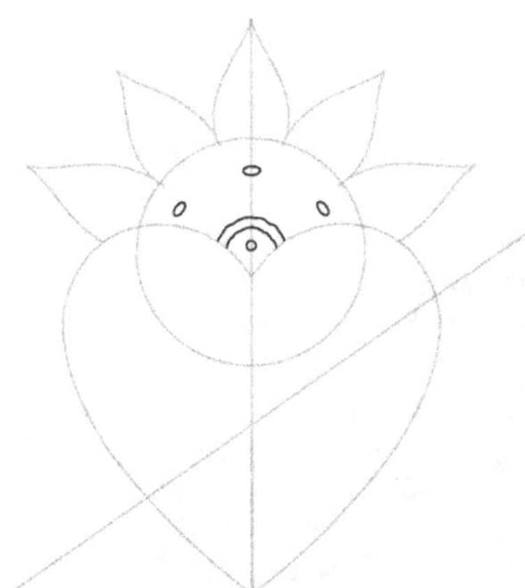

05

06

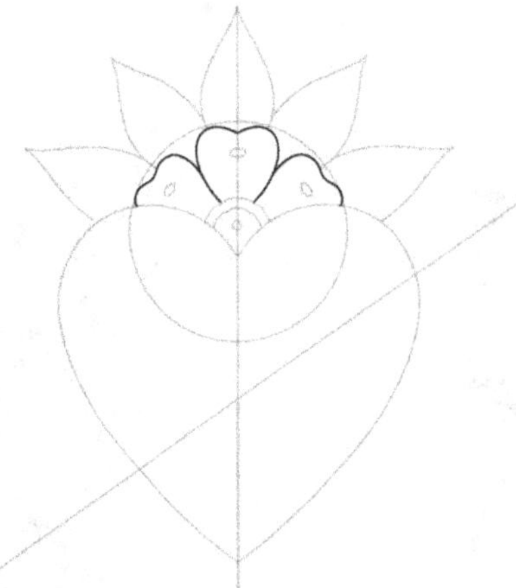

07

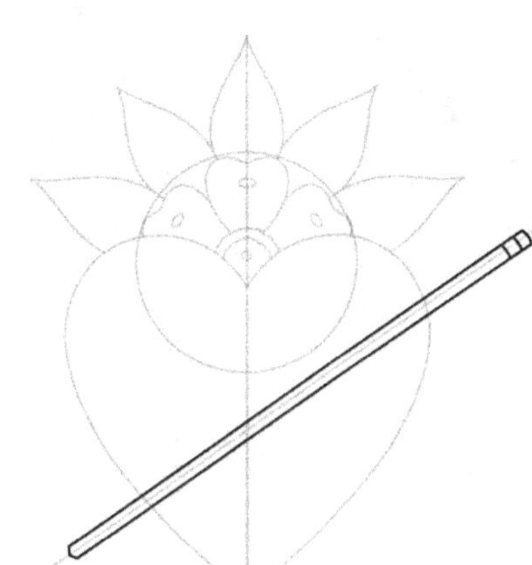

08

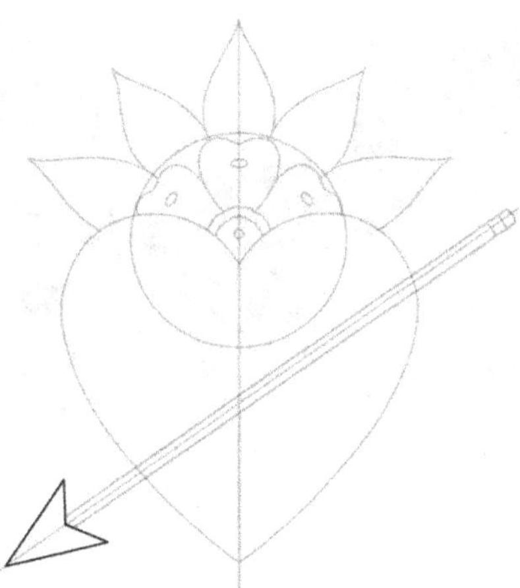

09

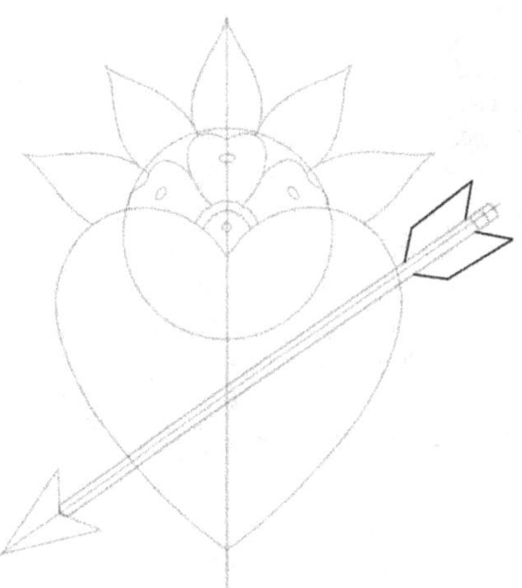

HOW TO DRAW TATTOO FLASH

10

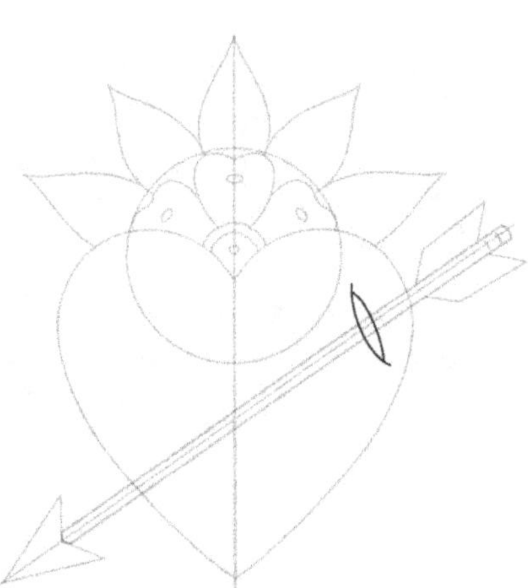

11

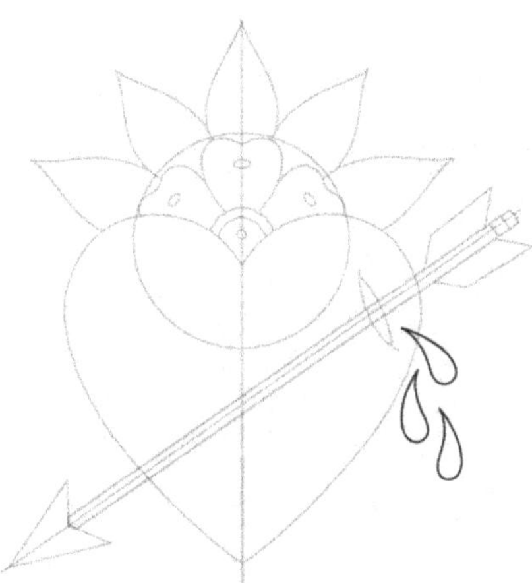

12

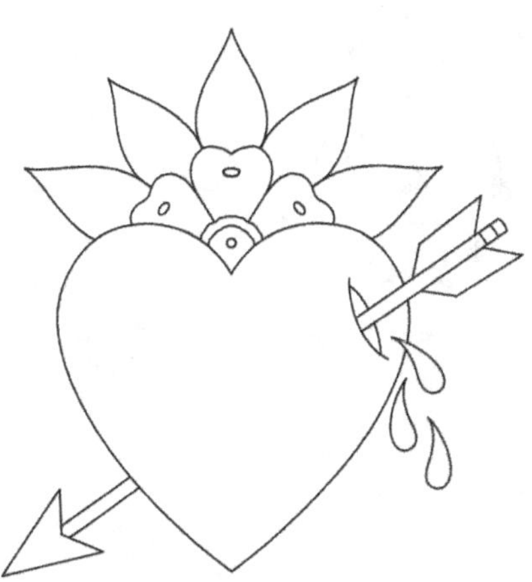

HOW TO DRAW TATTOO FLASH

HEART & BANNER

A heart and banner tattoo symbolises love, devotion, or remembrance, with the heart representing affection or passion and the banner often featuring a name or phrase to honour a loved one or a meaningful sentiment.

01   **02**   **03**

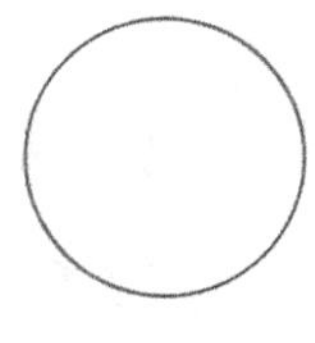

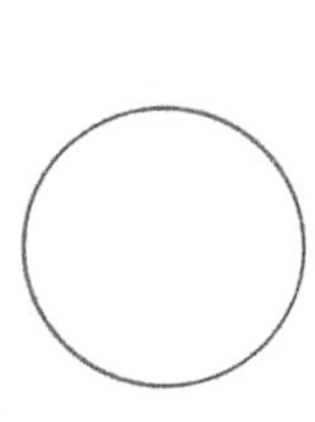

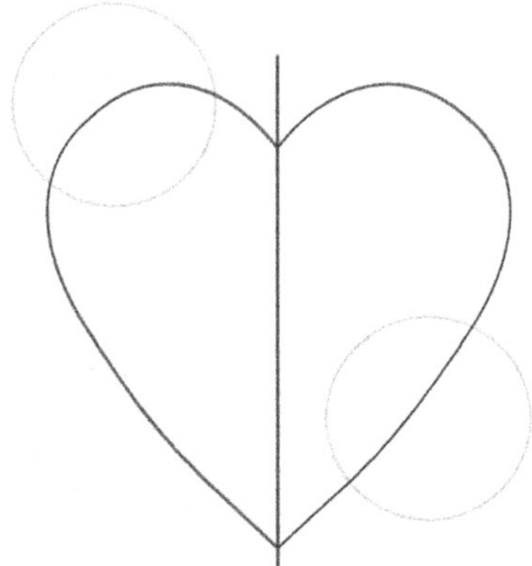

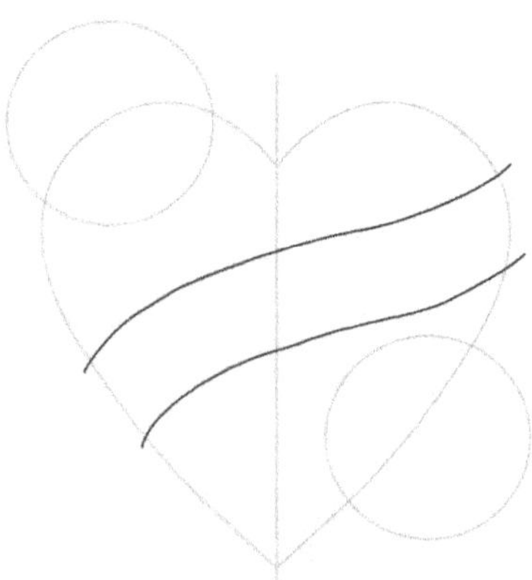

04

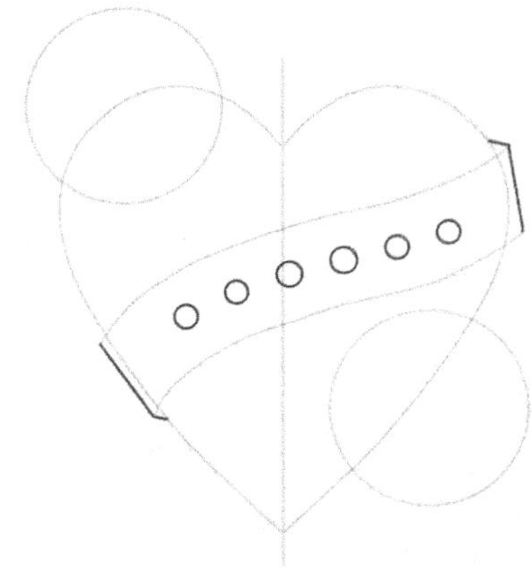

05

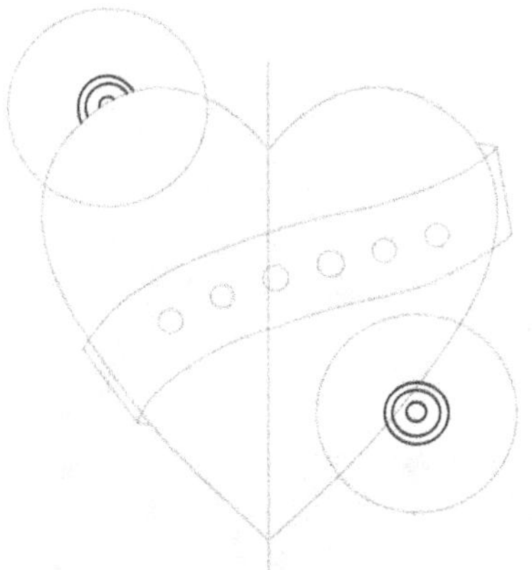

06

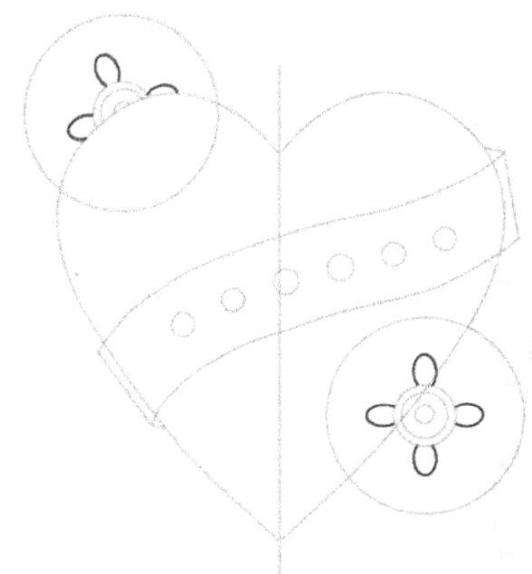

07

08

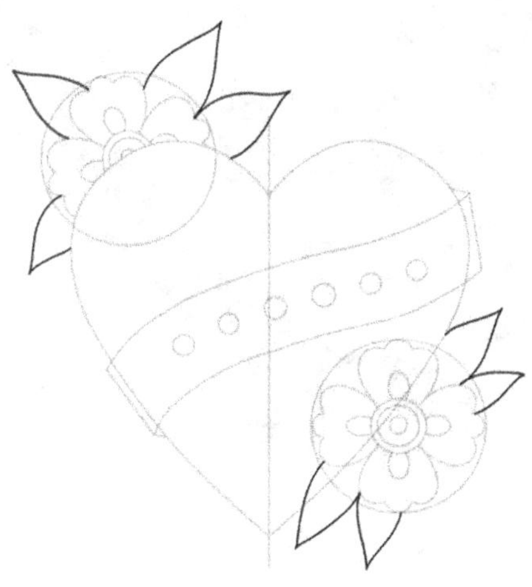

09

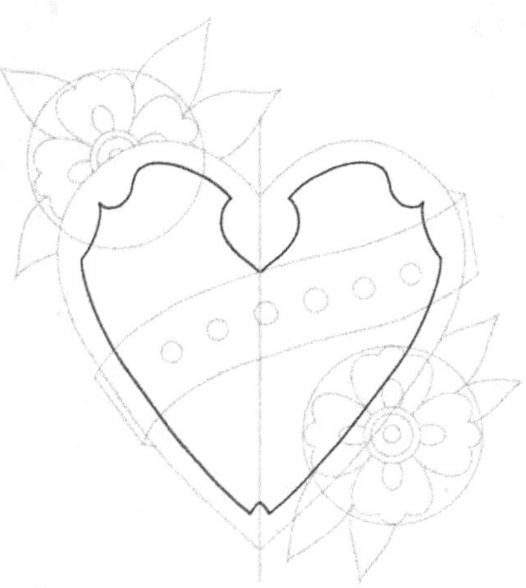

10

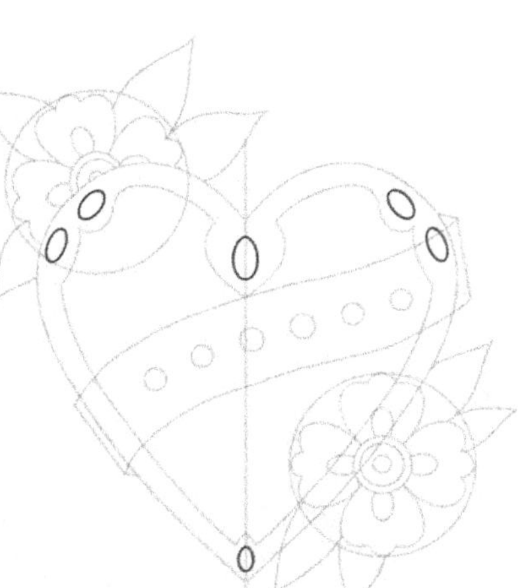

11

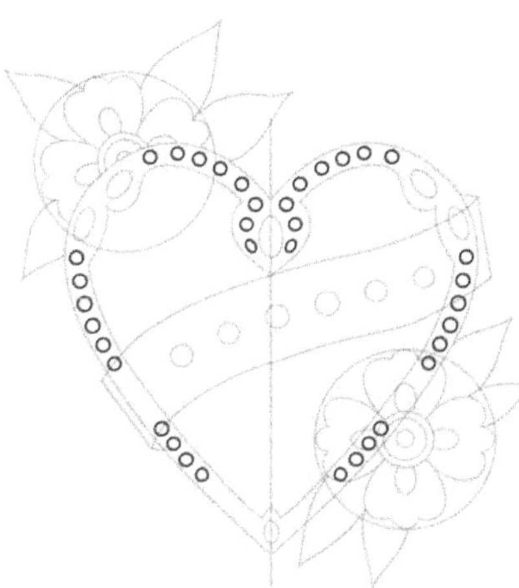

12

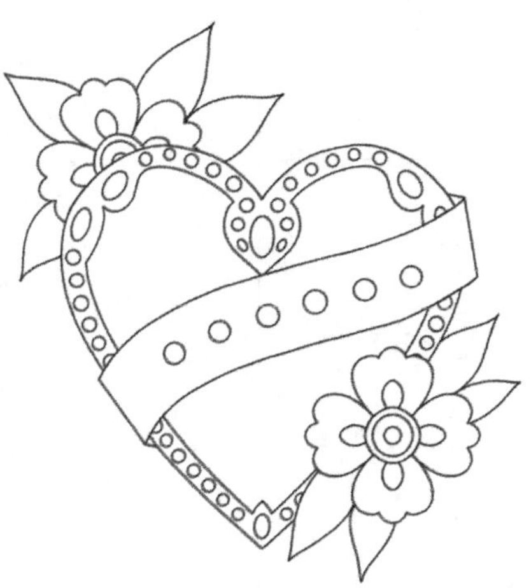

HOW TO DRAW TATTOO FLASH

VAULTEDITIONS.COM

HEART LOCKET

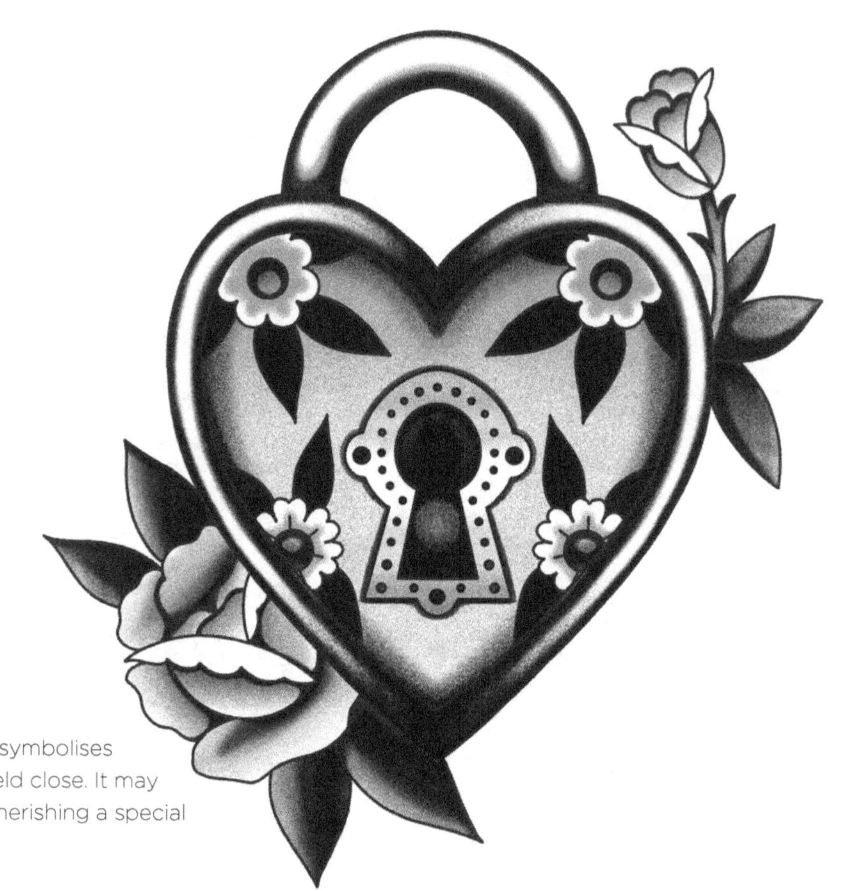

A heart locket tattoo symbolises love and memories held close. It may represent someone cherishing a special bond or relationship.

01   **02**   **03**

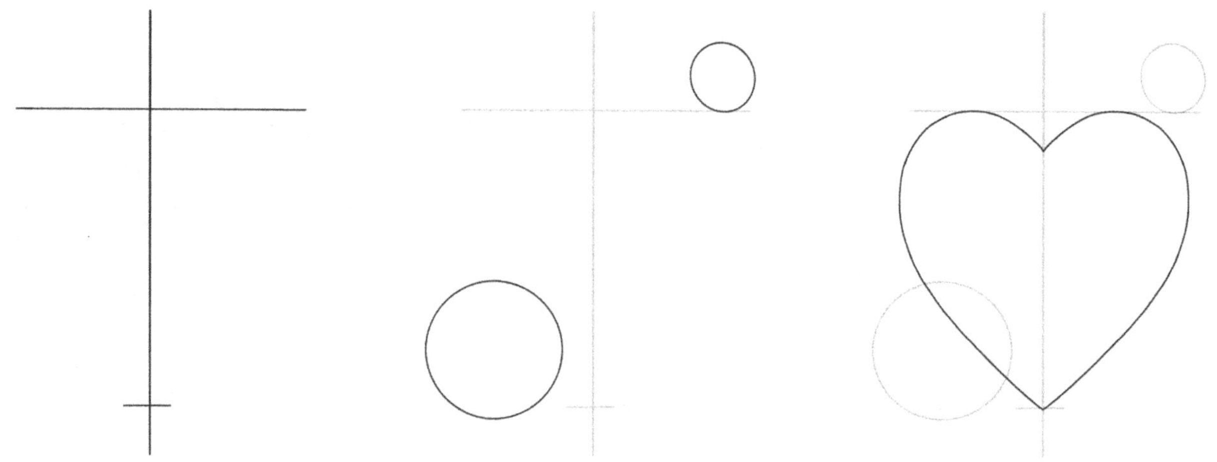

04

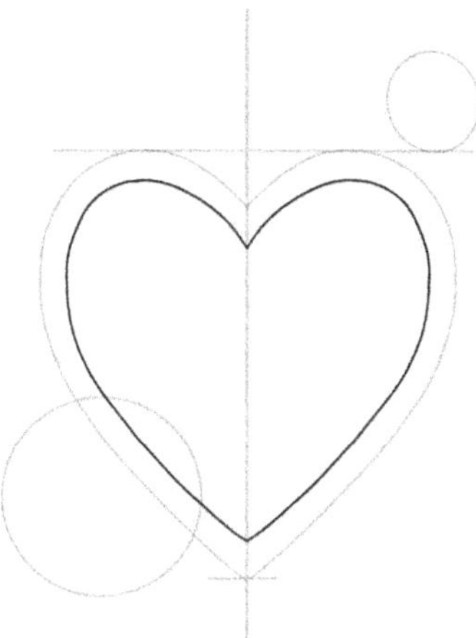

05

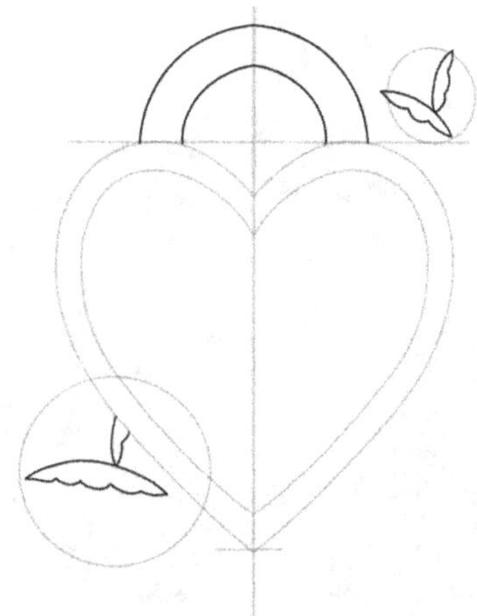

06

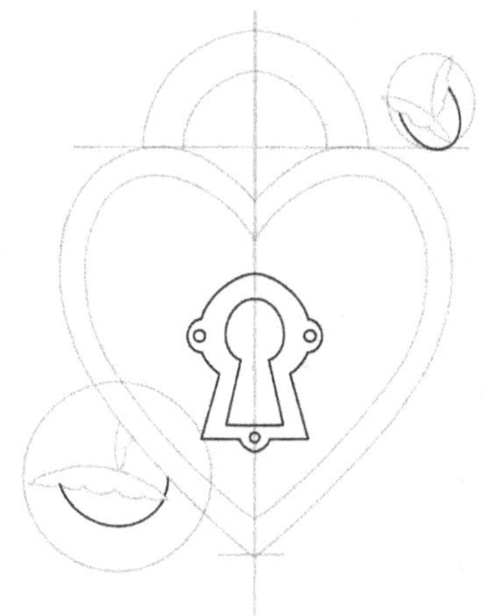

07

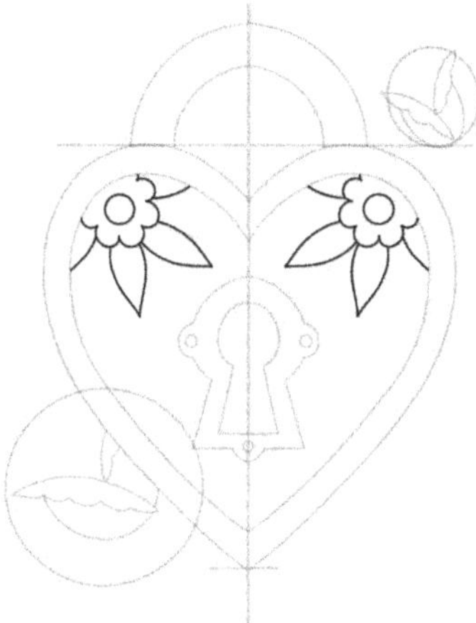

08

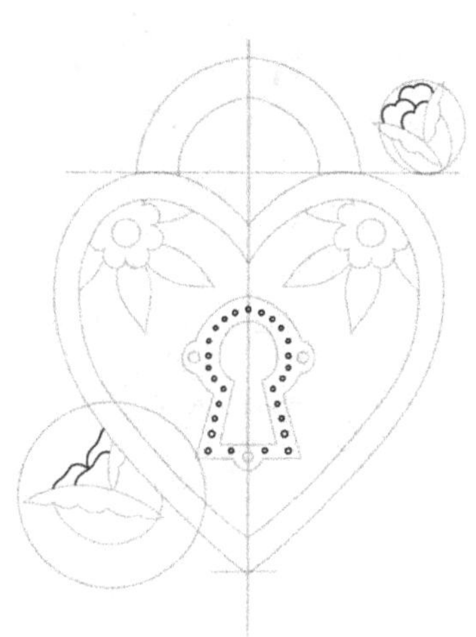

09

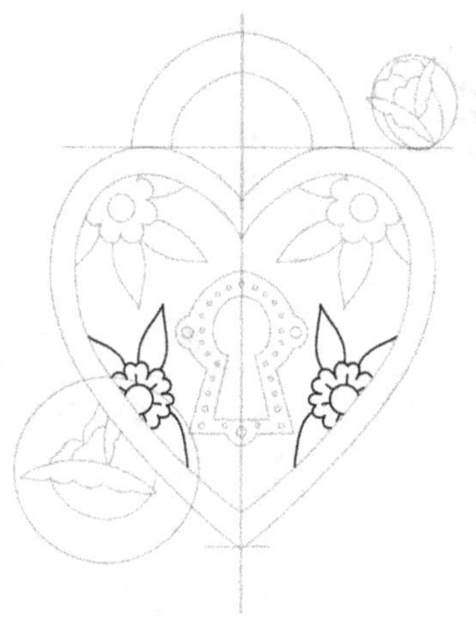

10

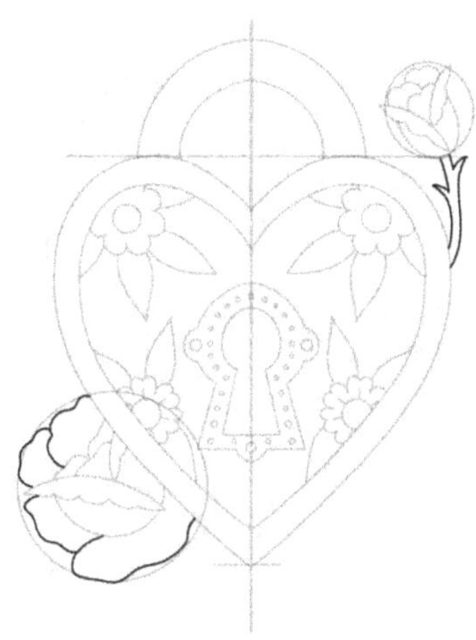

11

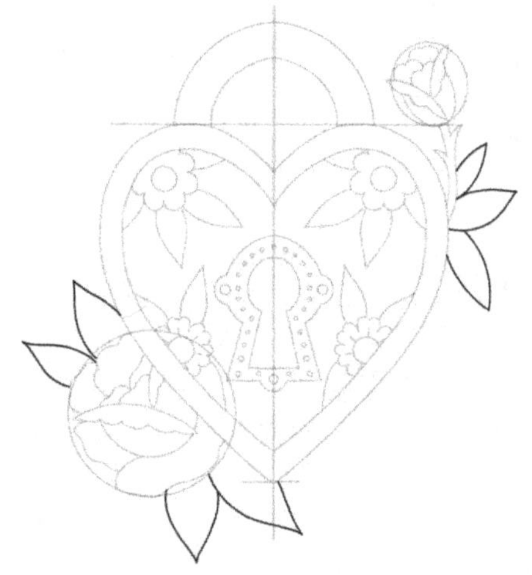

12

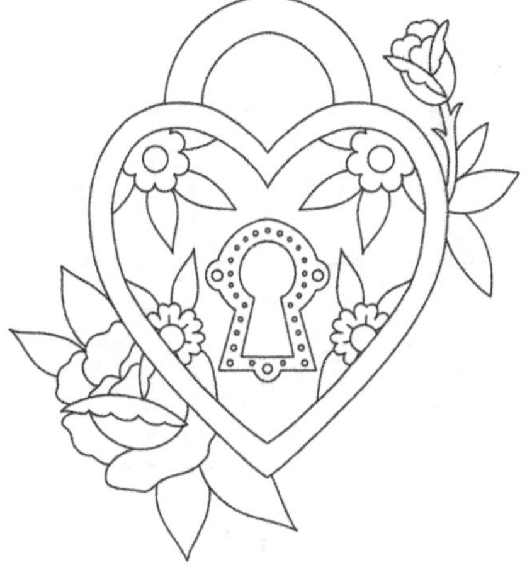

HOW TO DRAW TATTOO FLASH

HOT AIR BALLOON

The hot air balloon represents freedom, adventure, and a desire to rise above challenges. It can symbolise a dreamer's spirit or a journey toward self-discovery.

01

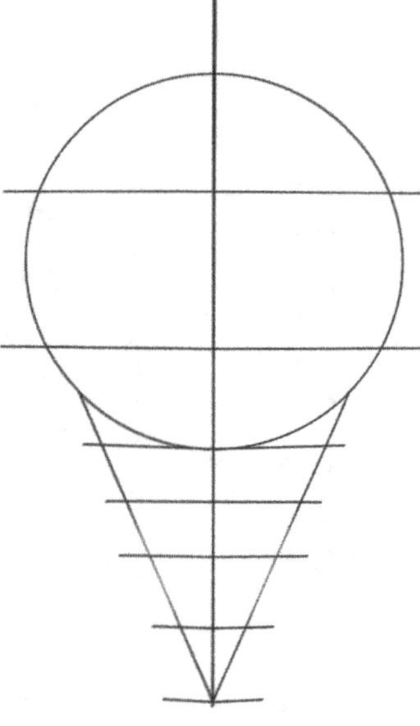

02

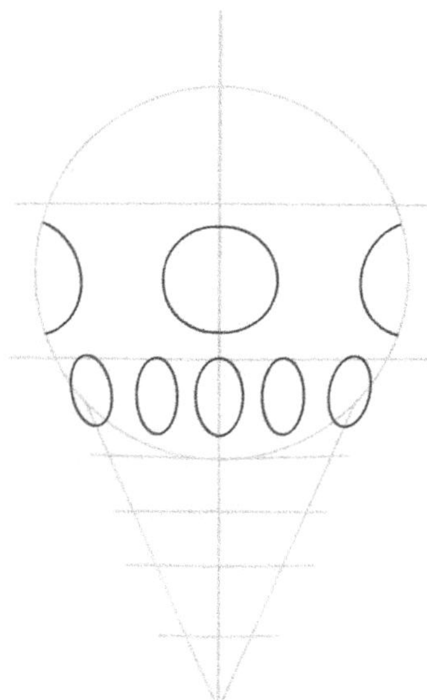

03

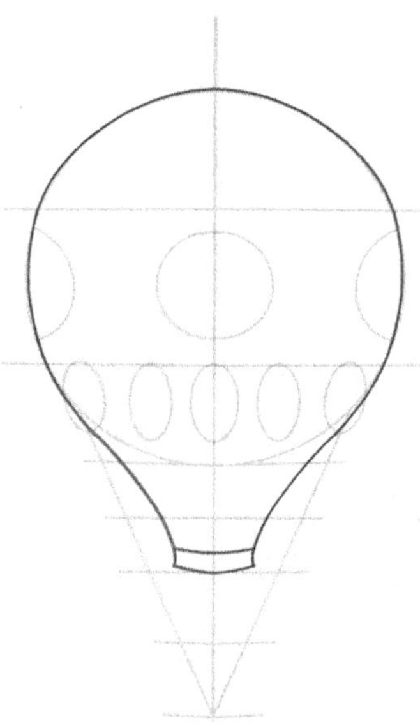

04

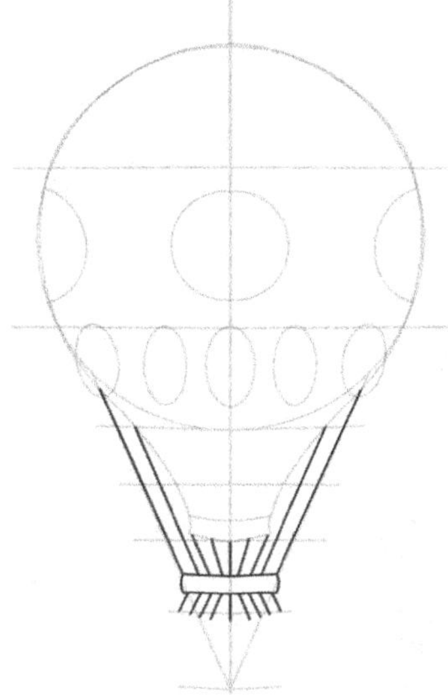

05

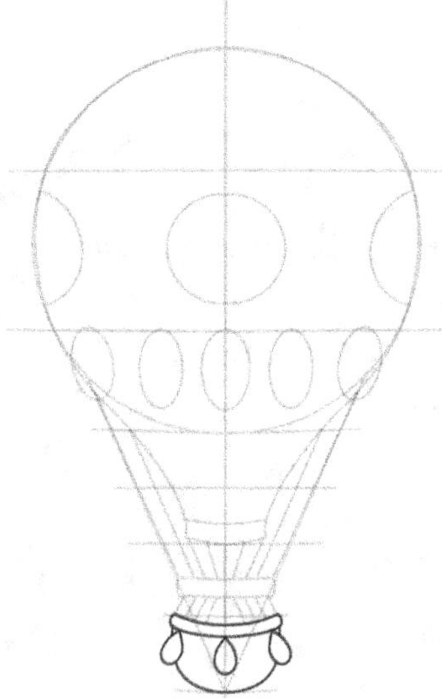

06

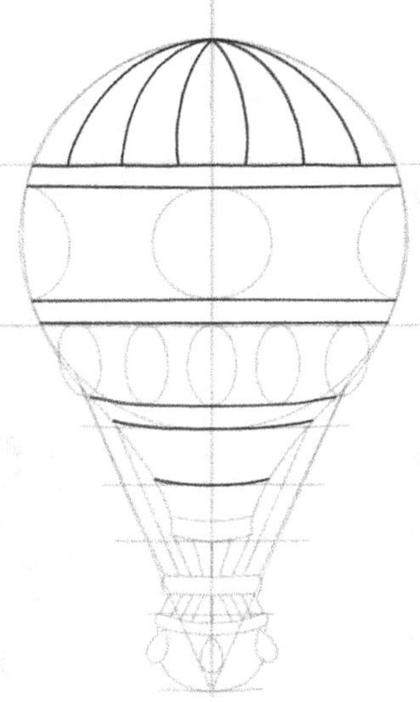

07

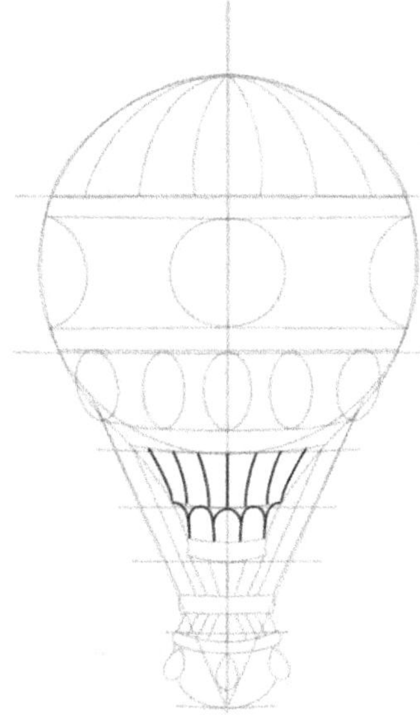

08

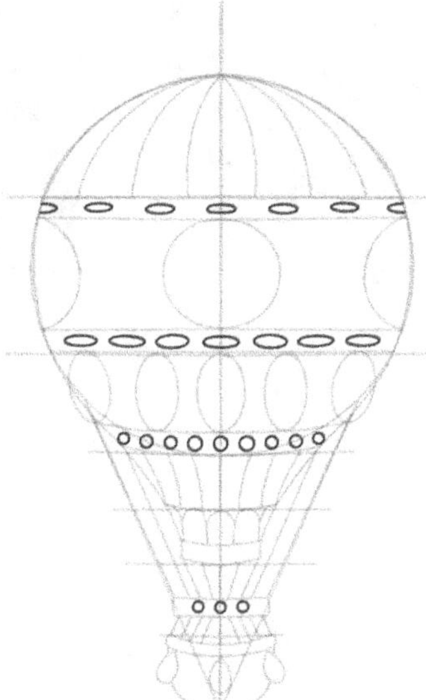

09

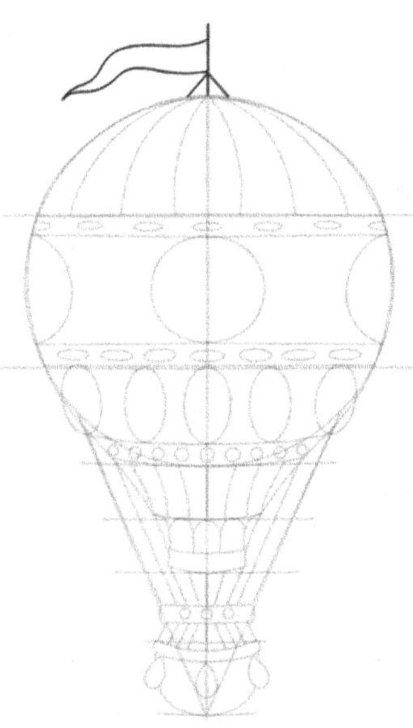

10

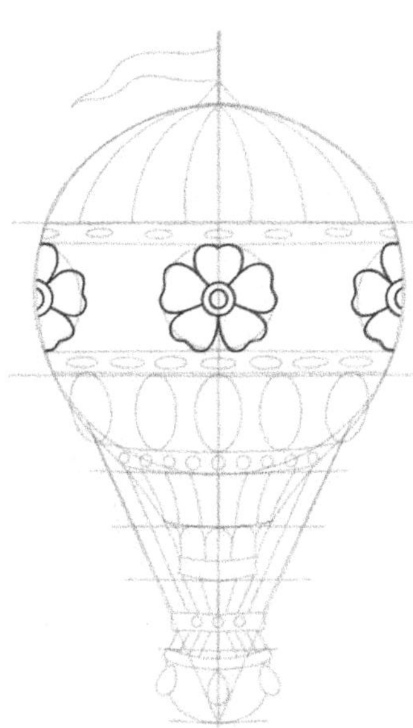

11

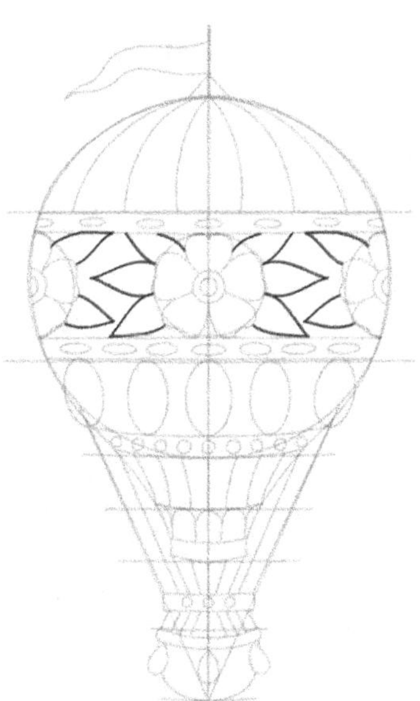

12

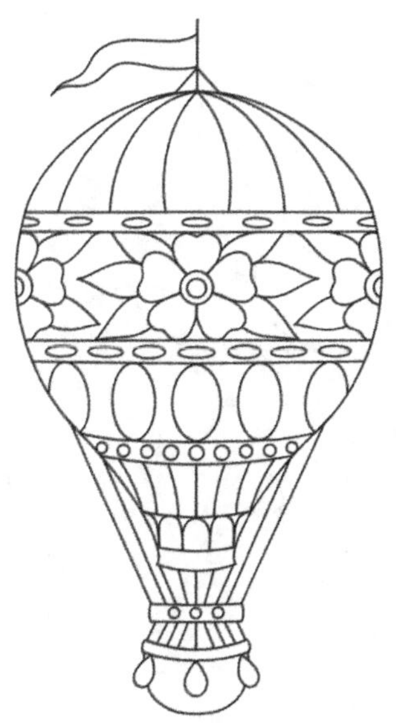

HOW TO DRAW TATTOO FLASH

PHARAOH'S HORSES

HOW TO DRAW TATTOO FLASH

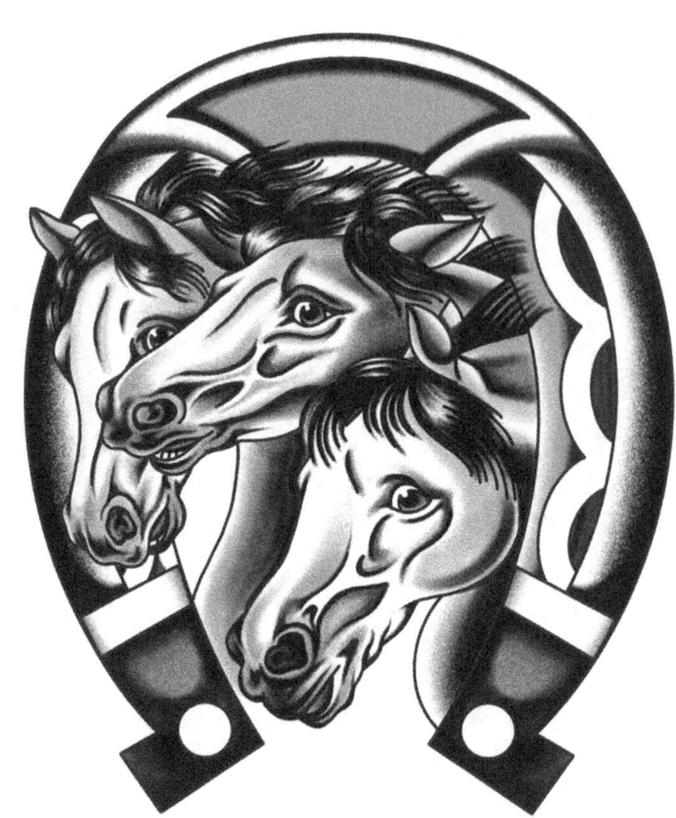

The pharaoh's horses tattoo symbolises power, nobility, and control, often representing someone's desire for strength and wisdom.

01

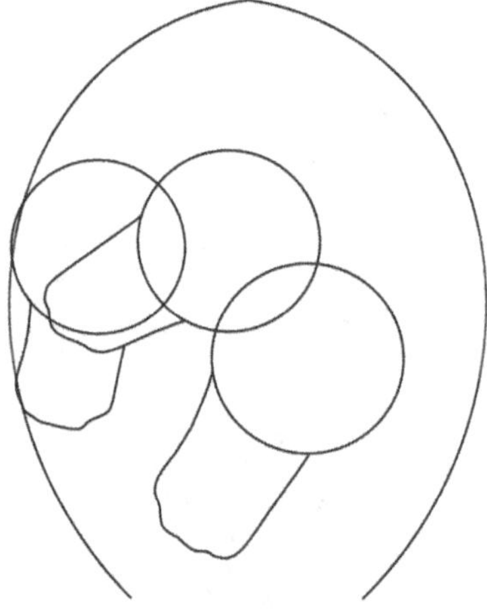

02

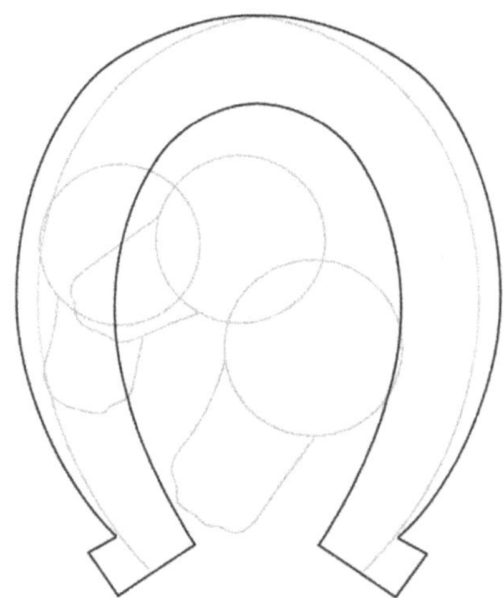

03

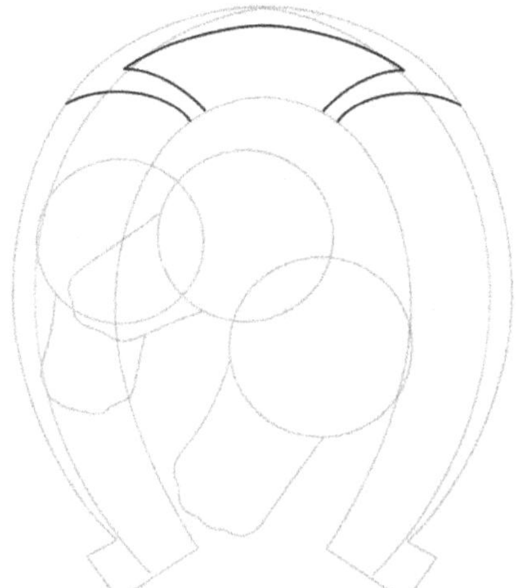

04

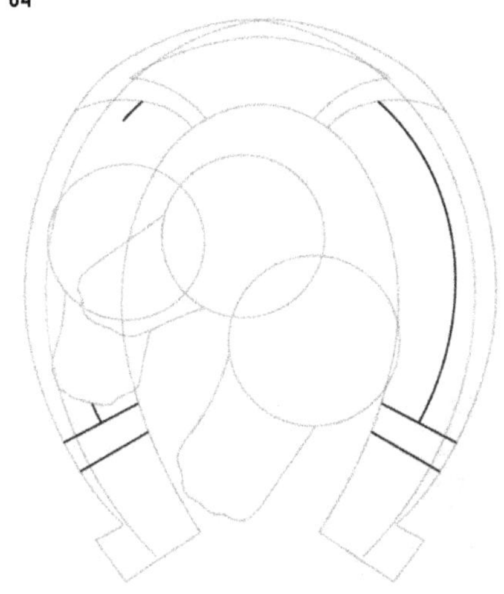

05

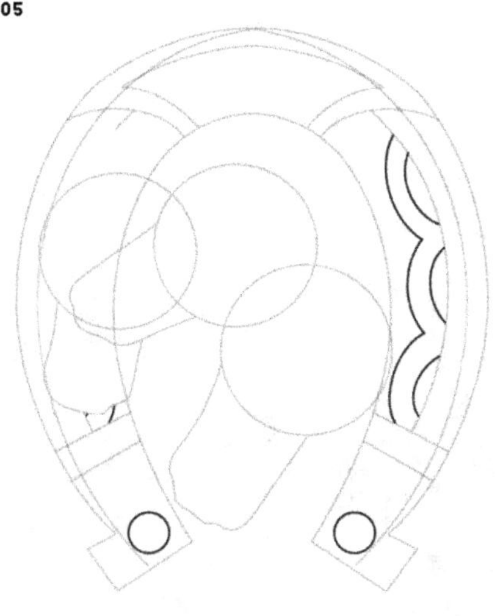

06

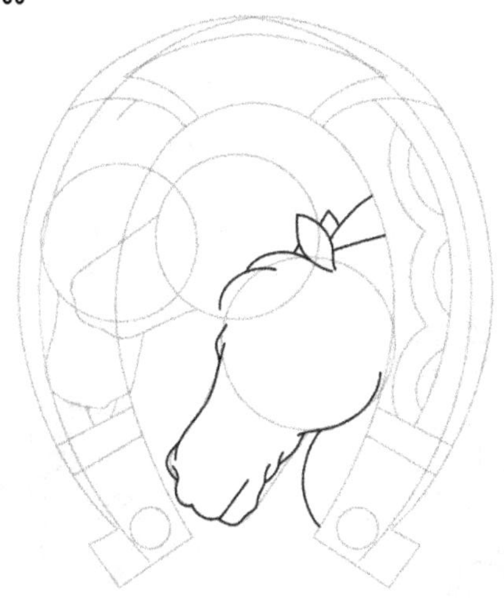

07

08

09

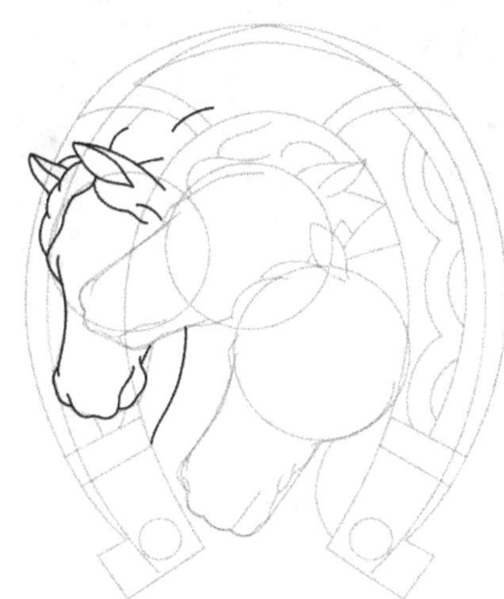

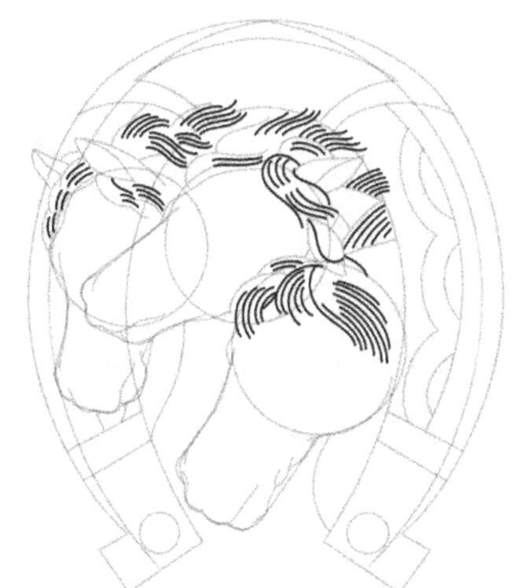

10

11

12

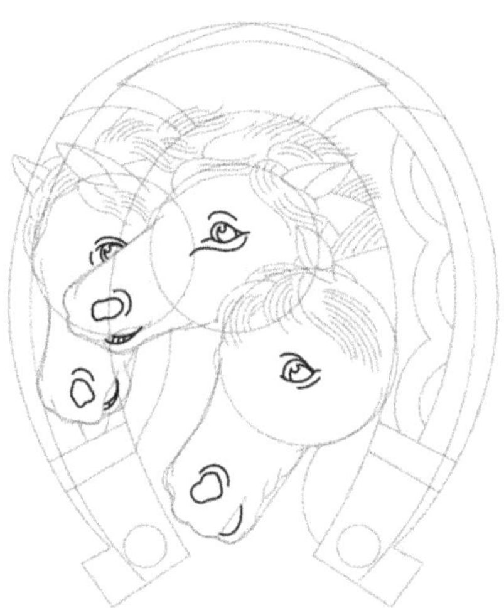

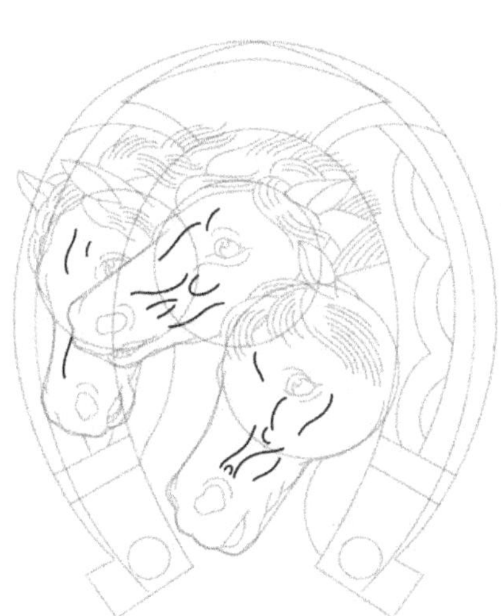

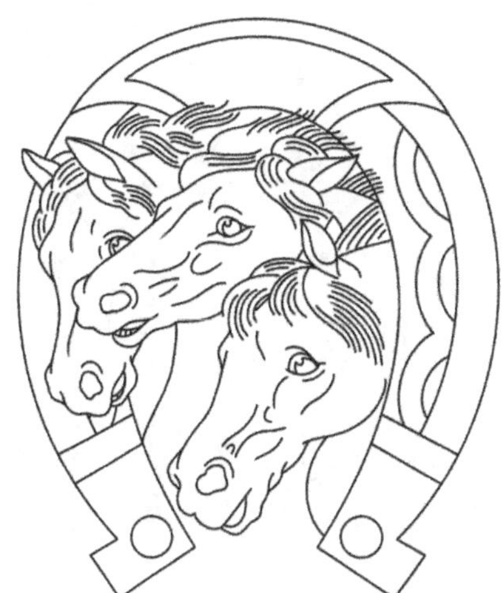

HOW TO DRAW TATTOO FLASH

HORSESHOE

A horseshoe tattoo is a classic symbol of luck and protection. Those who want to invite good fortune into their lives often choose it.

01

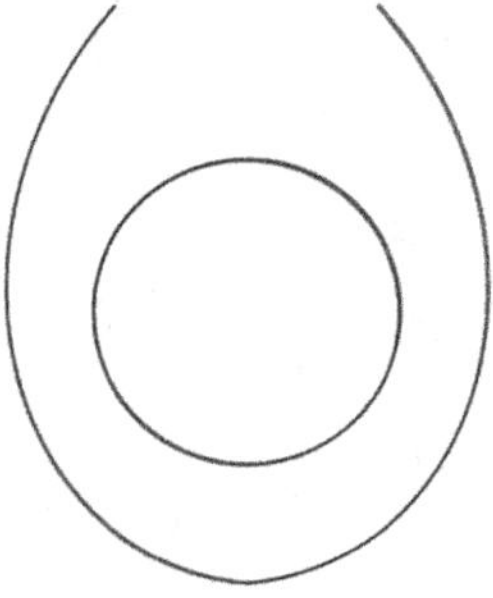

02

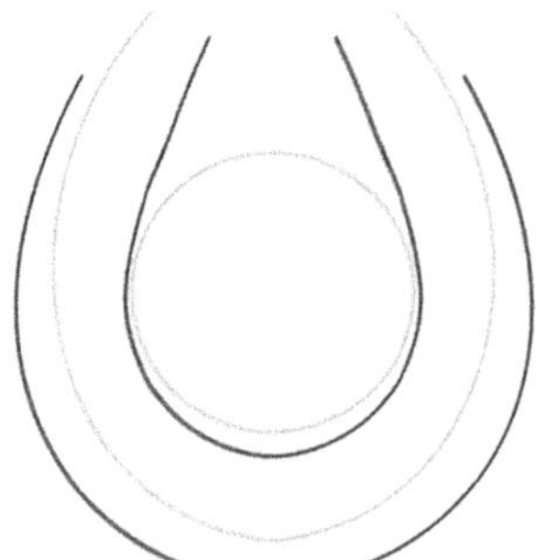

03

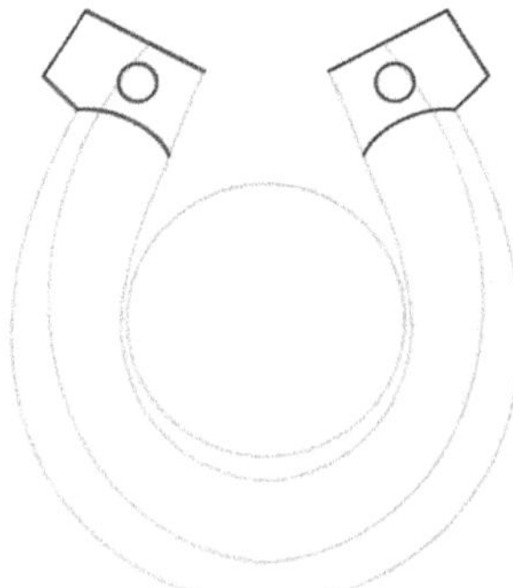

04

05

06

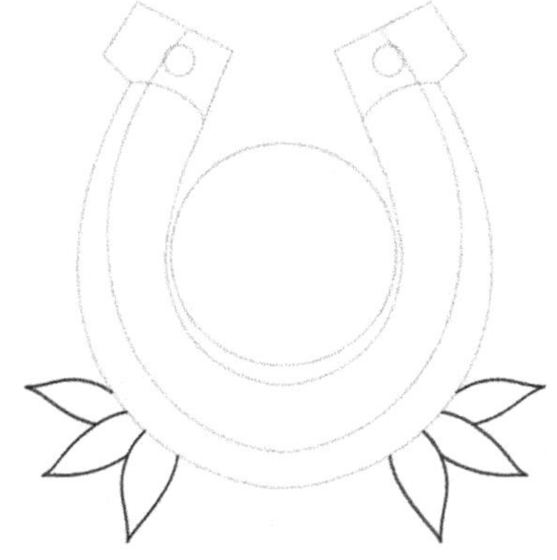

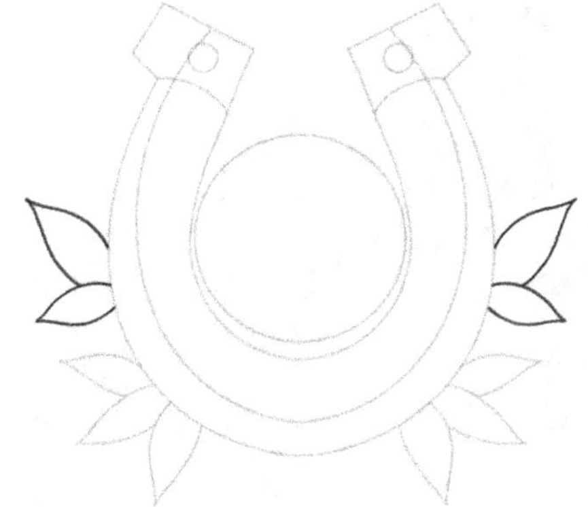

07

08

09

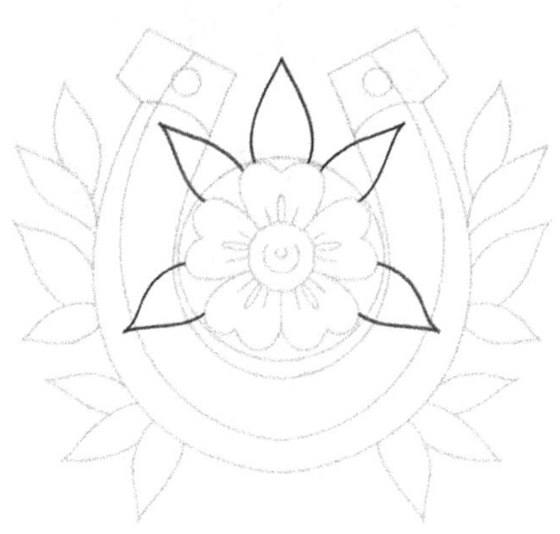

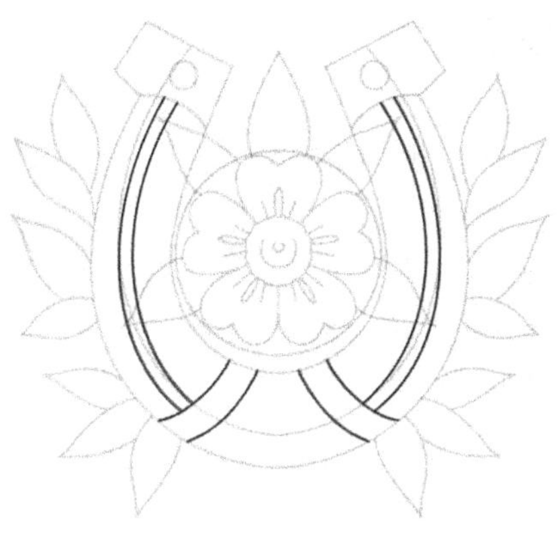

10

11

12

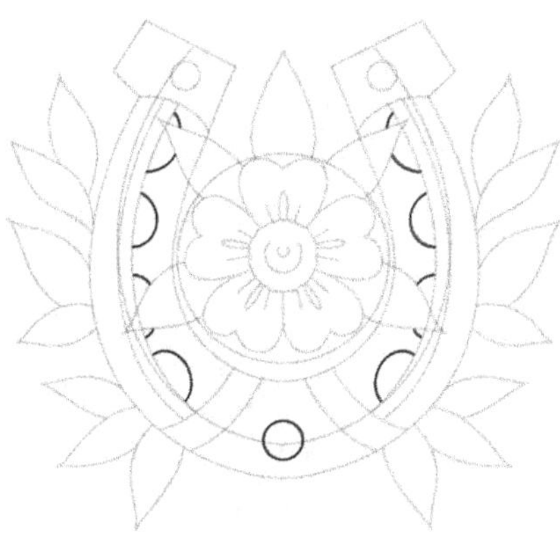

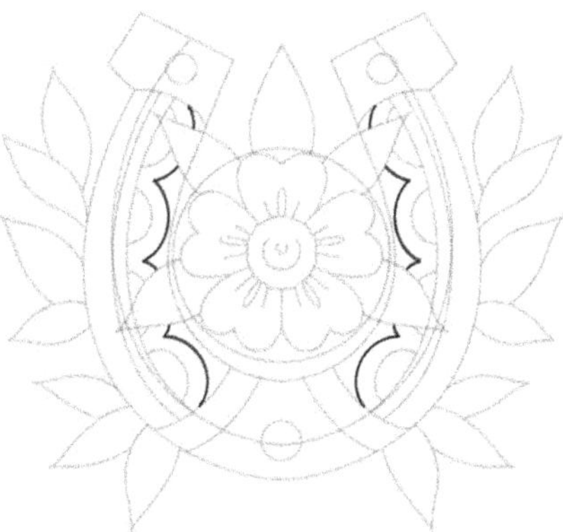

HOW TO DRAW TATTOO FLASH

BUTTERFLY LADY

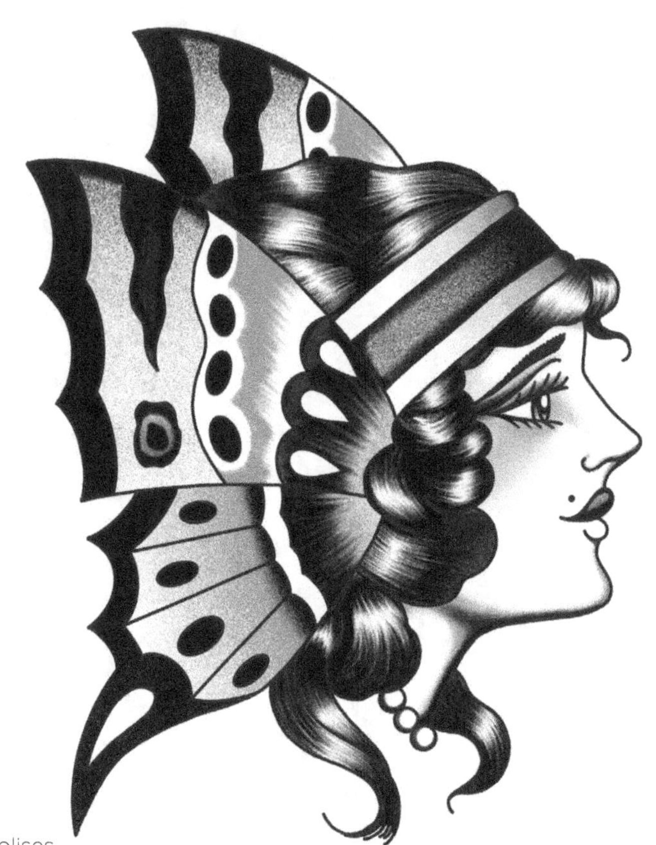

The butterfly lady tattoo symbolises transformation, beauty, grace and feminine strength.

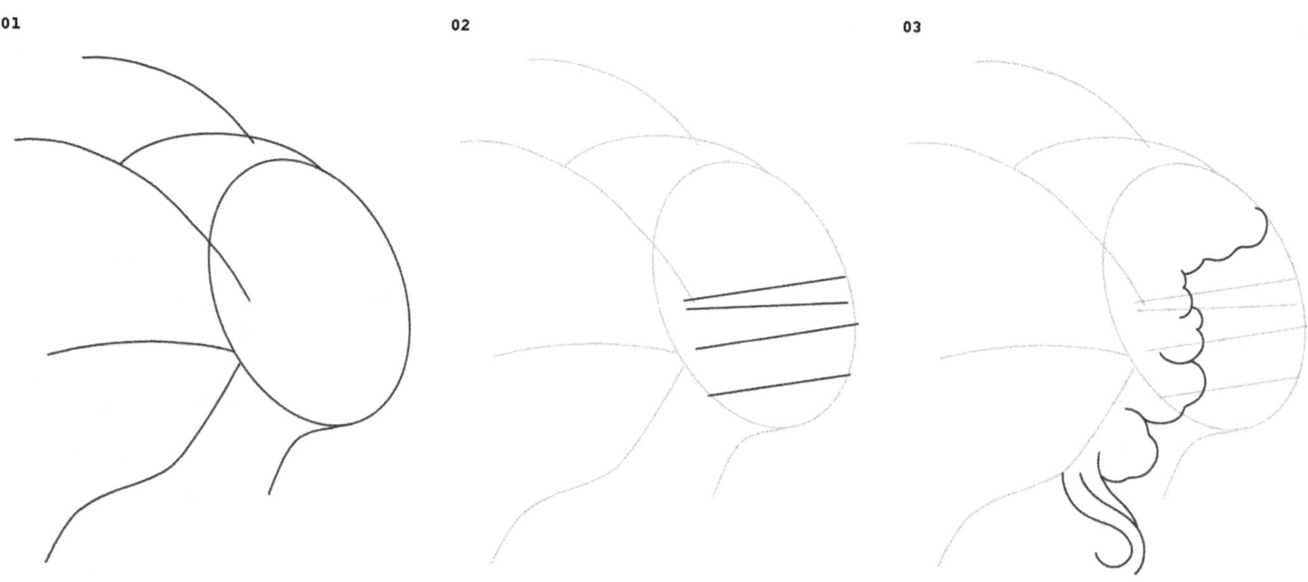

01

02

03

04

05

06

07

08

09

10

11

12

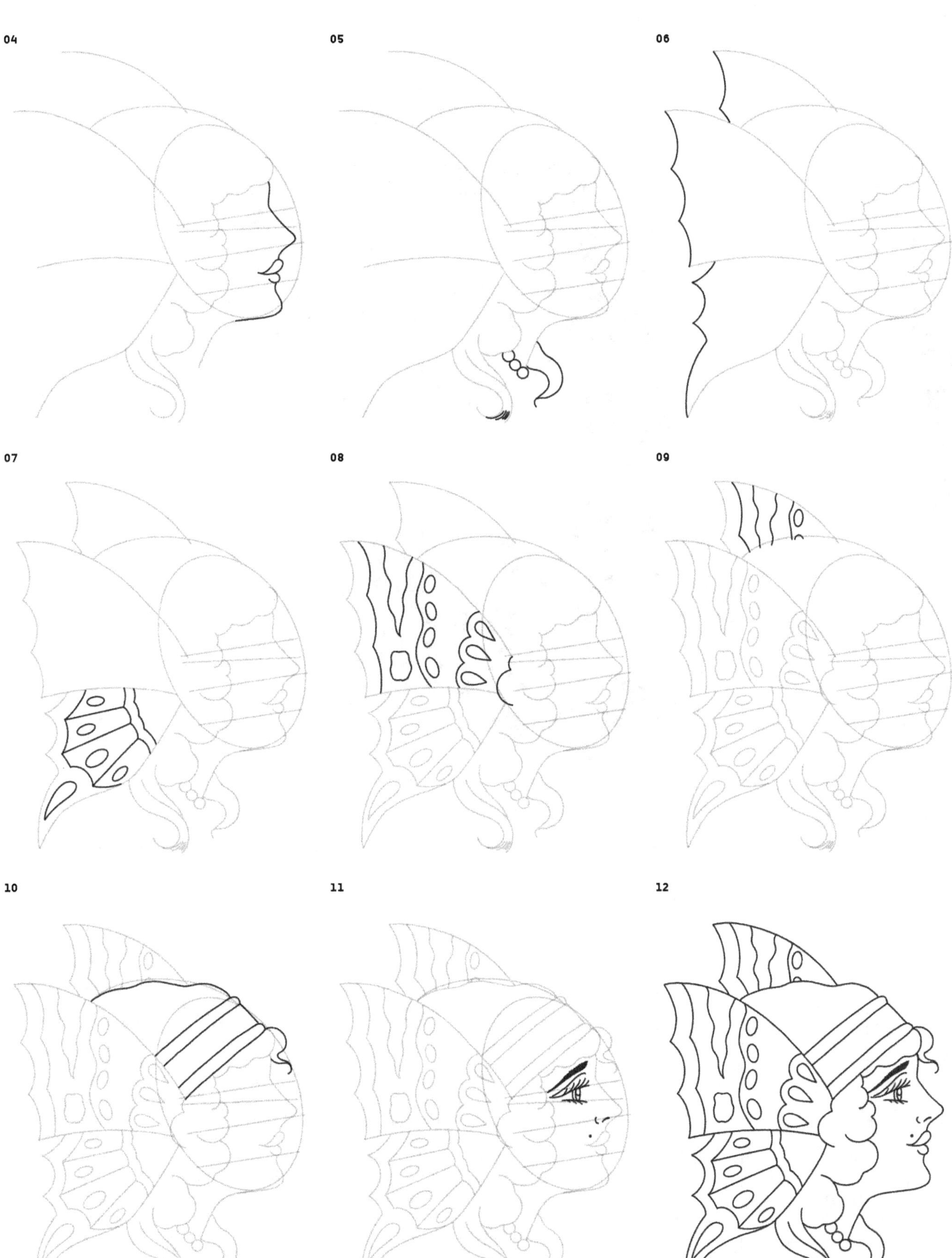

HOW TO DRAW TATTOO FLASH

HOURGLASS

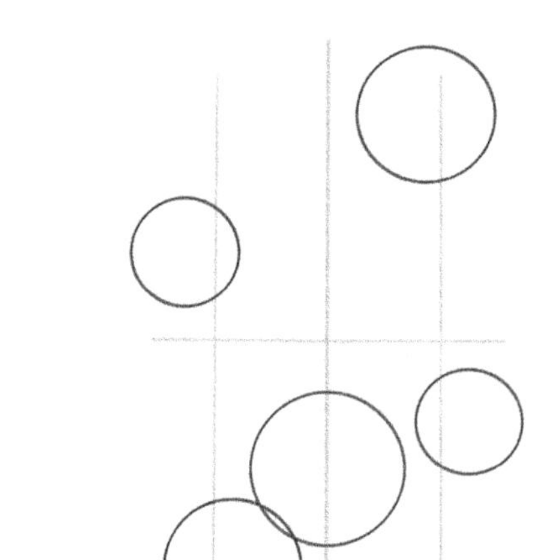

The hourglass represents the passage of time and the finite nature of life. It's often chosen as a reminder to make the most of the present, symbolising mortality, urgency, and the inevitable flow of time.

01   **02**   **03**

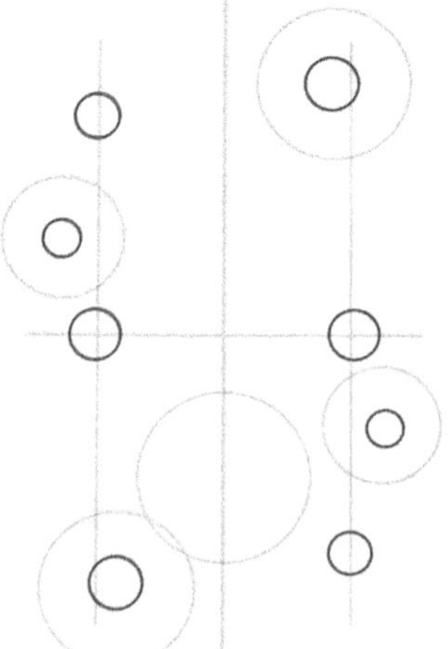

04

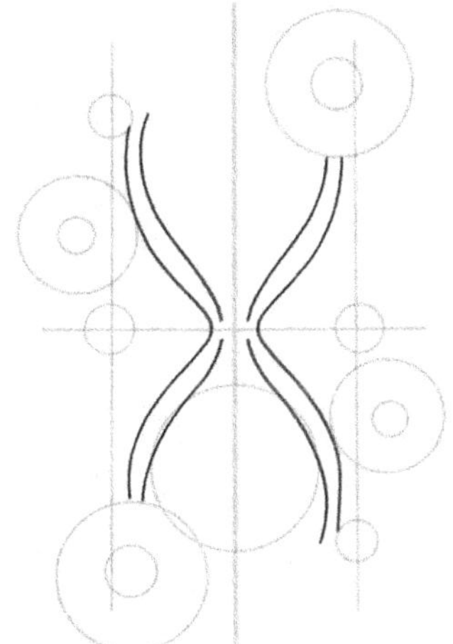

05

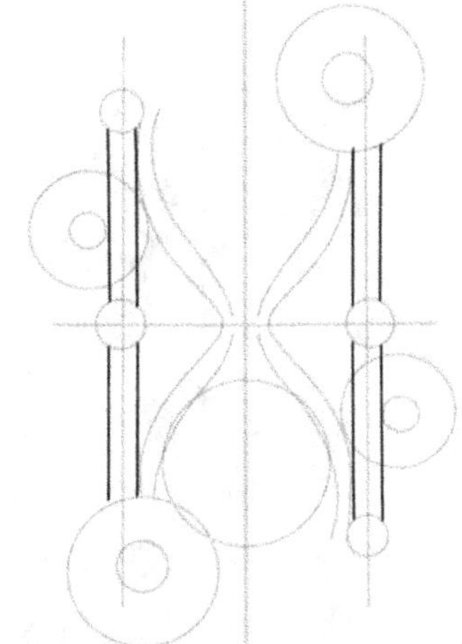

06

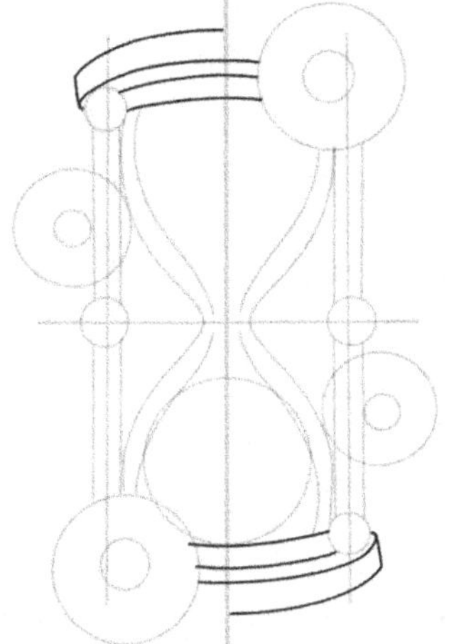

07

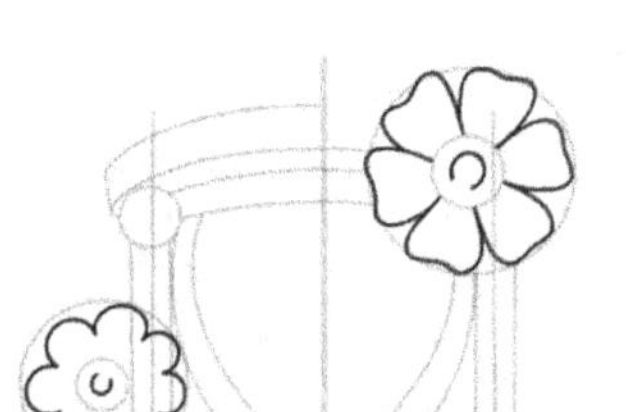

08

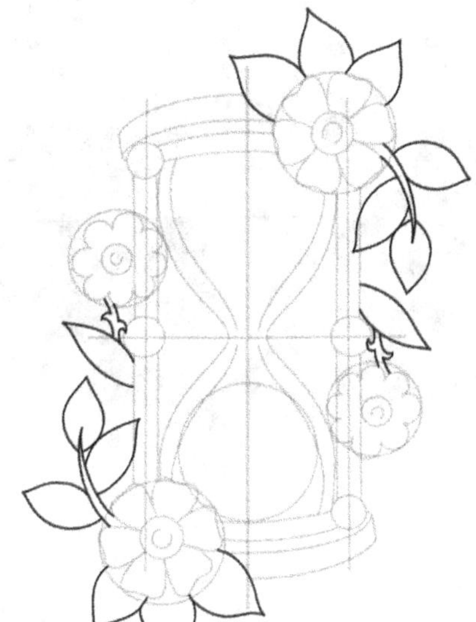

09

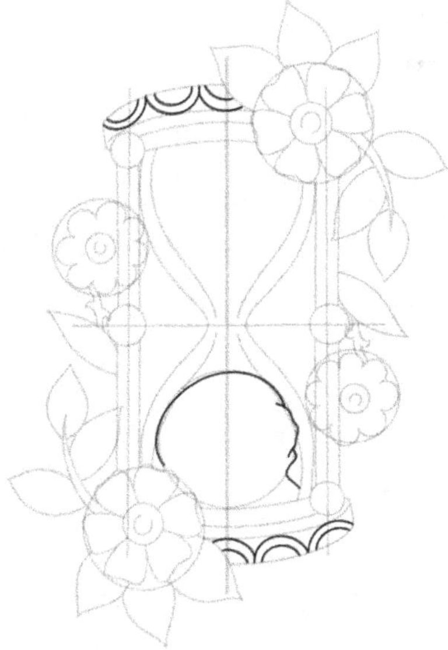

10

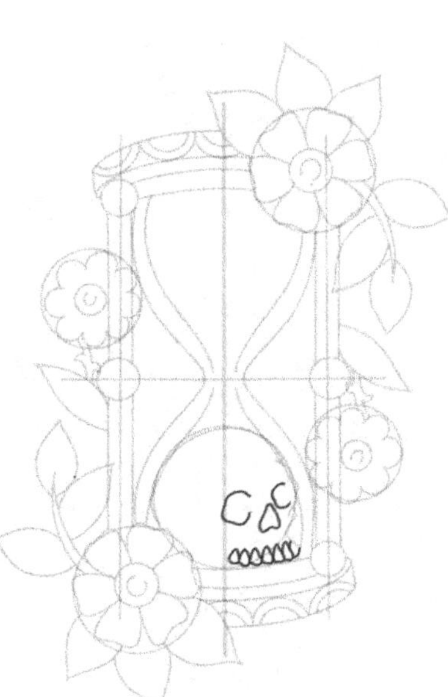

11

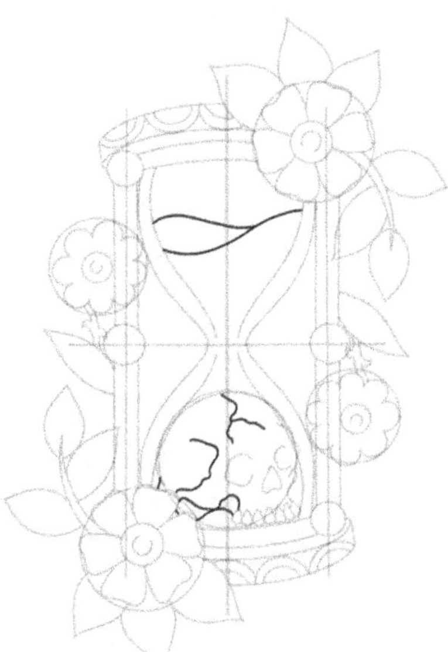

12

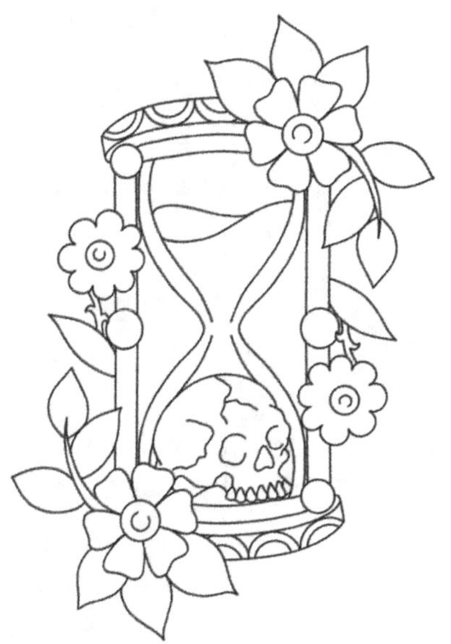

HOW TO DRAW TATTOO FLASH

LIGHTHOUSE

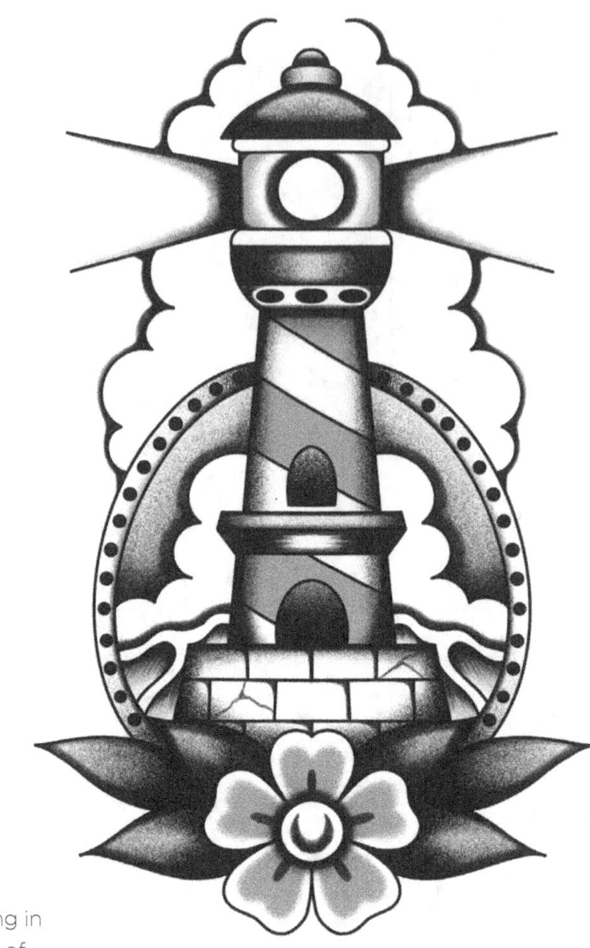

A lighthouse tattoo commonly symbolises guidance, safety, and hope. It's a reminder to stay strong in turbulent times and be a beacon of light for others.

01

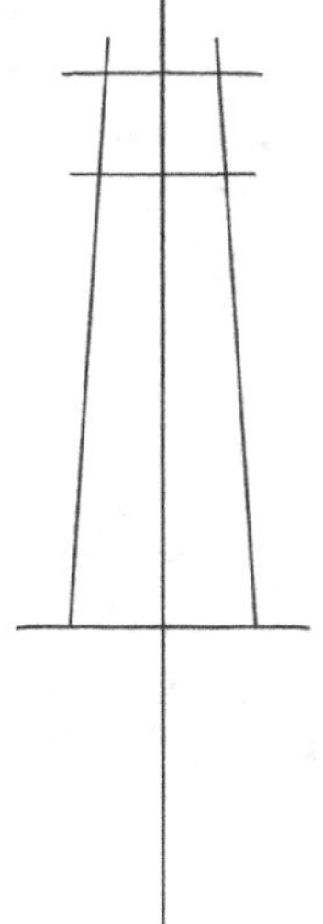

02

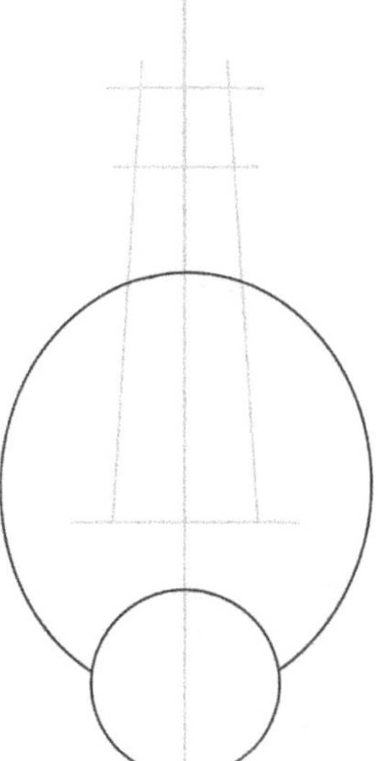

03

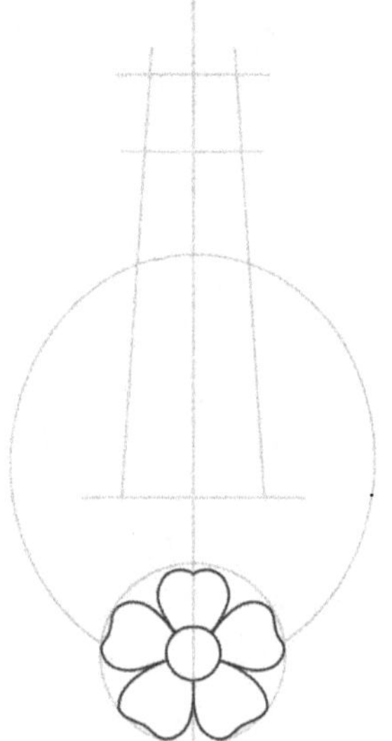

04

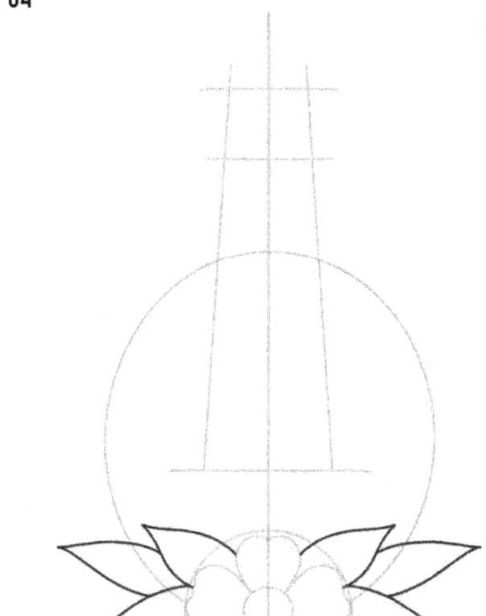

05

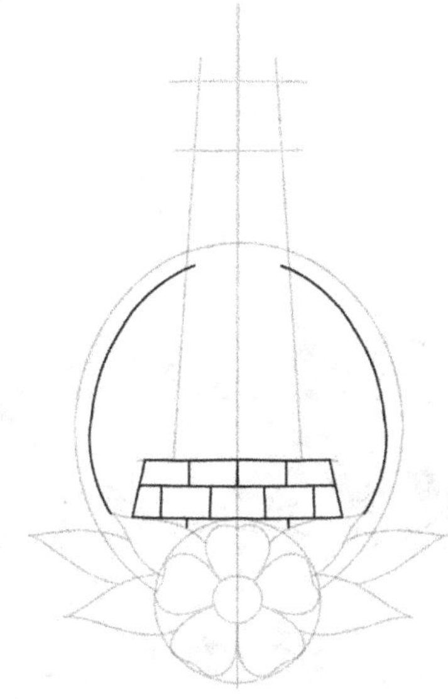

06

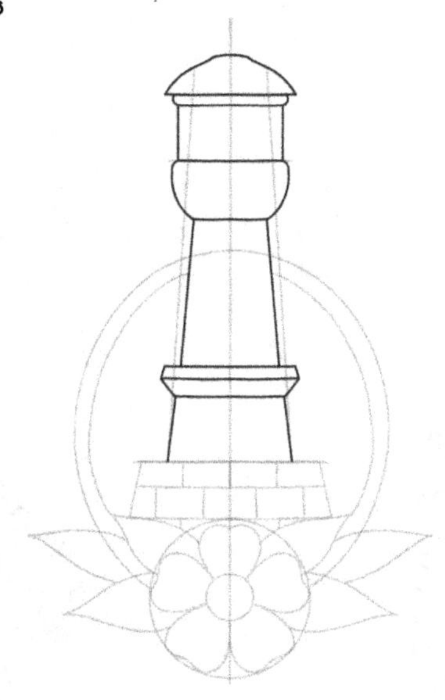

07

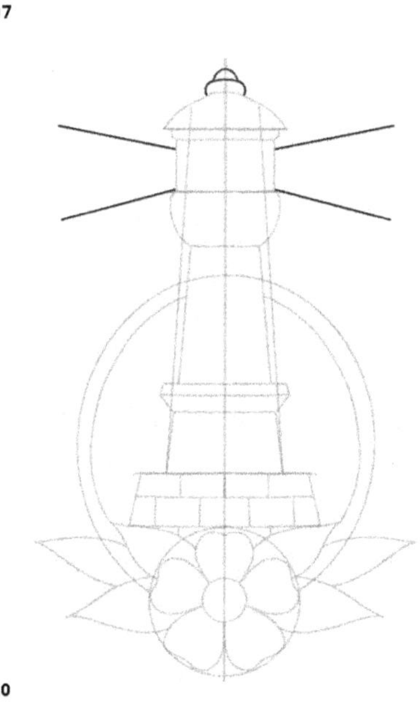

08

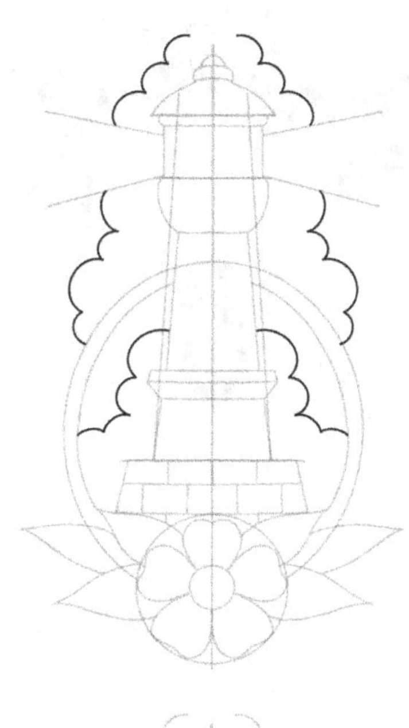

09

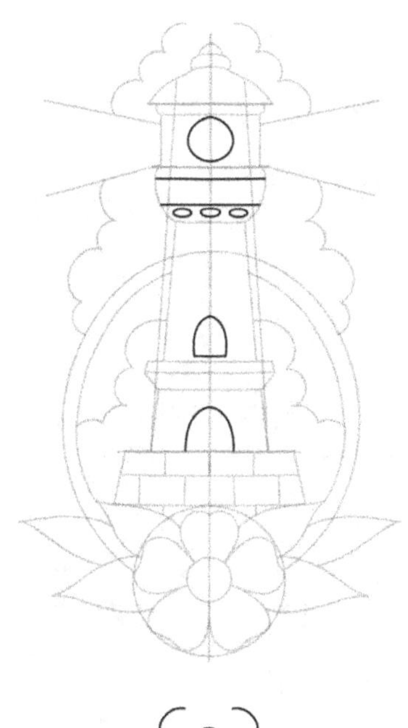

10

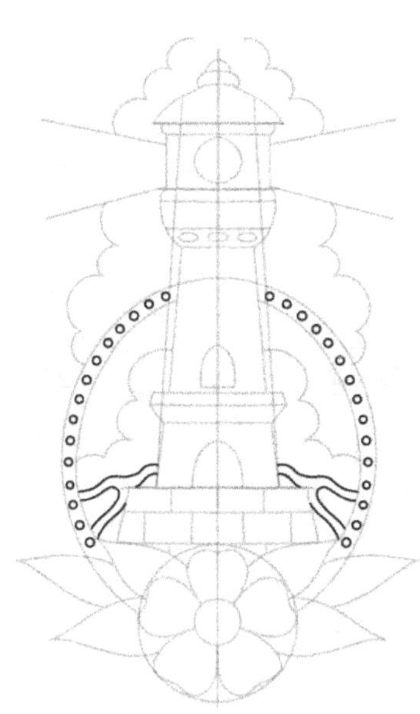

11

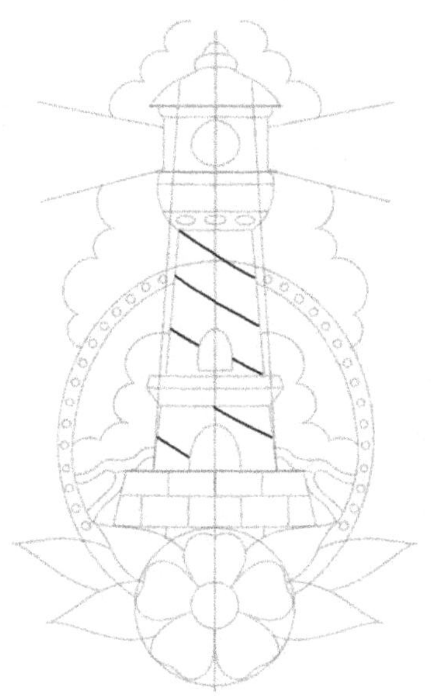

12

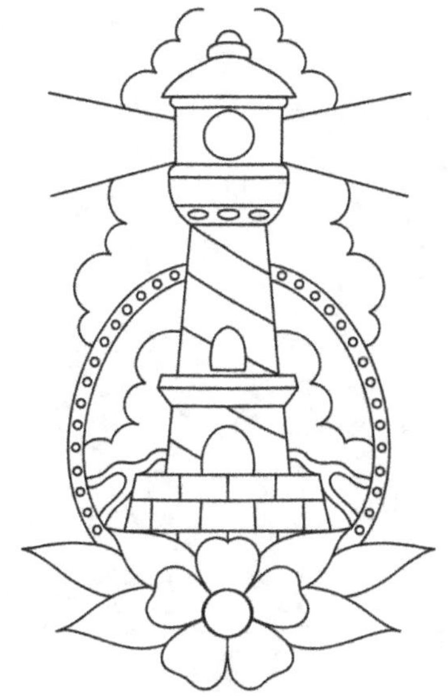

FANGS

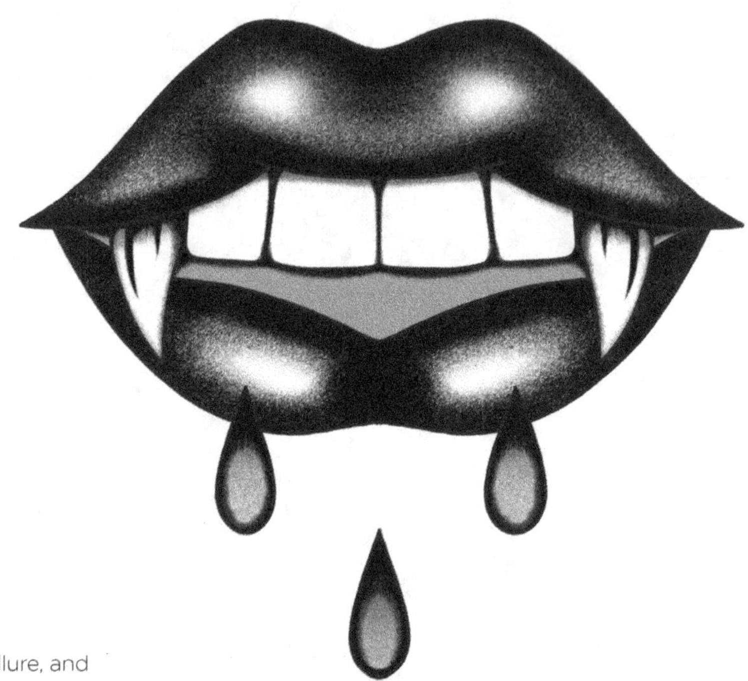

Fangs represent danger, allure, and mystery. This tattoo might appeal to someone drawn to the darker side of life or who embraces their wild, untamed nature.

01   **02**   **03**

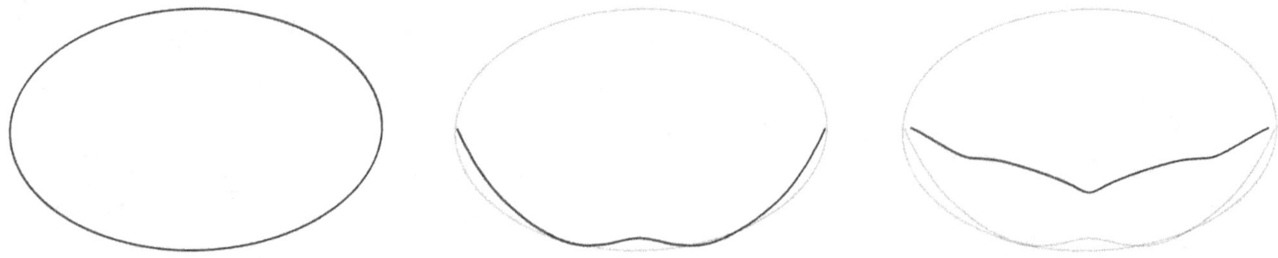

04

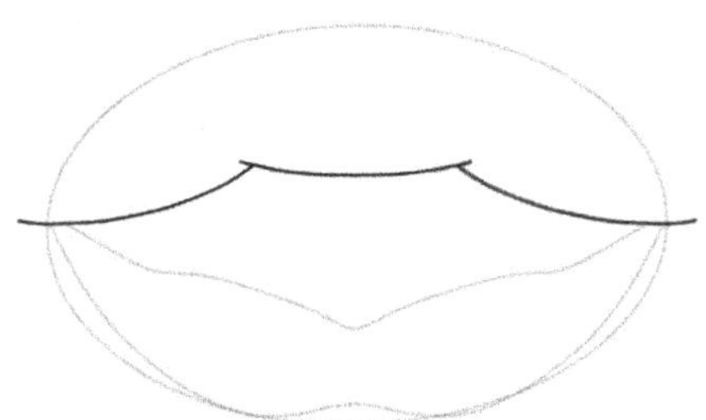

05

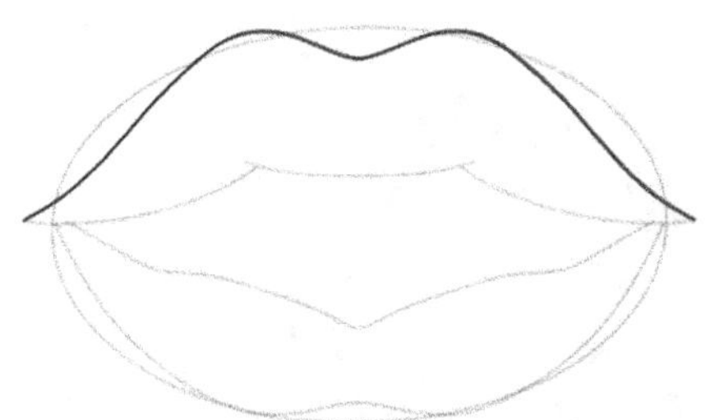

06

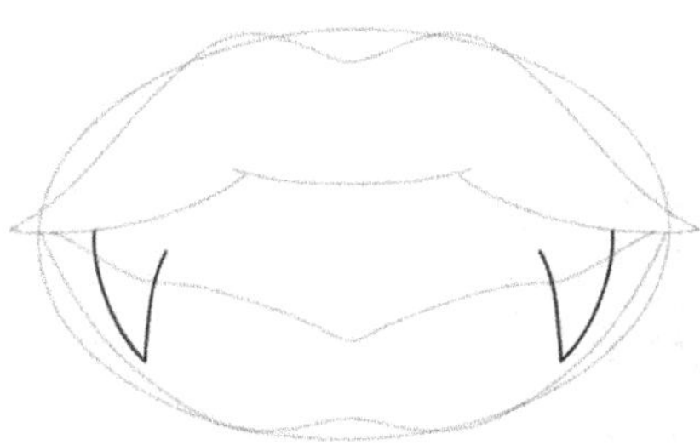

07

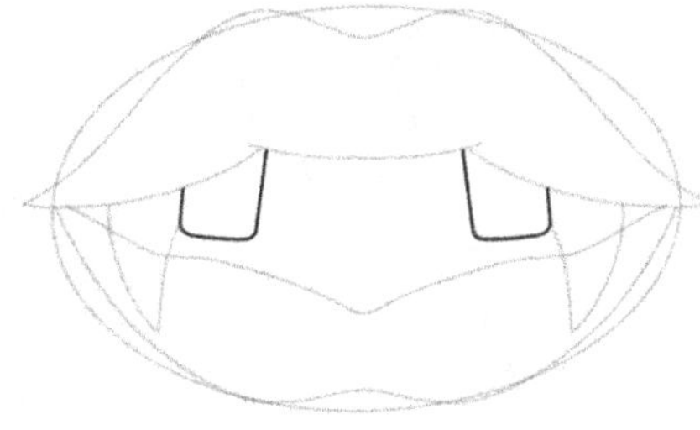

08

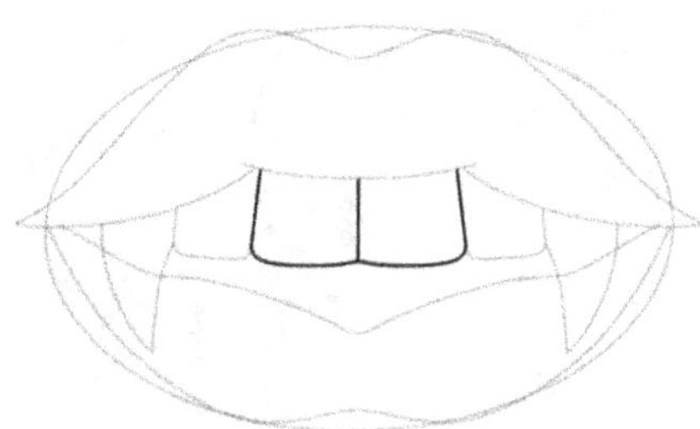

09

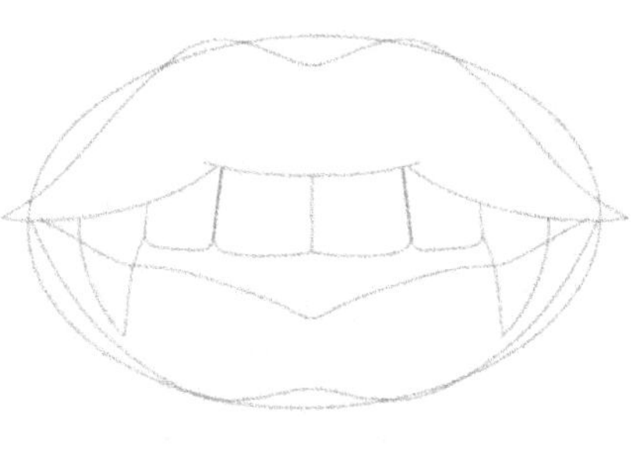

HOW TO DRAW TATTOO FLASH

10

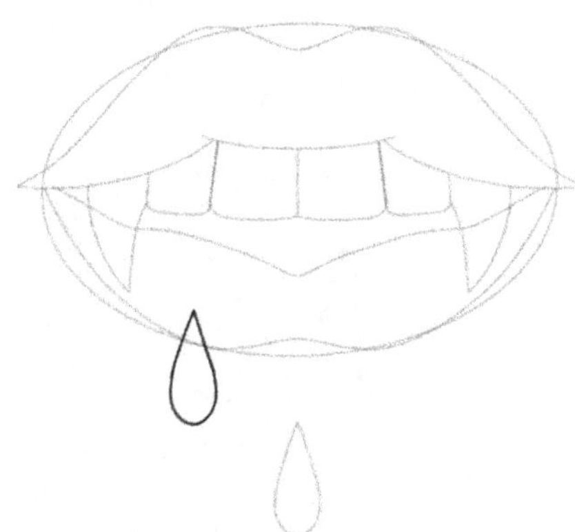

11

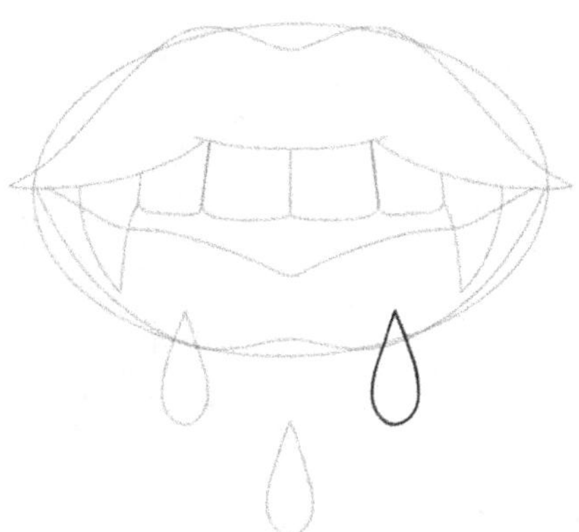

12

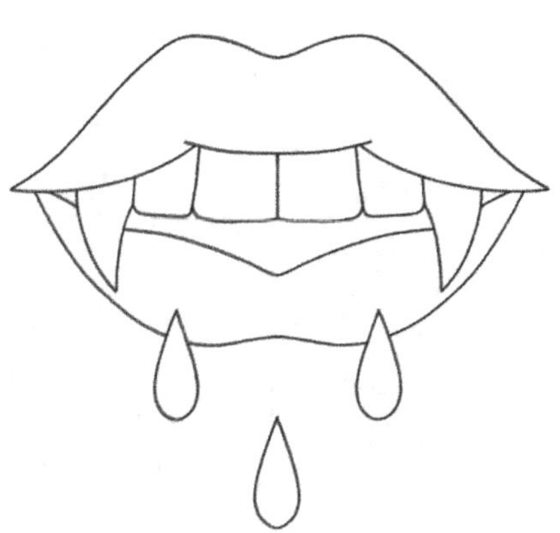

RABBIT'S FOOT

HOW TO DRAW TATTOO FLASH

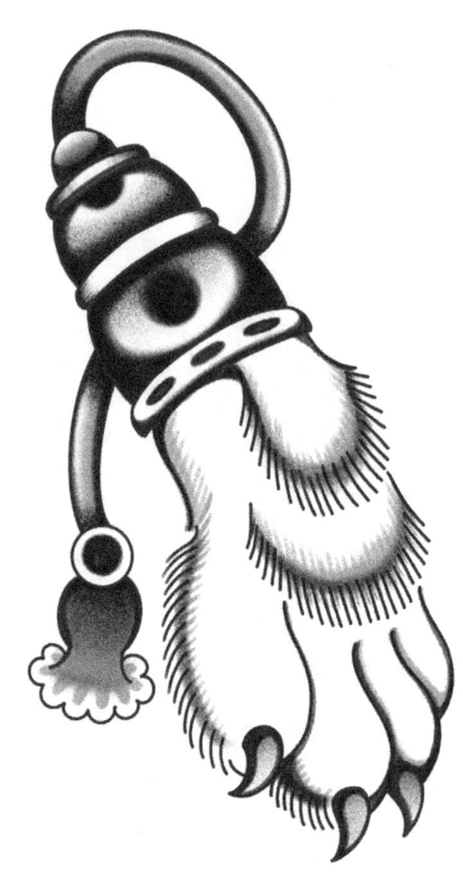

A rabbit's foot symbolises luck and protection. This tattoo is for those who want to carry a charm for good fortune wherever they go.

01

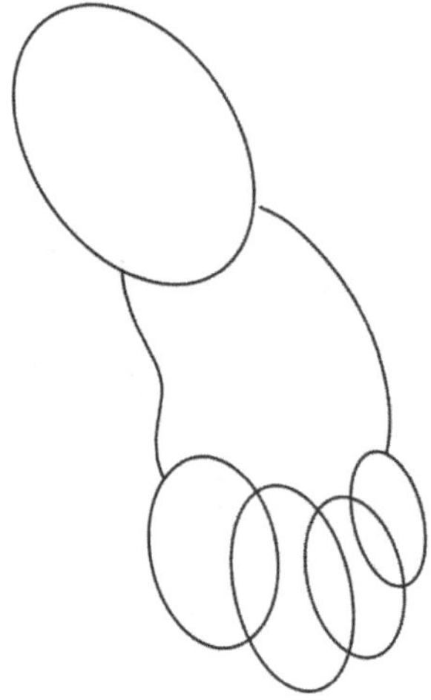

02

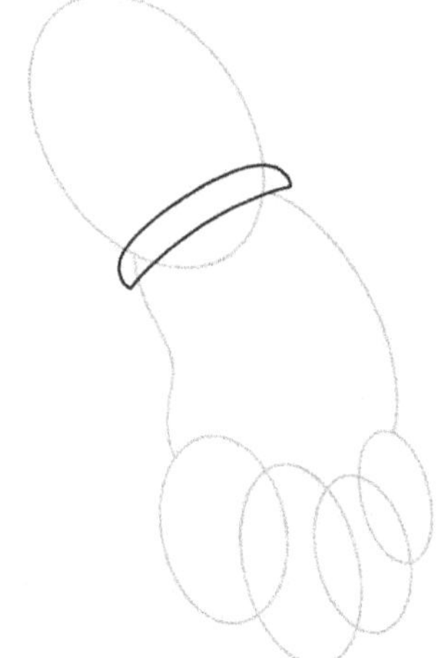

03

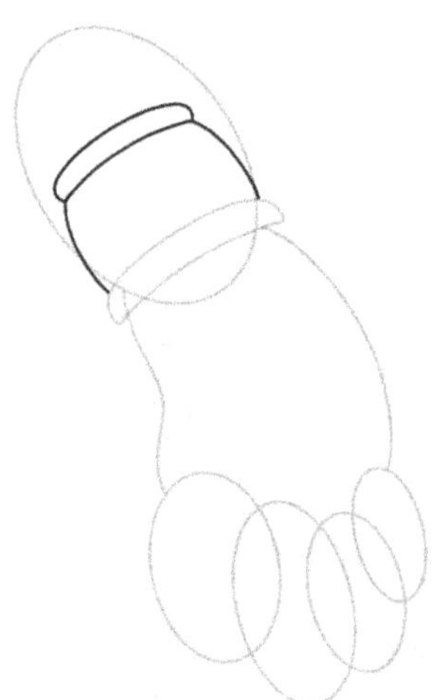

04

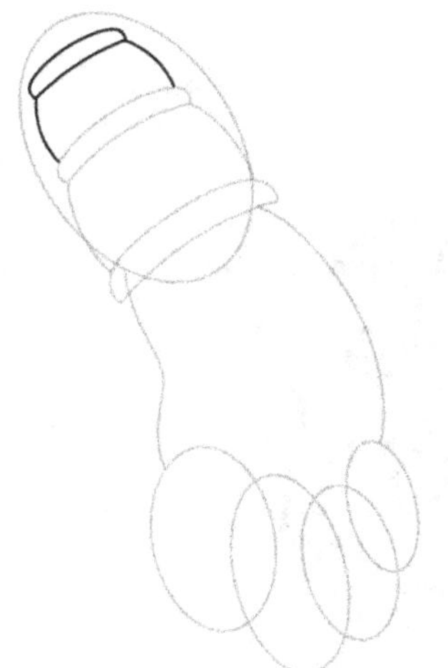

05

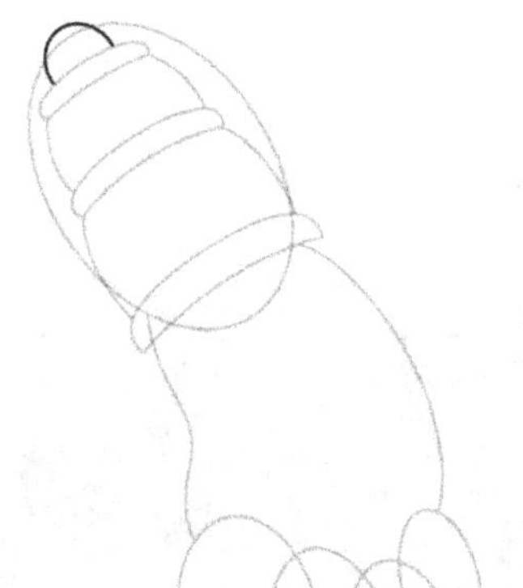

06

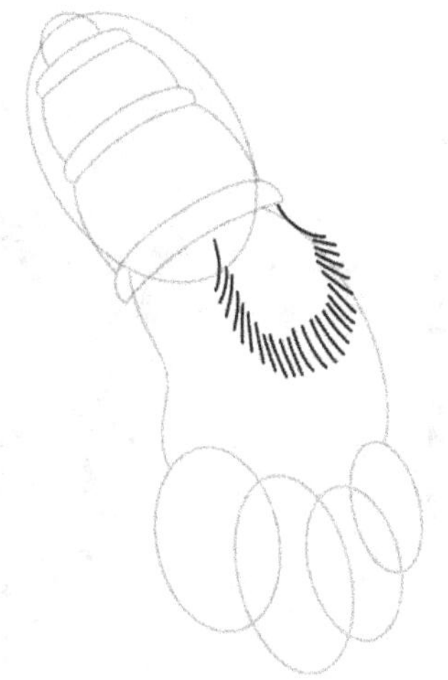

07

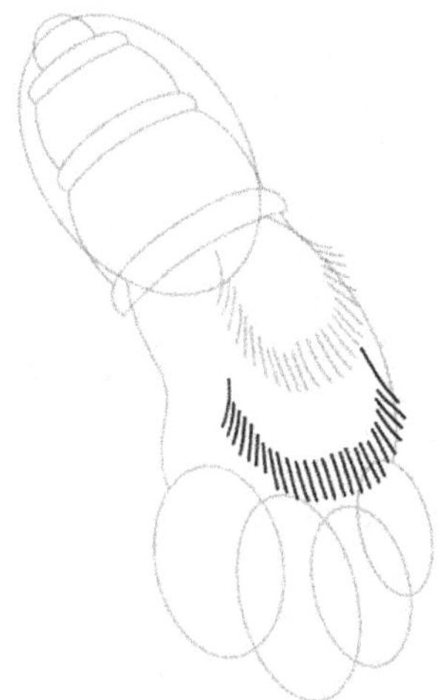

08

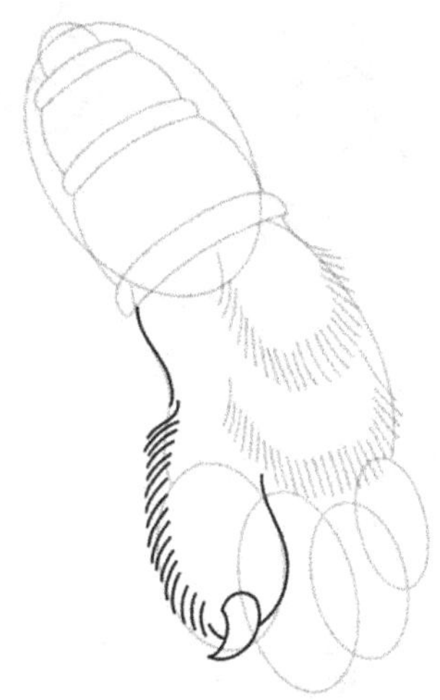

09

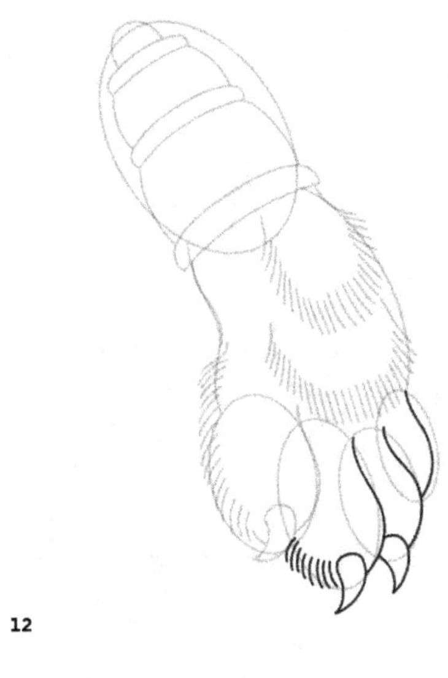

10

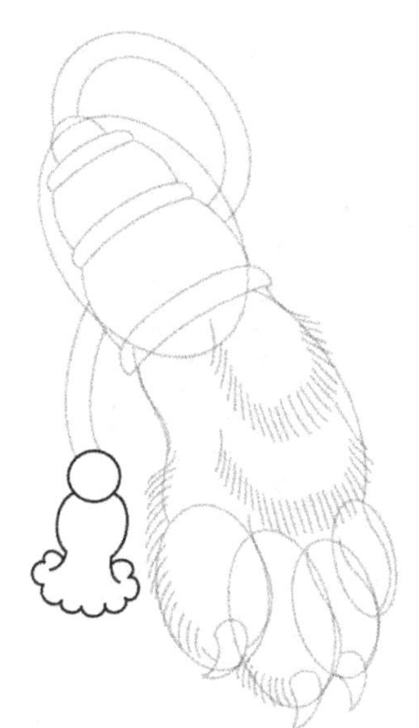

11

12

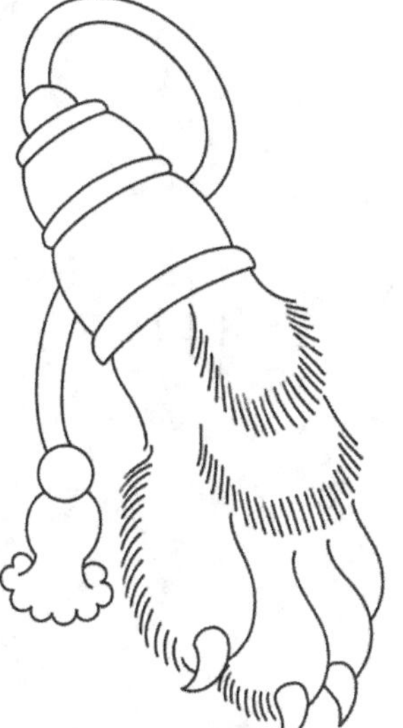

PANTHER BUTTERFLY

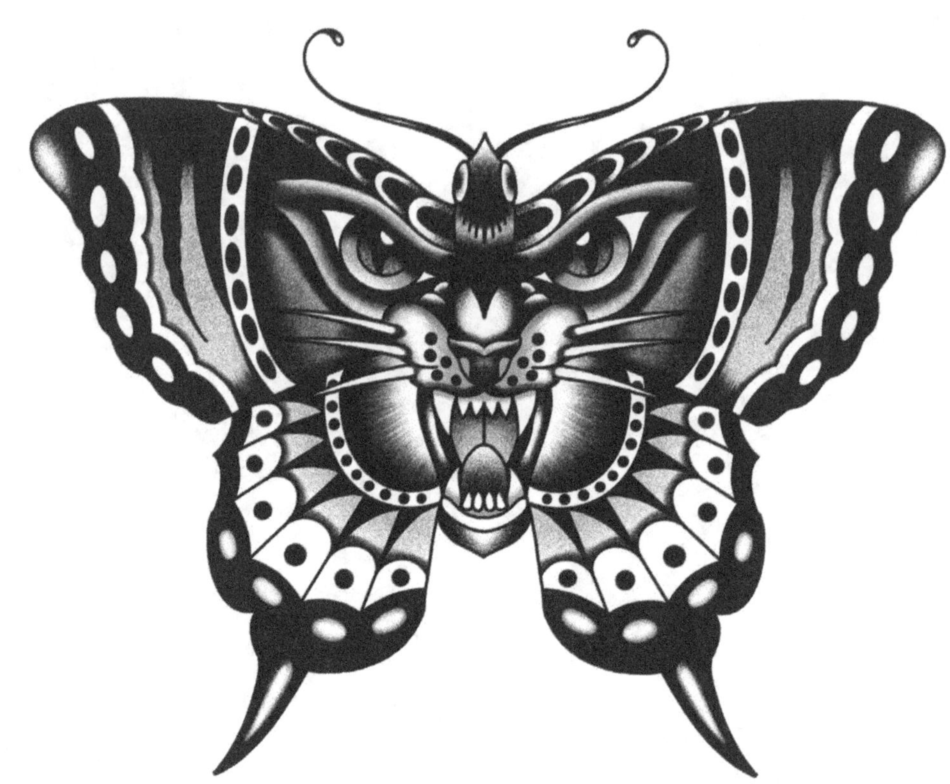

The panther butterfly tattoo commonly symbolises strength and transformation, with the panther representing resilience and the butterfly symbolising change and growth.

01

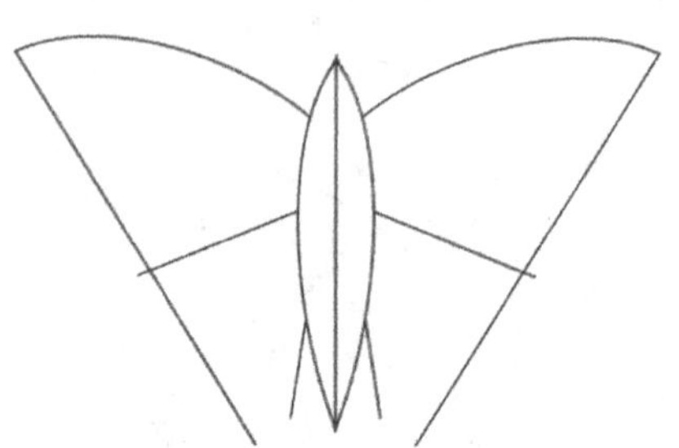

02

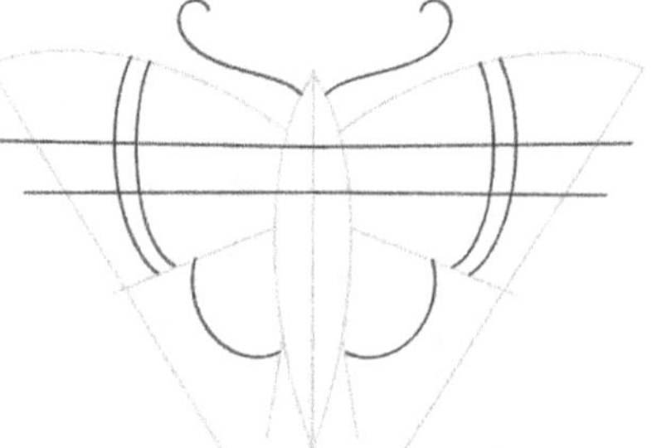

03

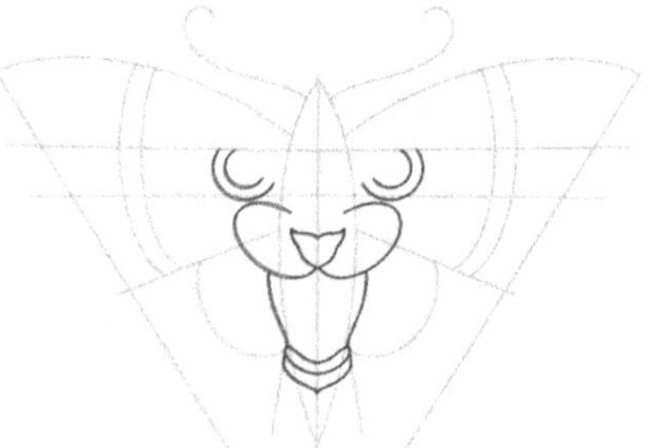

04

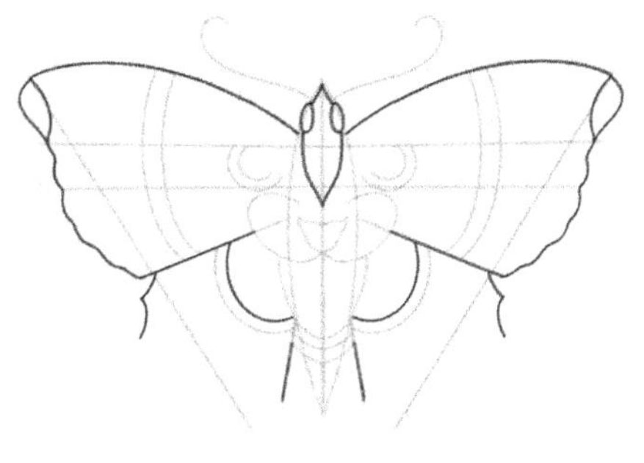

05

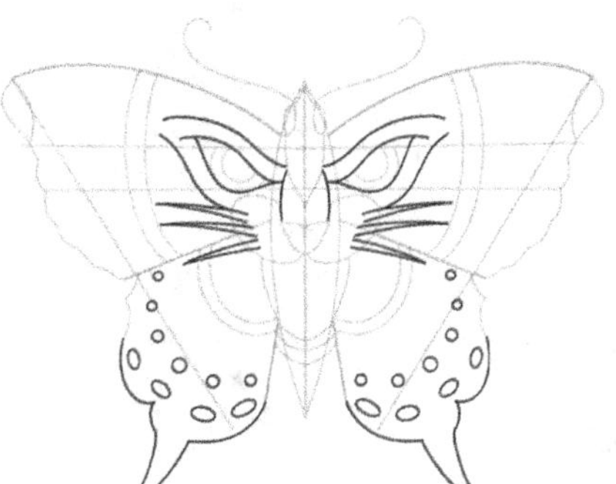

06

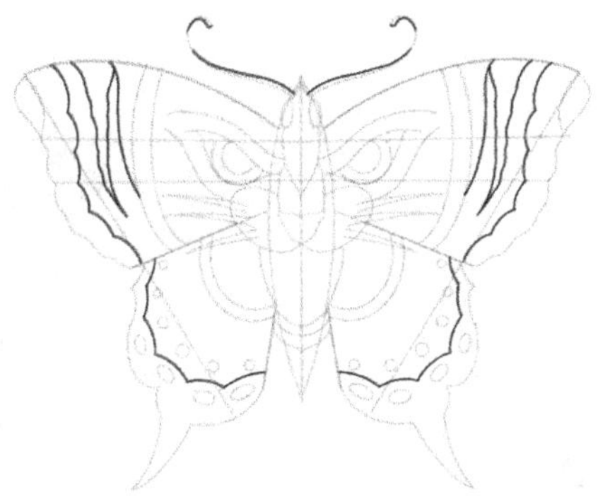

07

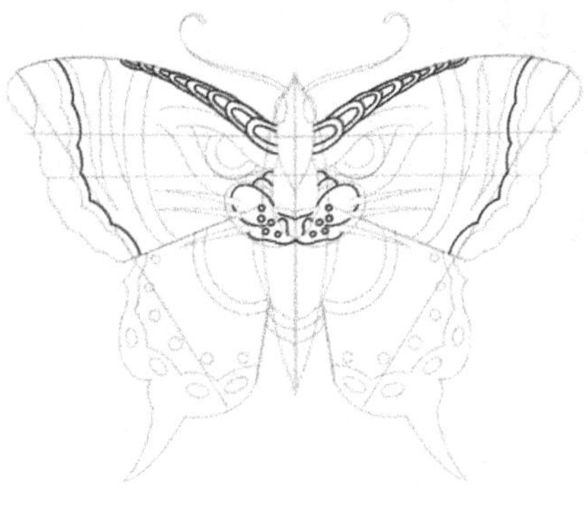

08

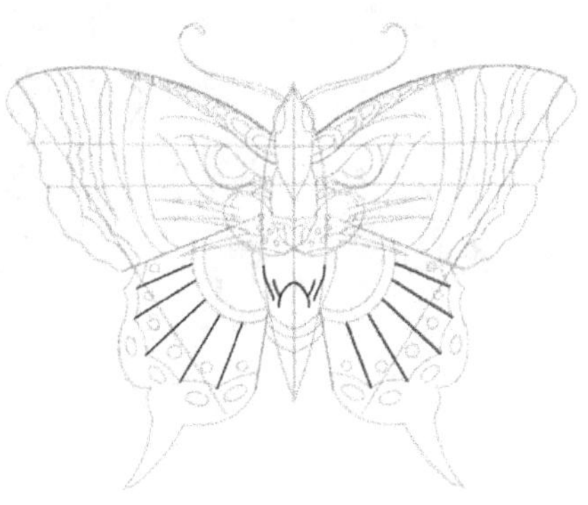

09

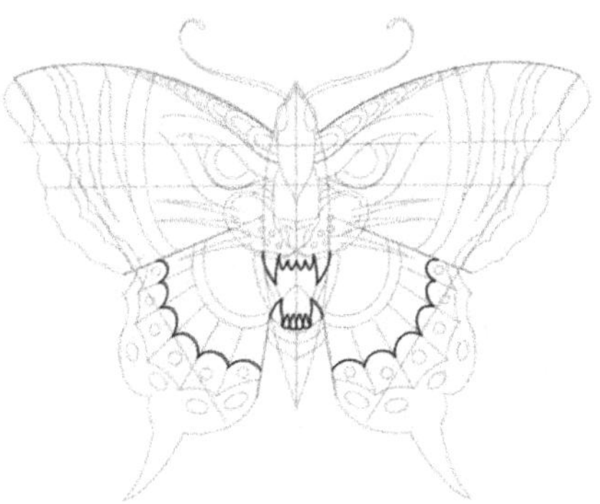

10

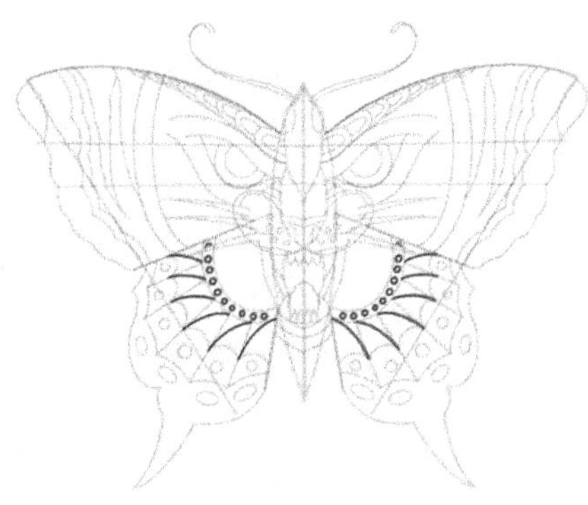

11

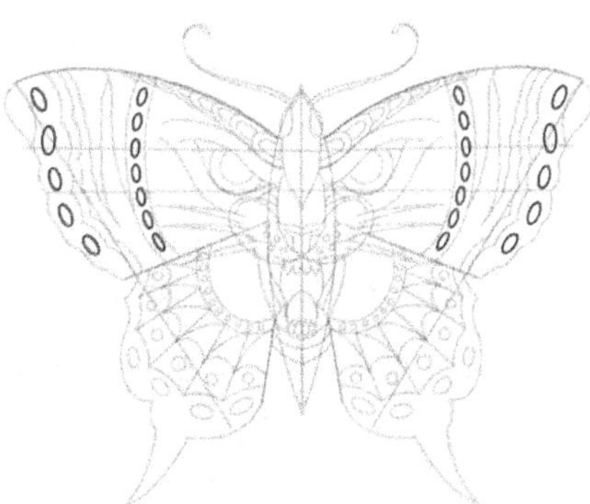

12

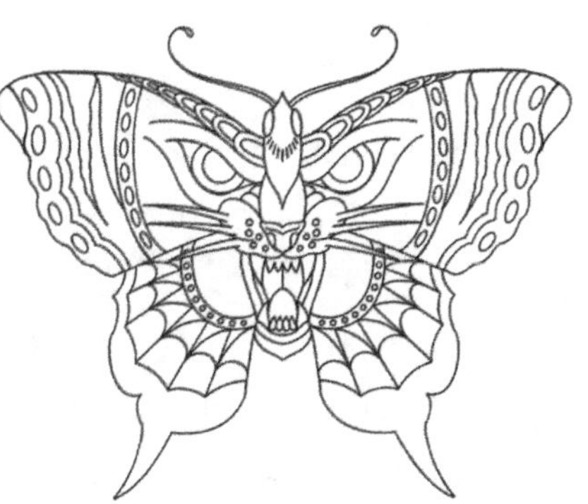

HOW TO DRAW TATTOO FLASH

HOW TO DRAW TATTOO FLASH

PIPE

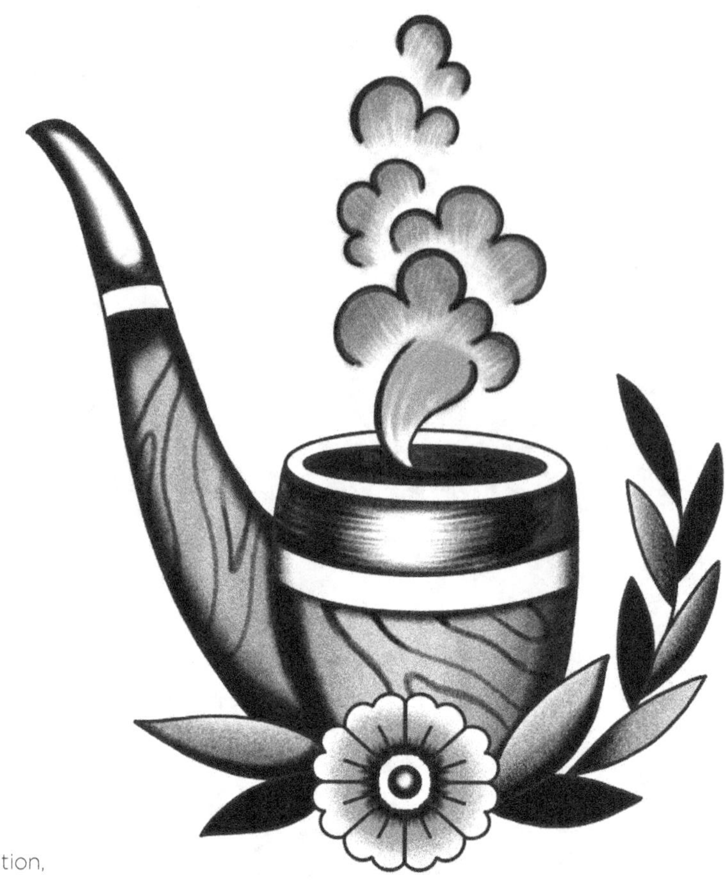

A pipe symbolises contemplation, wisdom, and relaxation, often associated with nostalgia and a reflective lifestyle.

01

02

03

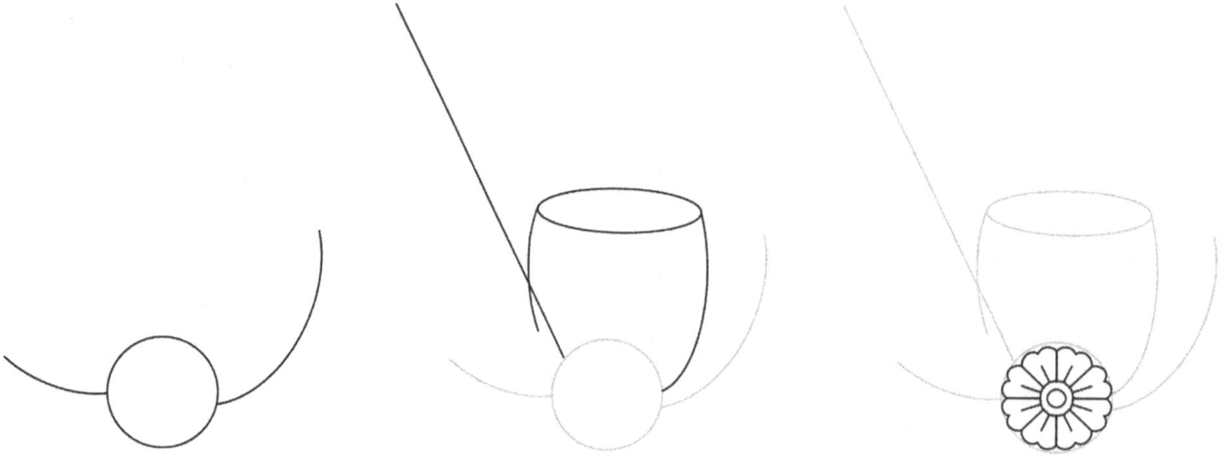

04

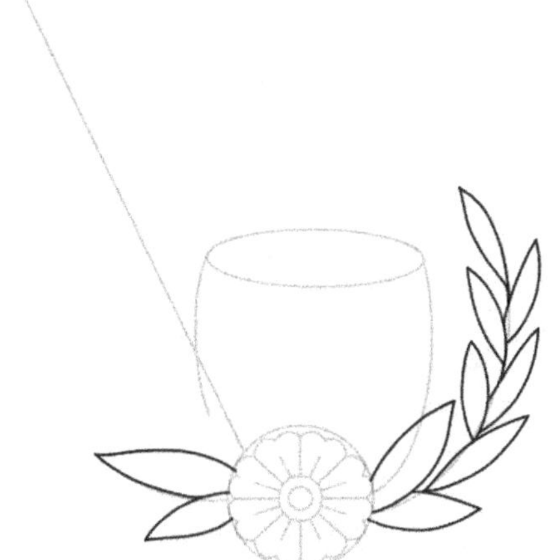

05

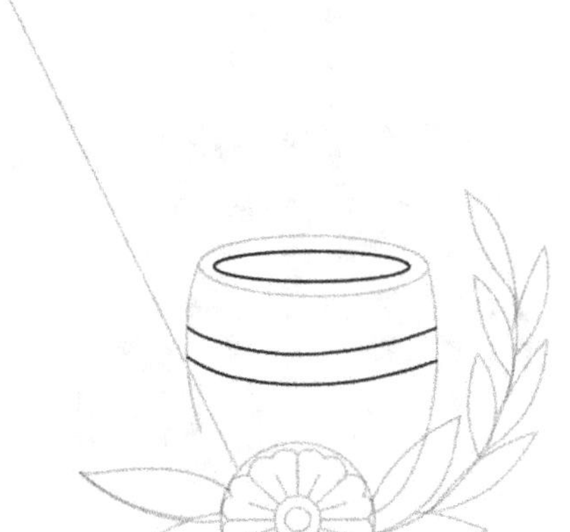

06

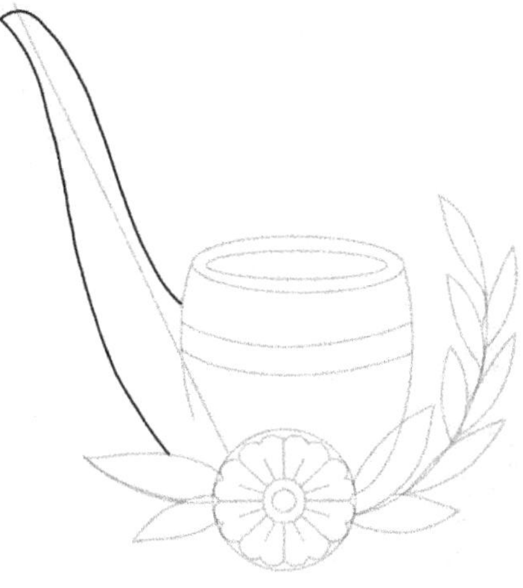

07

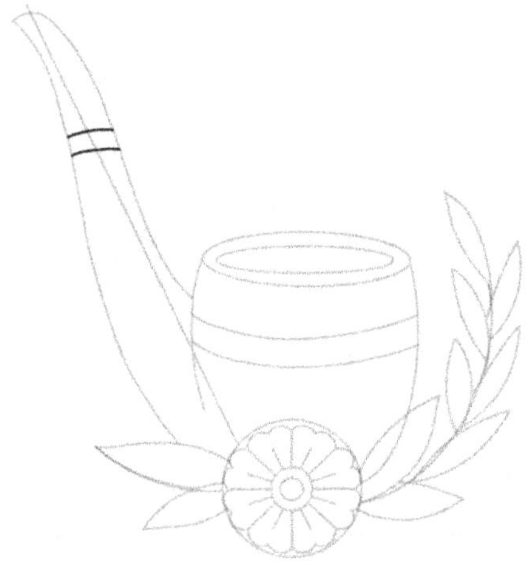

08

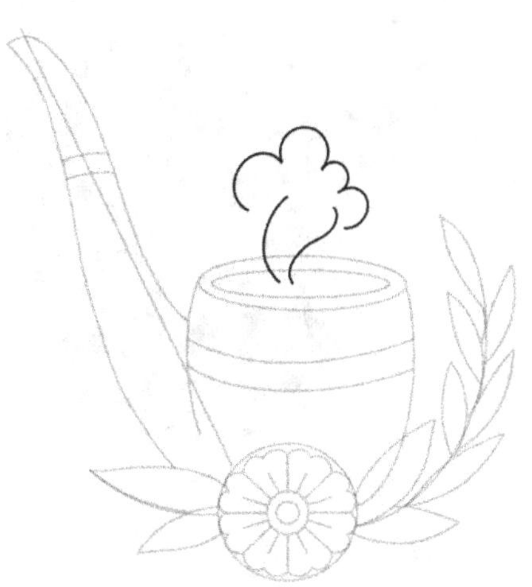

09

10

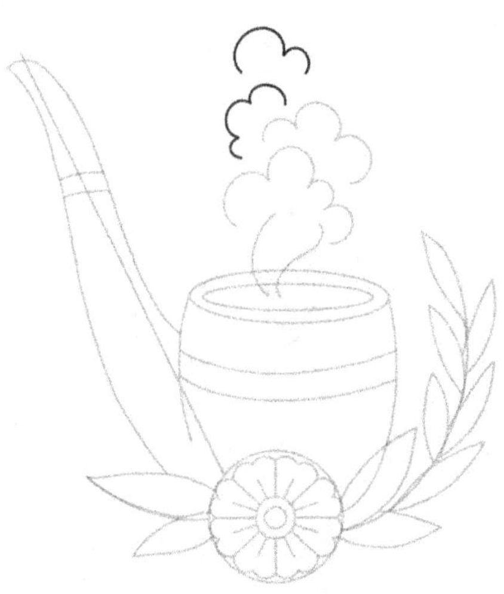

11

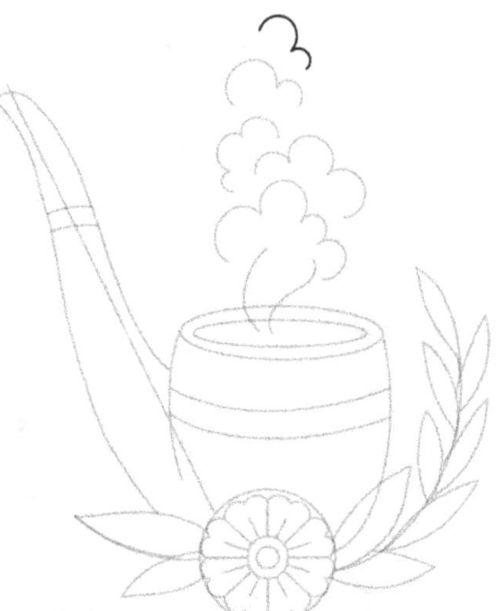

12

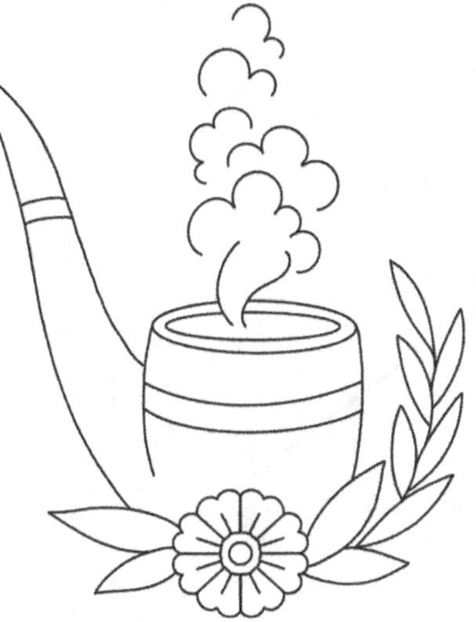

VAULTEDITIONS.COM

HOW TO DRAW TATTOO FLASH

RAVEN

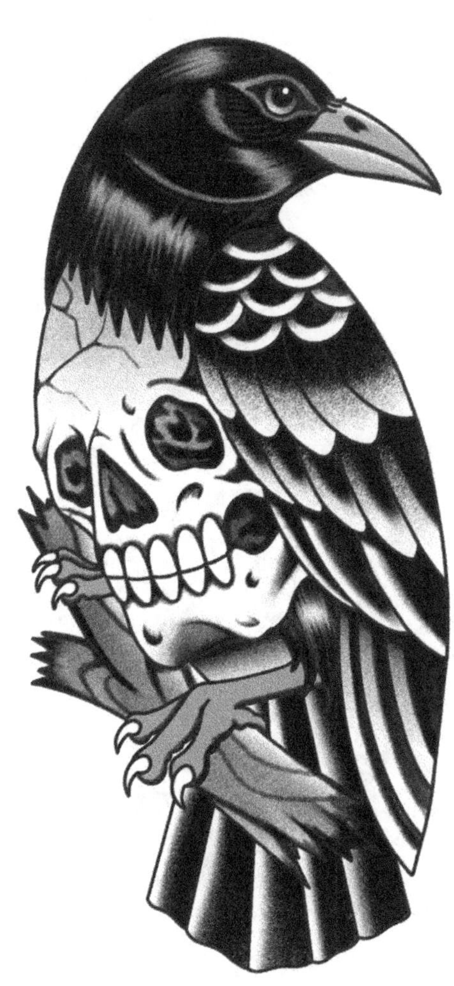

A raven tattoo symbolises mystery, intelligence, and transformation, often associated with omens, death, and rebirth, as well as wisdom and prophecy in various mythologies.

01

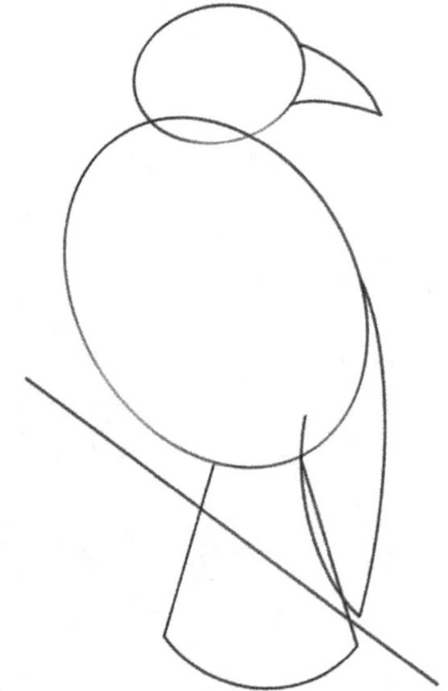

02

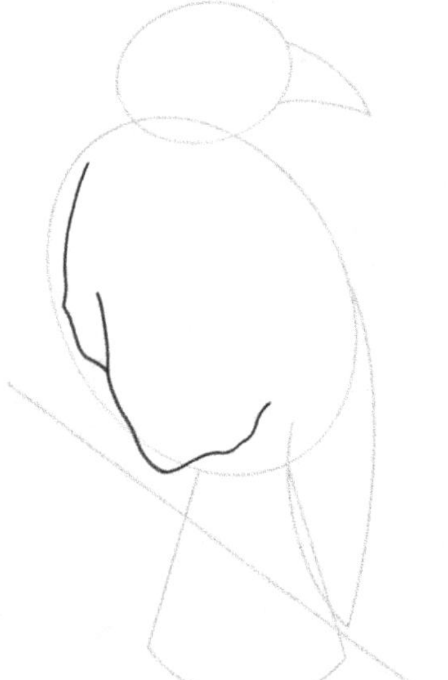

03

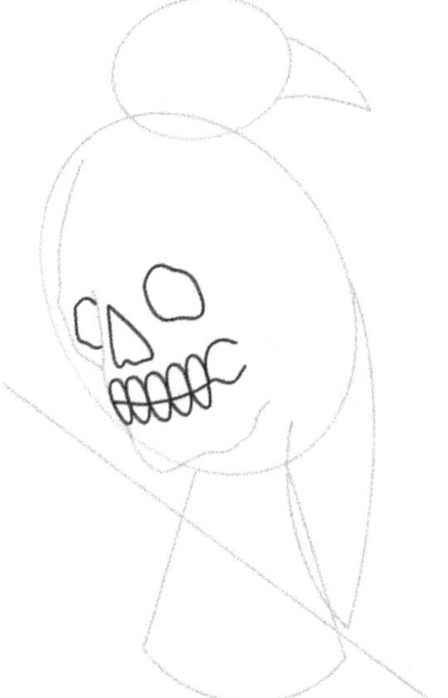

04

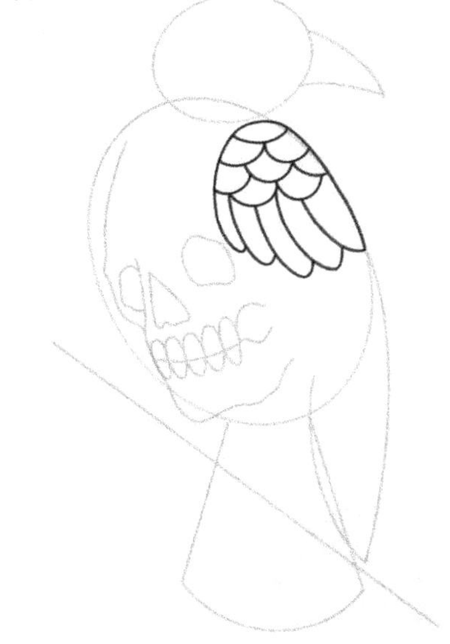

05

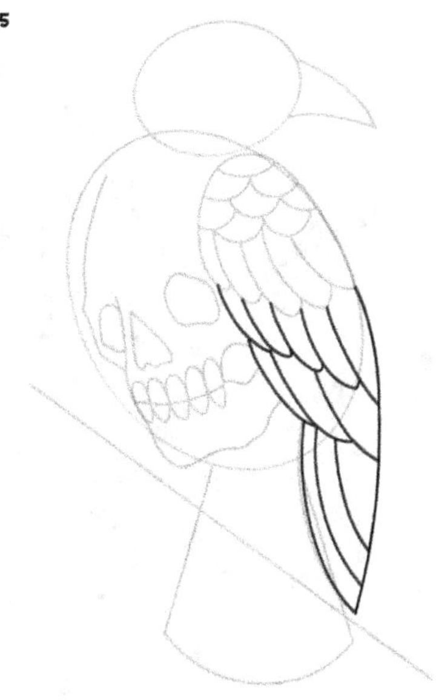

06

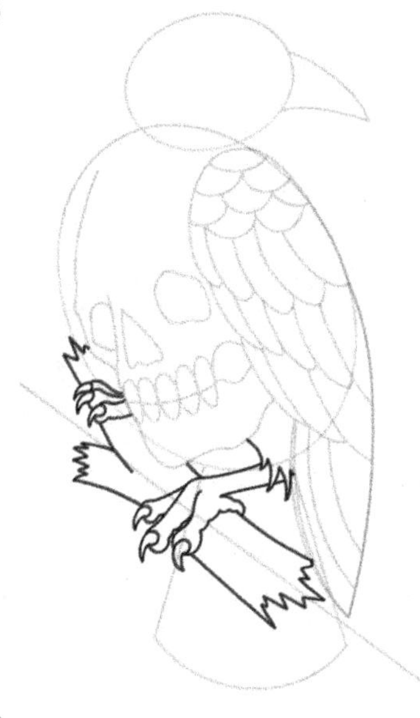

07

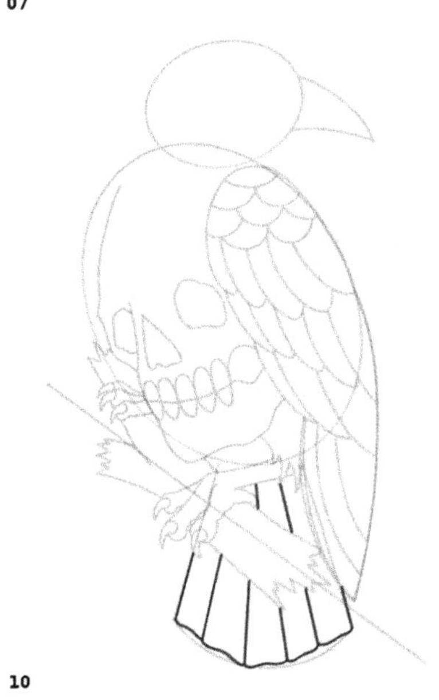

08

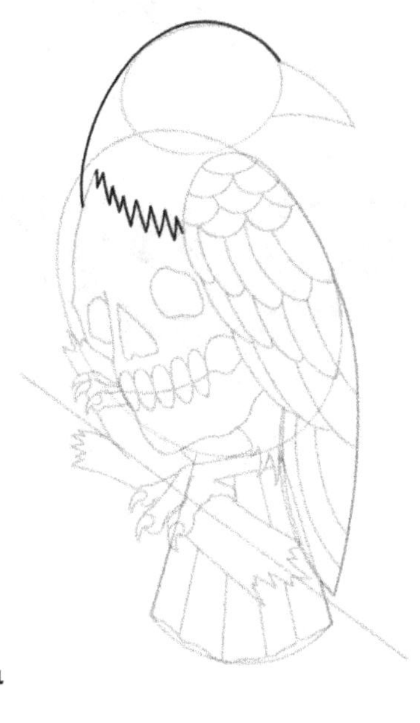

09

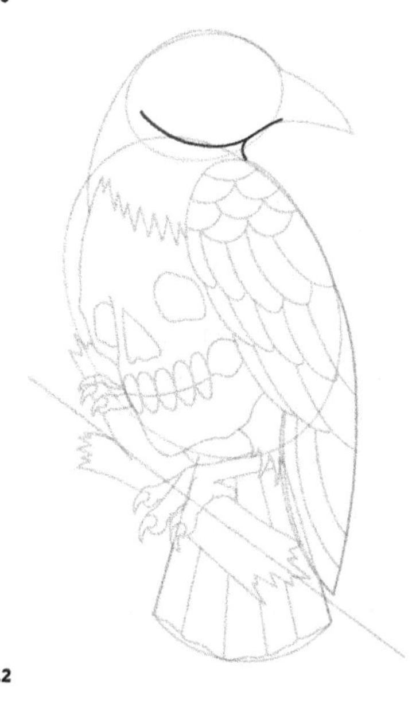

10

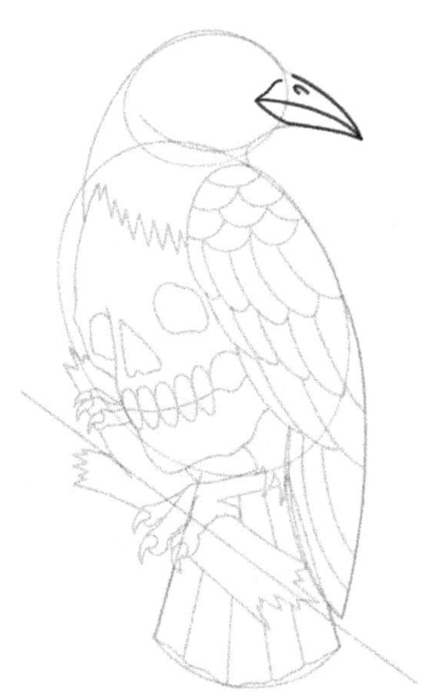

11

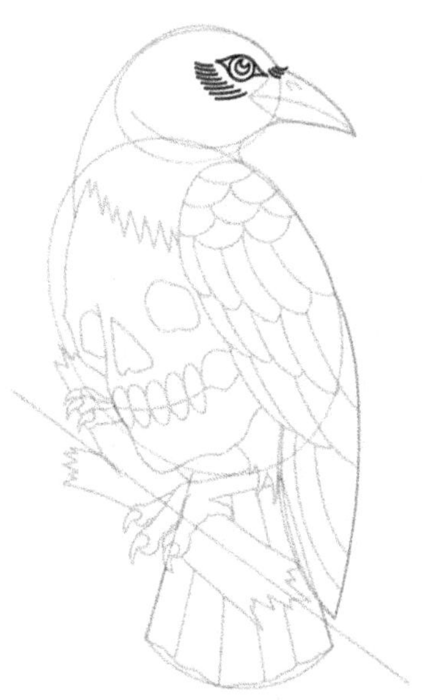

12

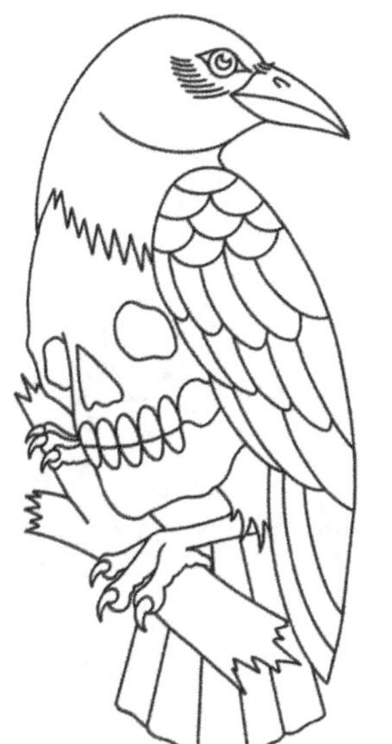

ROSE

HOW TO DRAW TATTOO FLASH

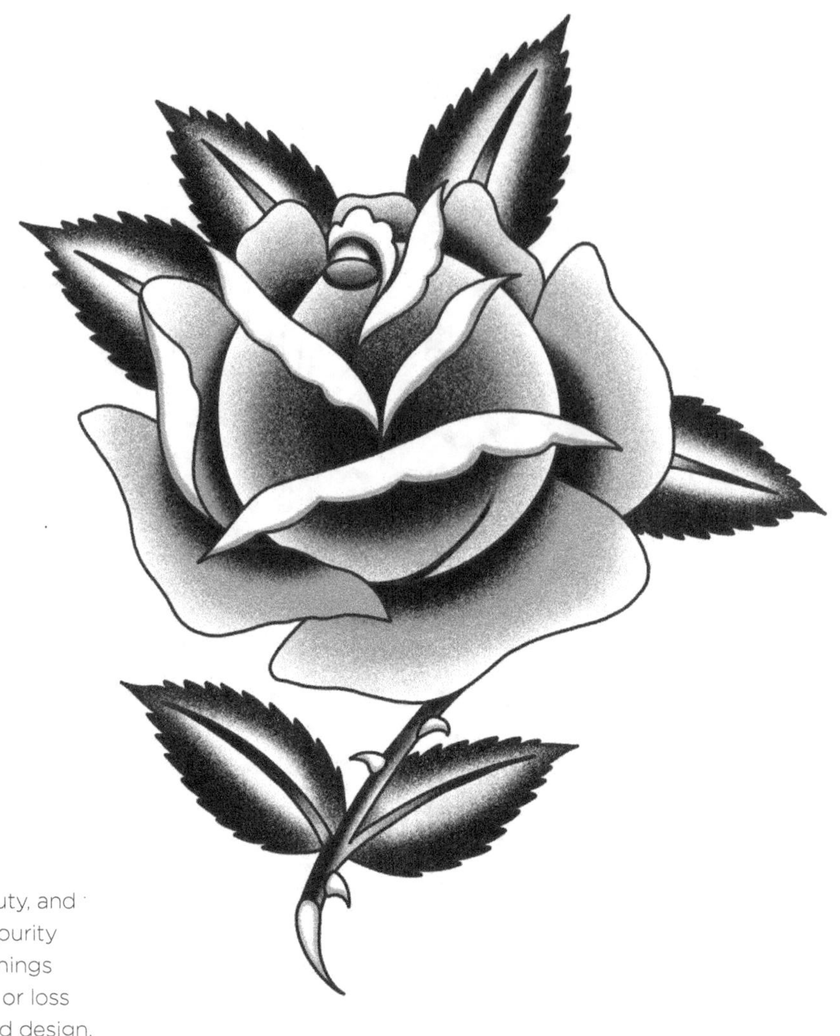

A rose symbolises love, beauty, and
passion, often representing purity
or desire. It also carries meanings
of balance, new beginnings, or loss
depending on the colour and design.

---

01   02   03

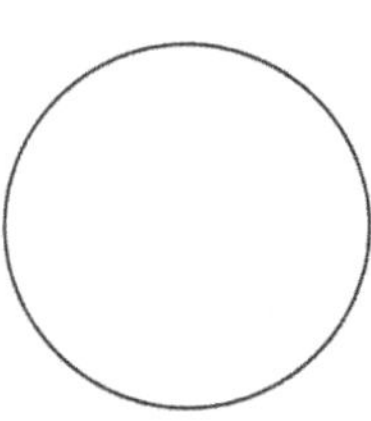

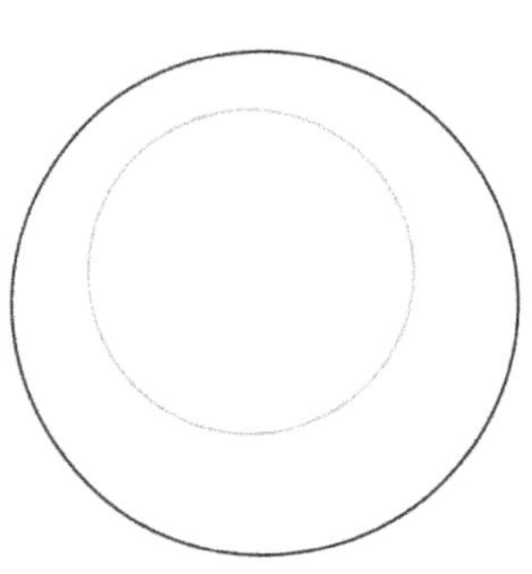

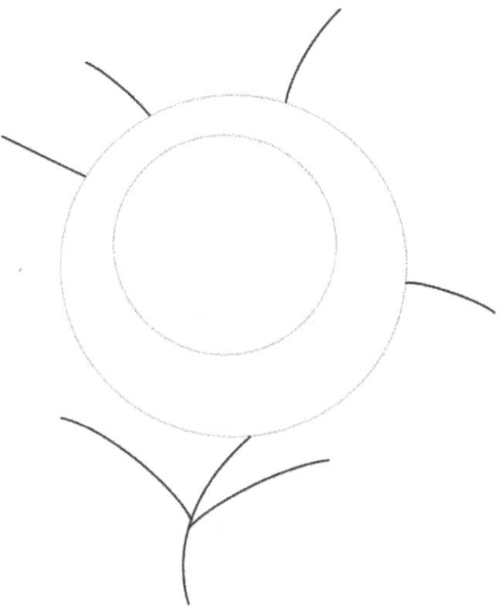

04

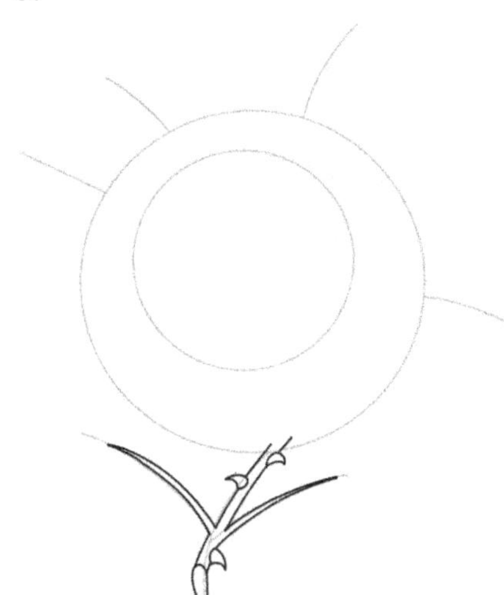

05

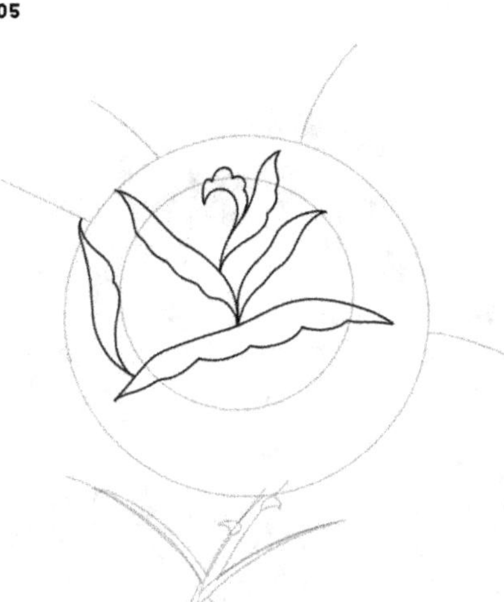

06

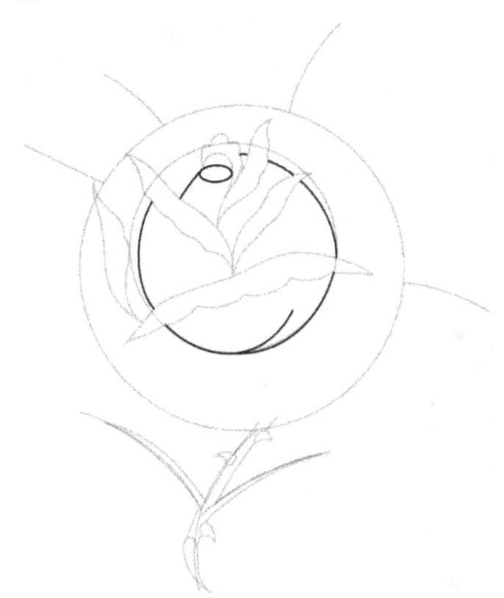

07

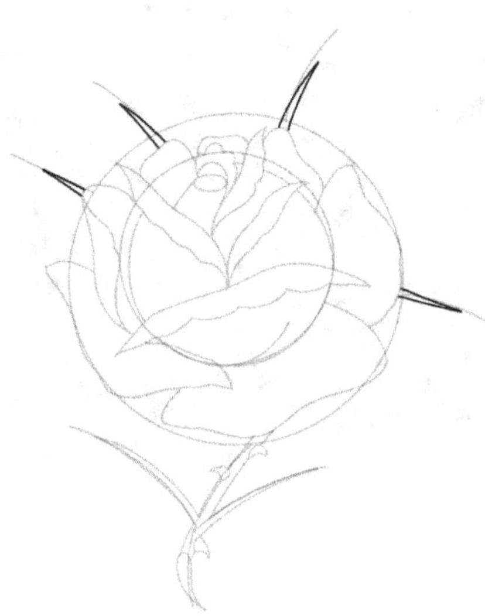

08

09

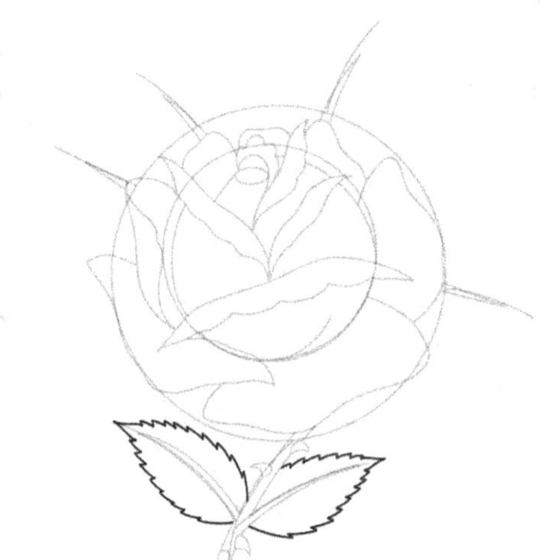

10

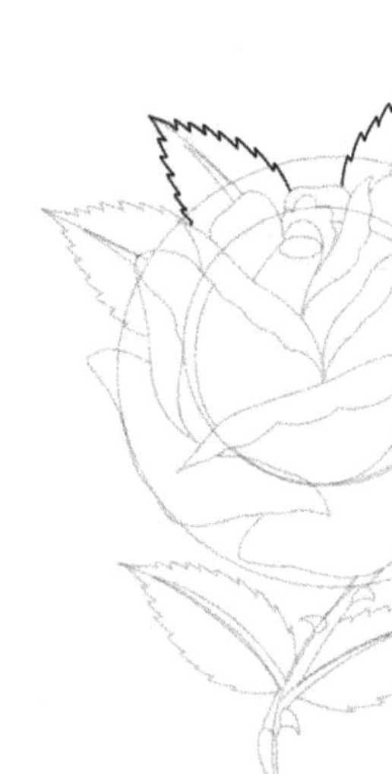

11

12

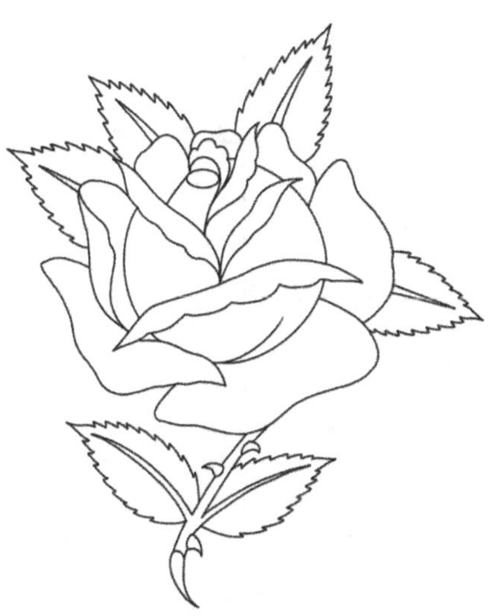

HOW TO DRAW TATTOO FLASH

RUSSIAN DOLL

HOW TO DRAW TATTOO FLASH

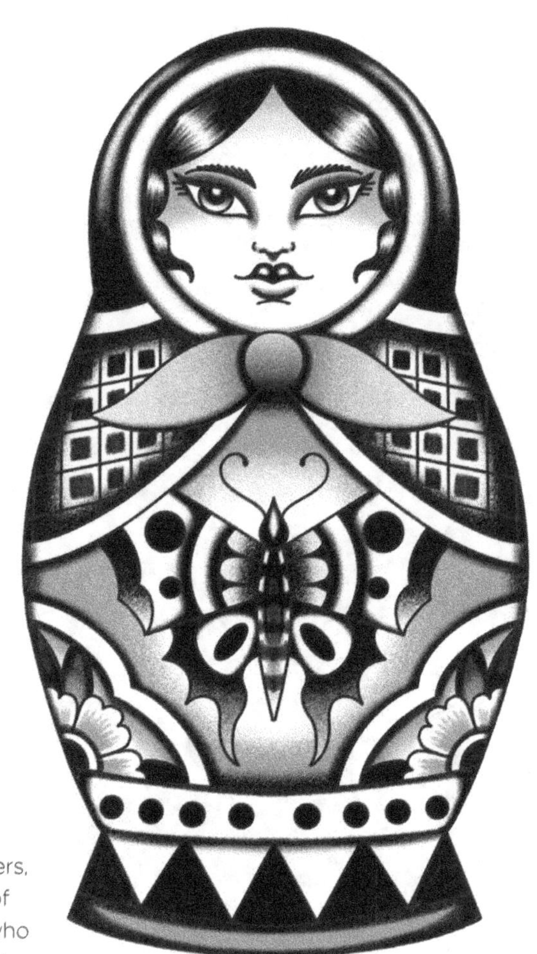

A Russian doll tattoo symbolises layers, hidden depths, and the complexity of self. It may be chosen by someone who feels there is more to them than meets the eye.

01

02

03

04
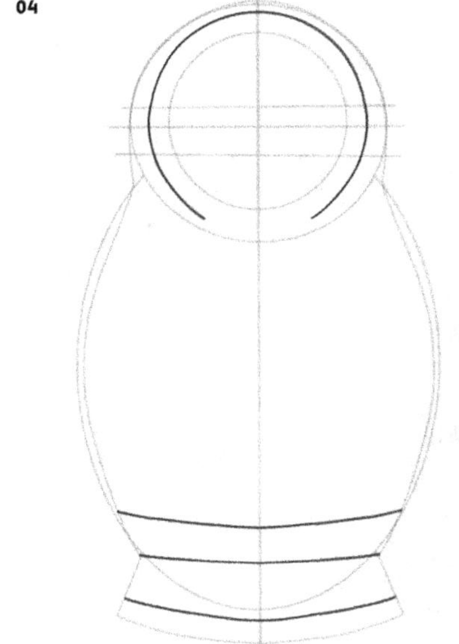

05
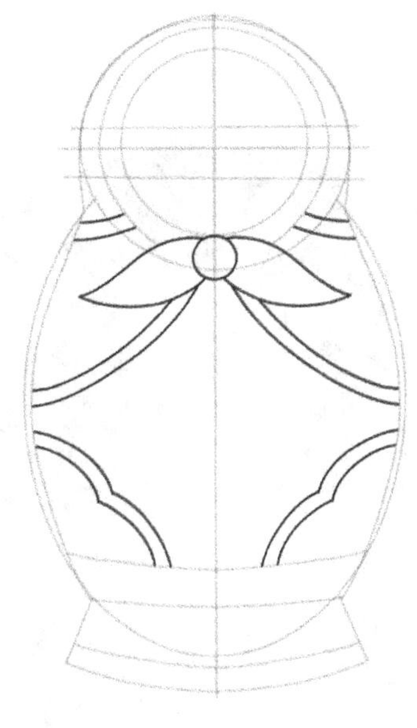

06
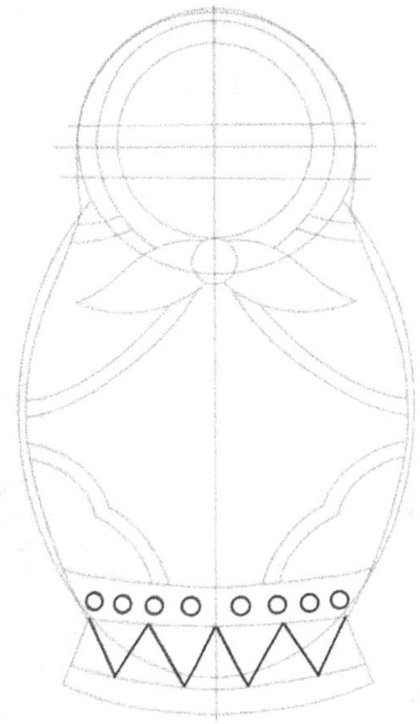

07
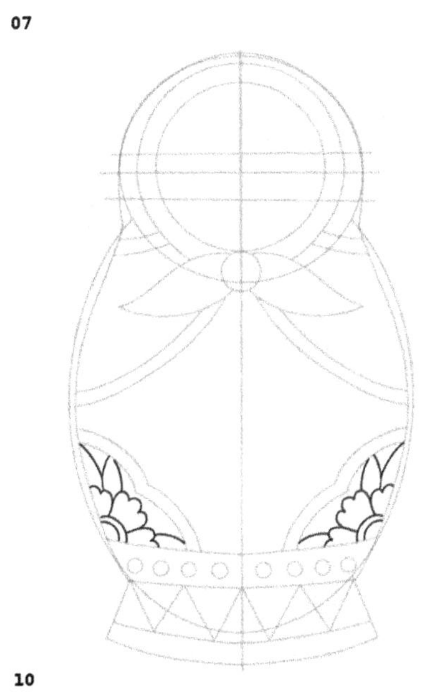

08
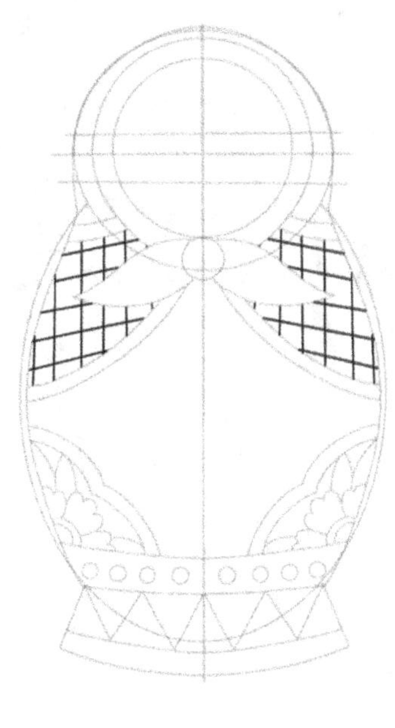

09
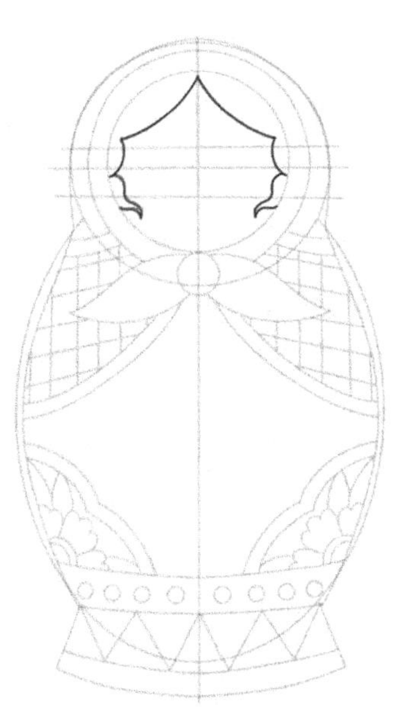

10
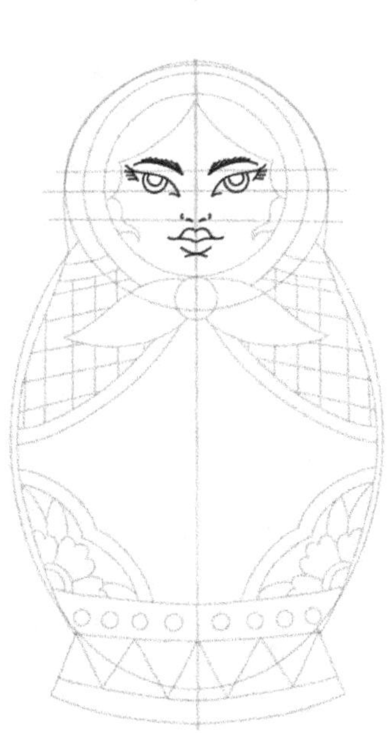

11
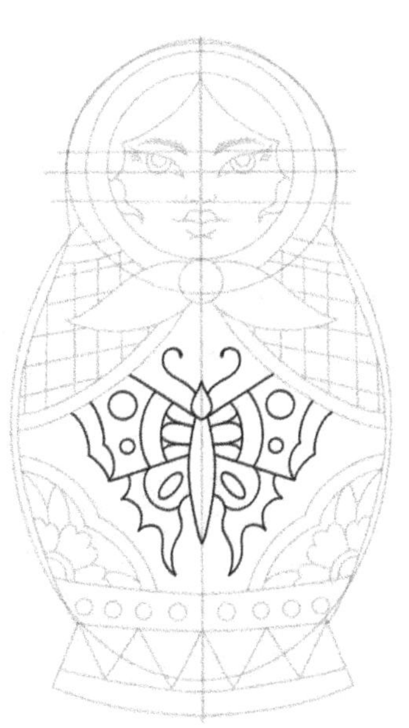

12
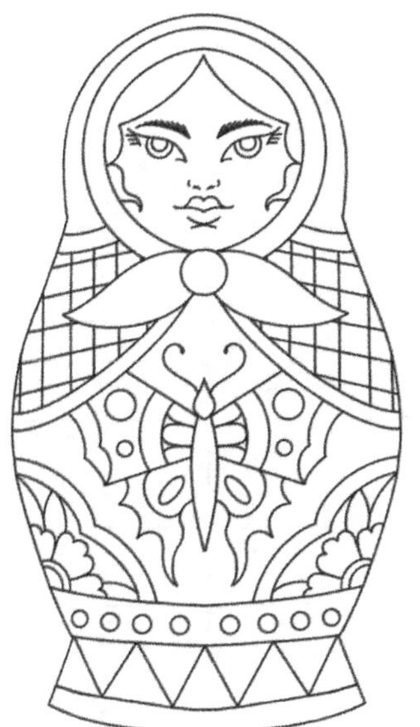

HOW TO DRAW TATTOO FLASH

SKULL

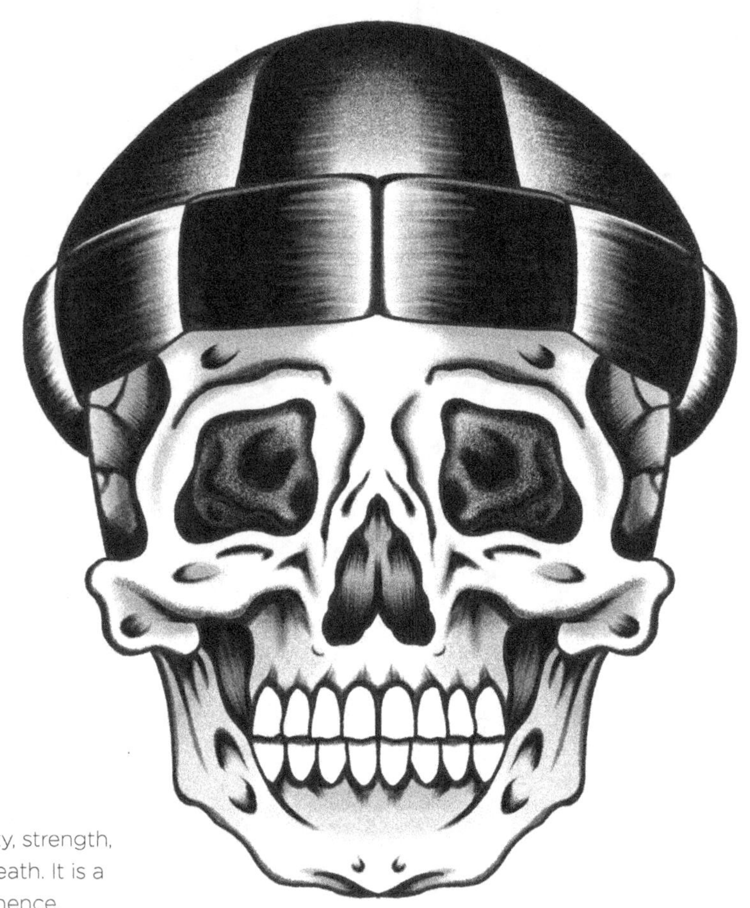

A skull symbolises mortality, strength, and the cycle of life and death. It is a reminder of life's impermanence.

01

02

03

04

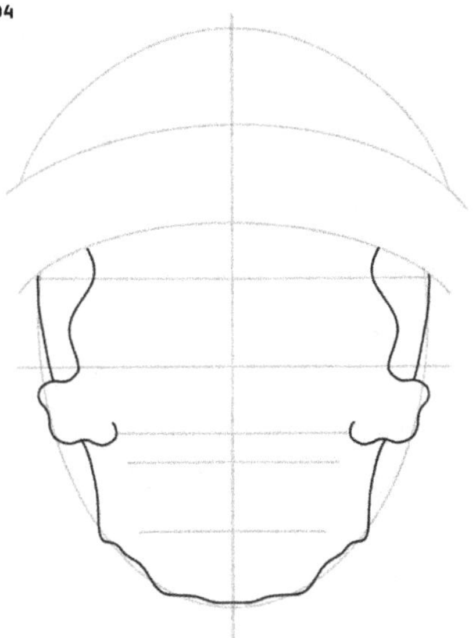

05

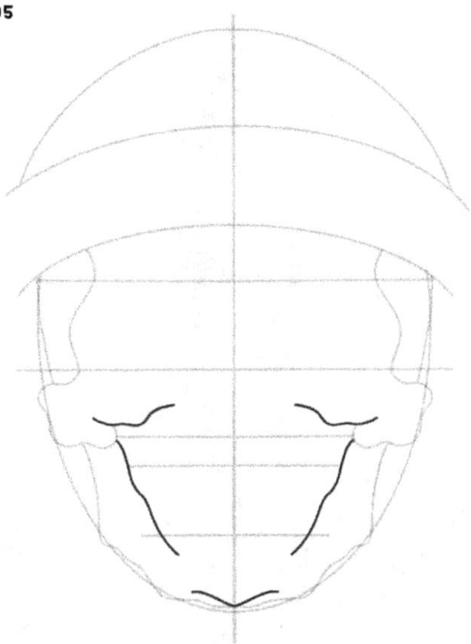

06

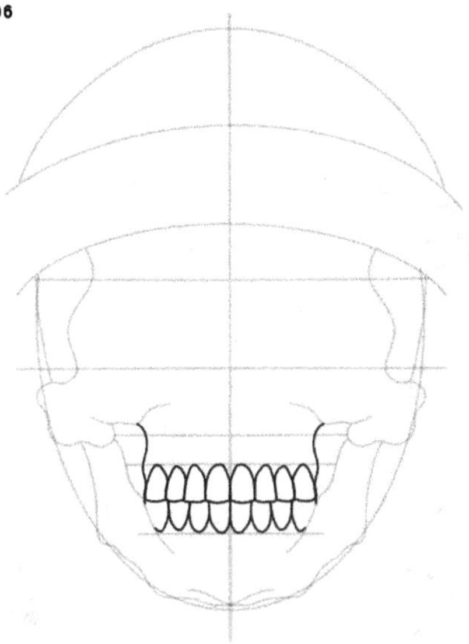

07

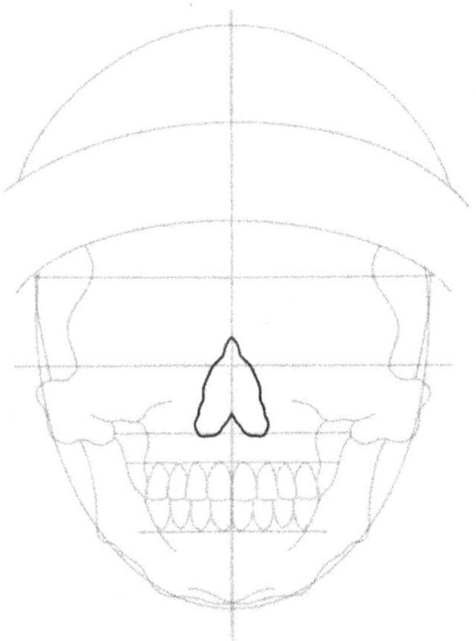

08

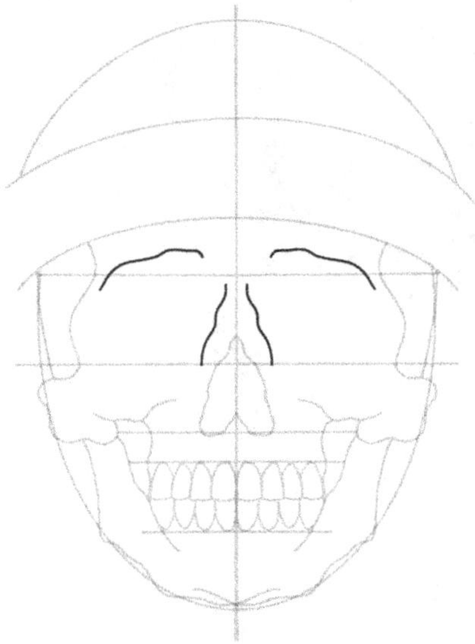

09

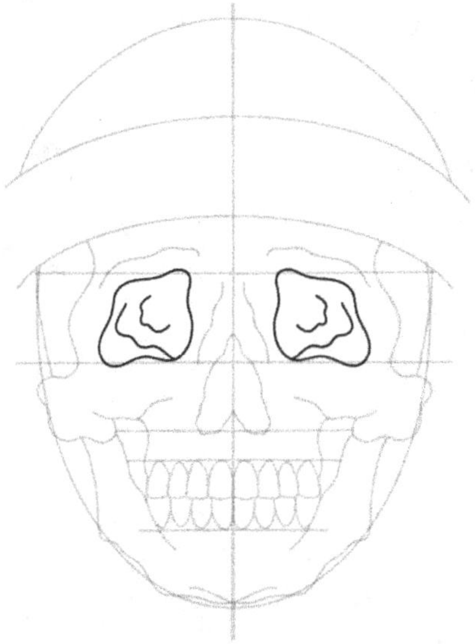

10

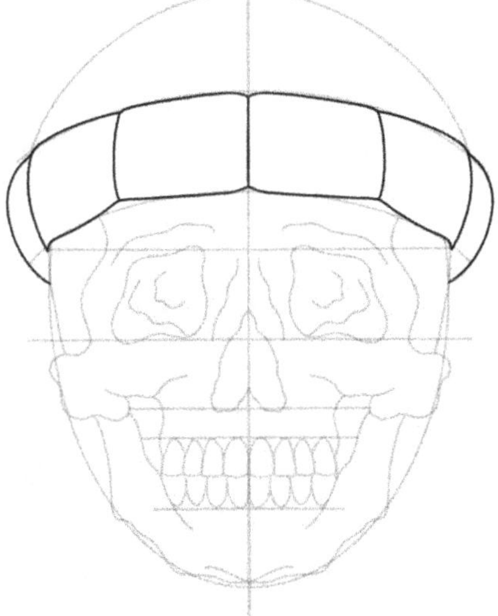

11

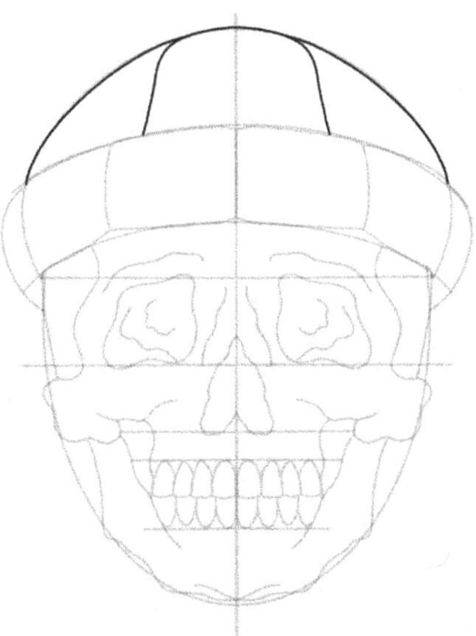

12

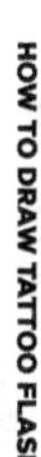

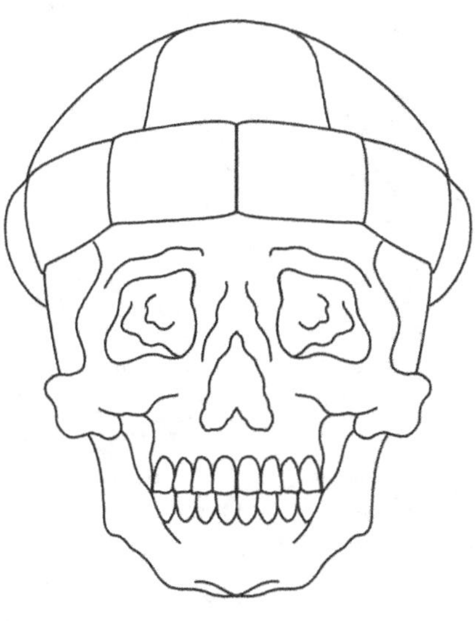

SNAKE & DAGGER

HOW TO DRAW TATTOO FLASH

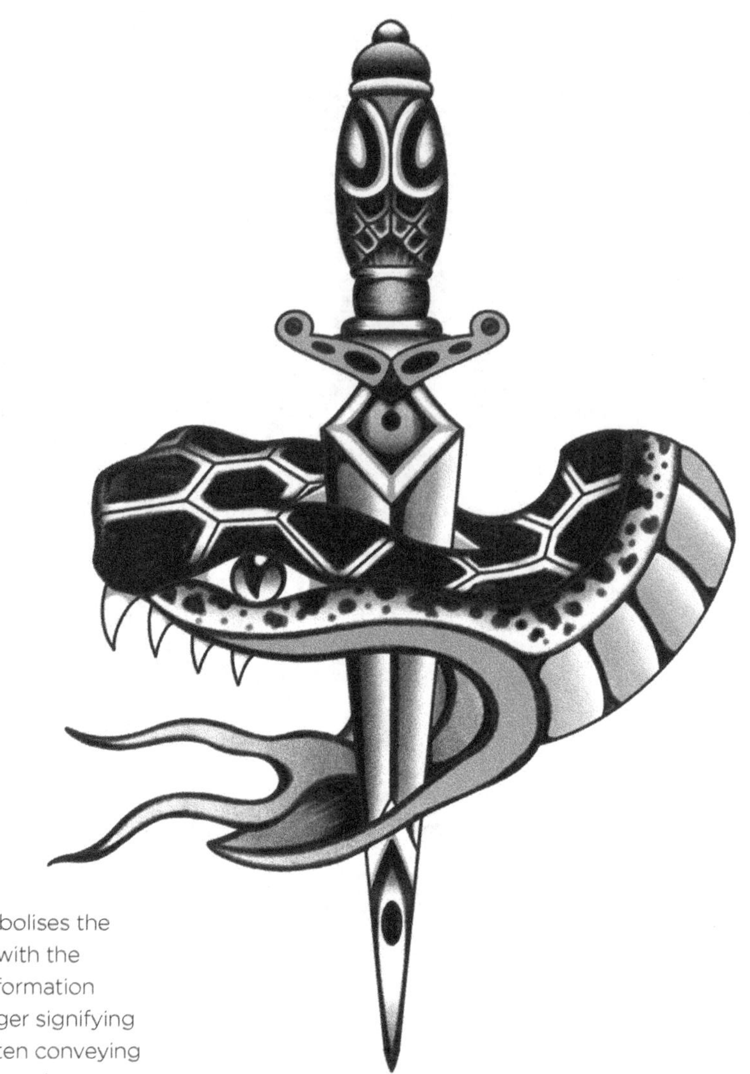

A snake and dagger symbolises the duality of life and death, with the snake representing transformation and danger, and the dagger signifying strength and sacrifice, often conveying themes of power and protection.

01   **02**   **03**

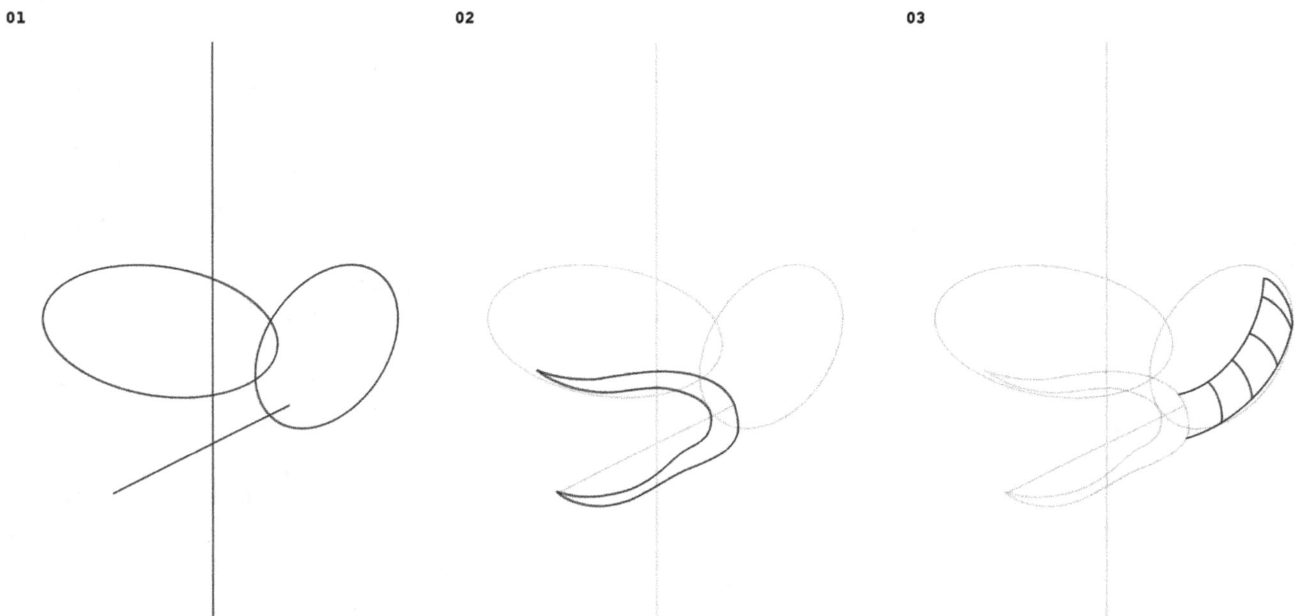

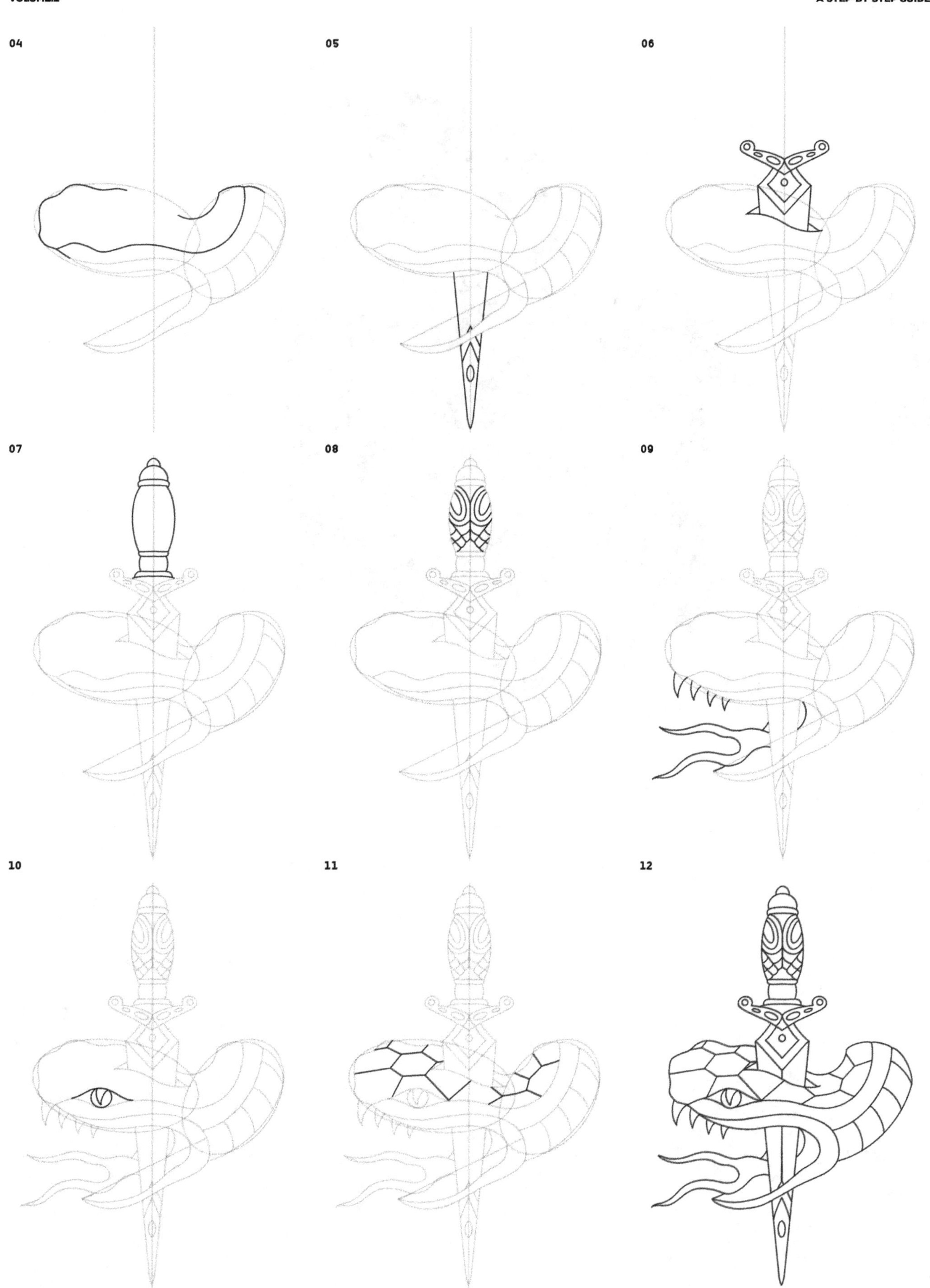

04
05
06
07
08
09
10
11
12
HOW TO DRAW TATTOO FLASH

HOW TO DRAW TATTOO FLASH

SNAKE

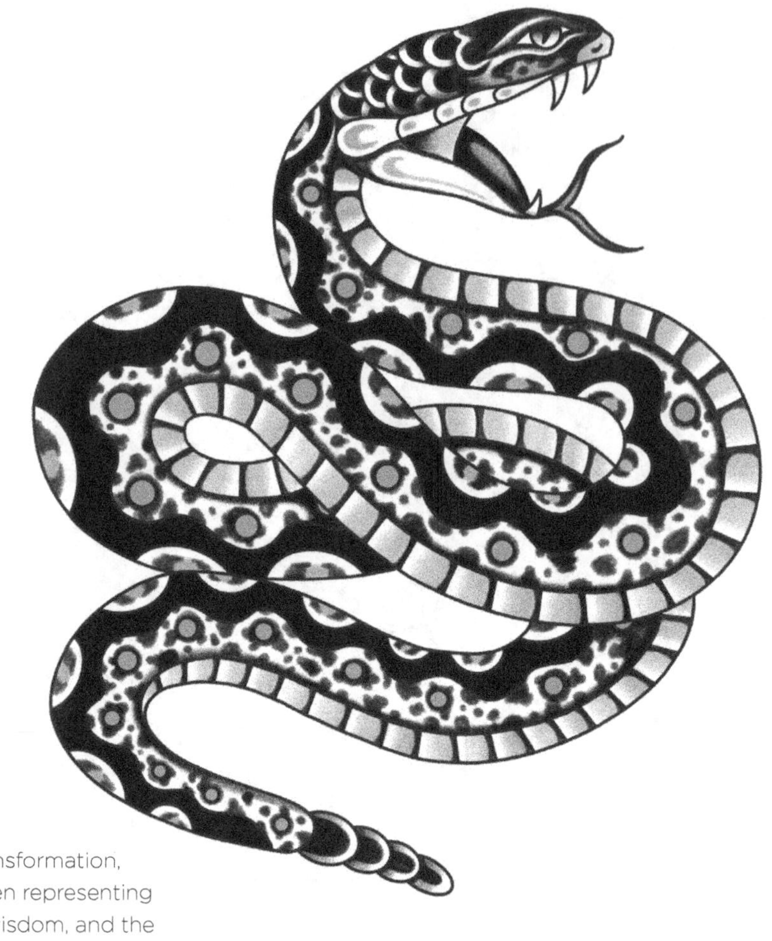

A snake symbolises transformation, rebirth, and danger, often representing themes of protection, wisdom, and the cyclical nature of life.

01

02

03

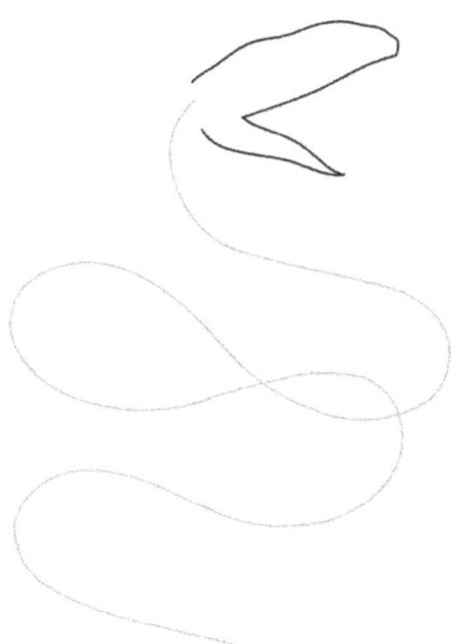

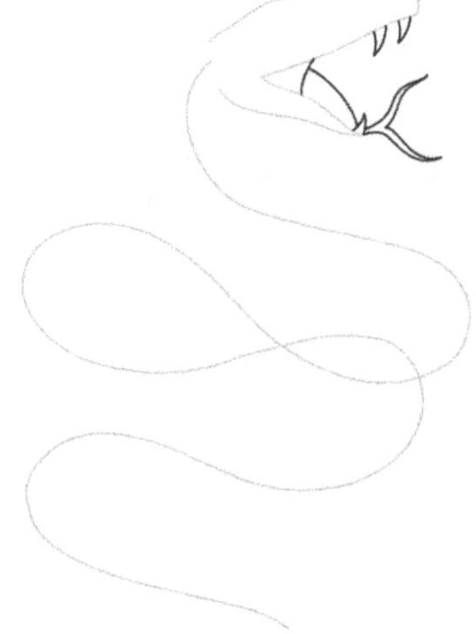

04

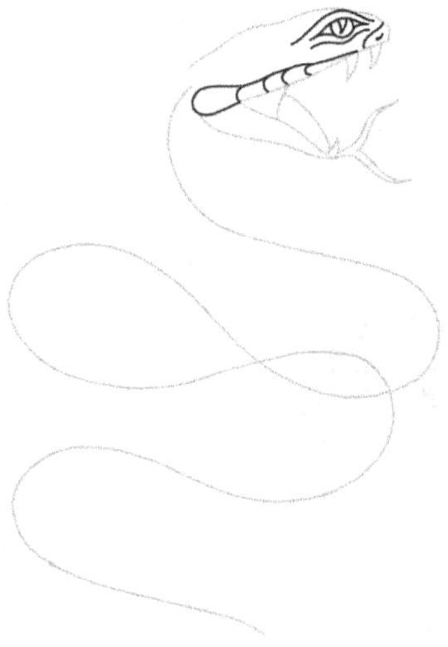

05

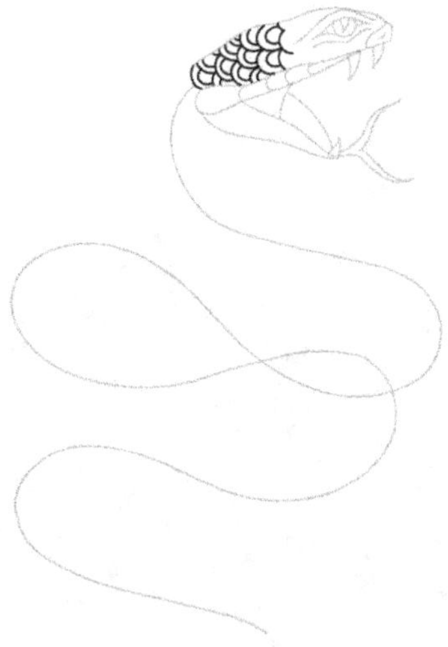

06

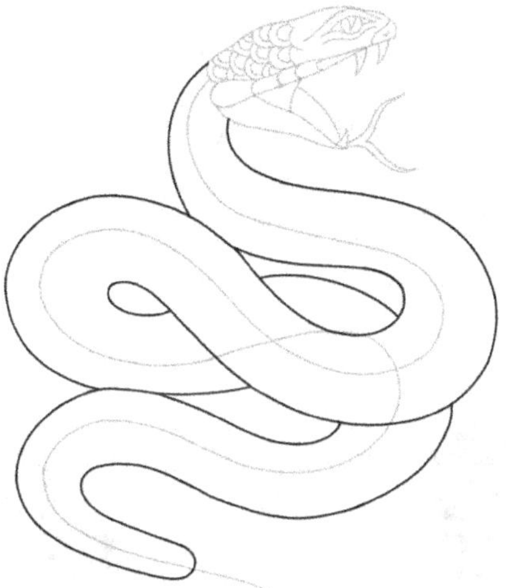

07

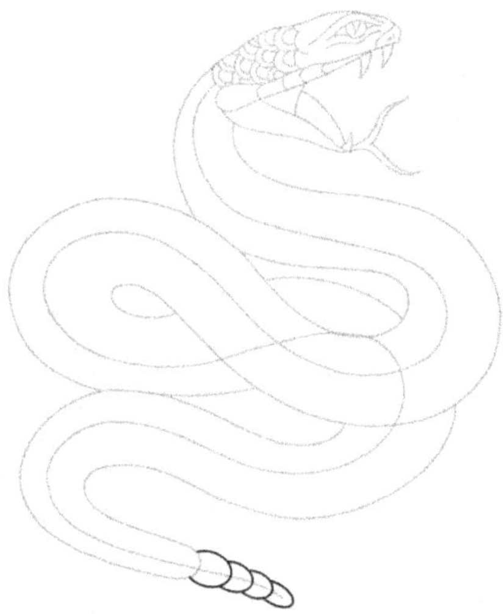

08

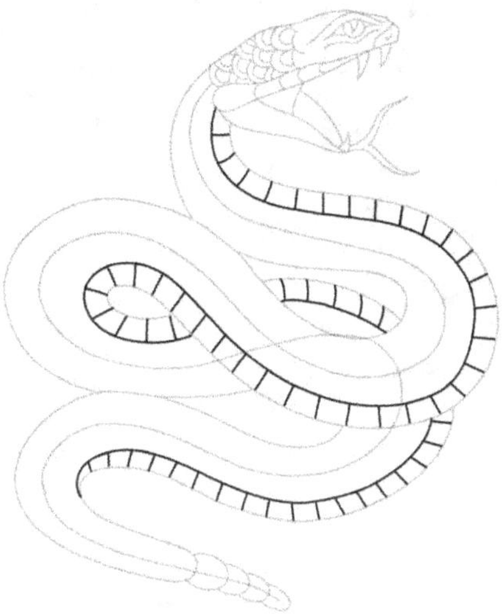

09

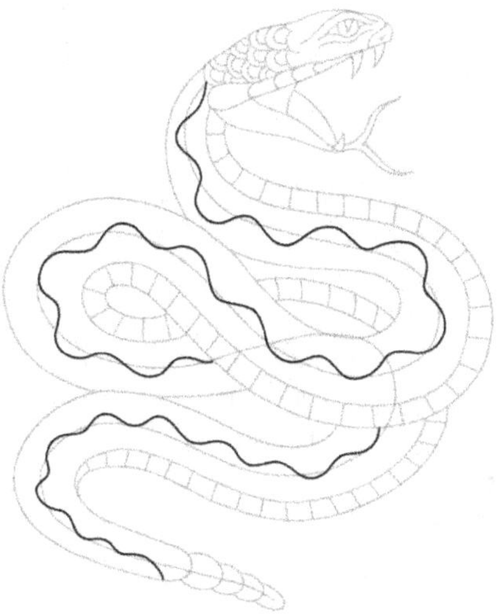

10

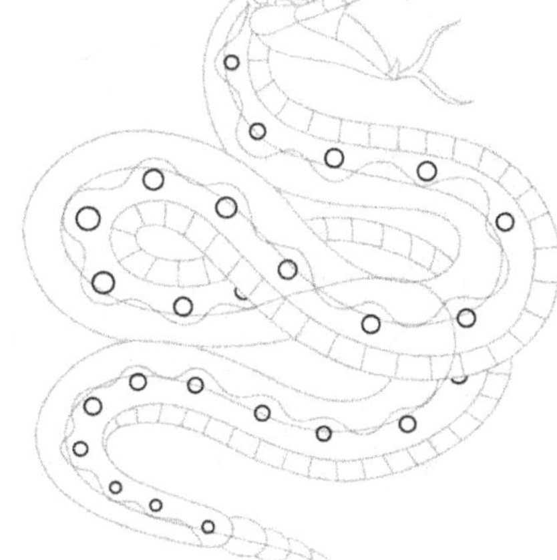

11

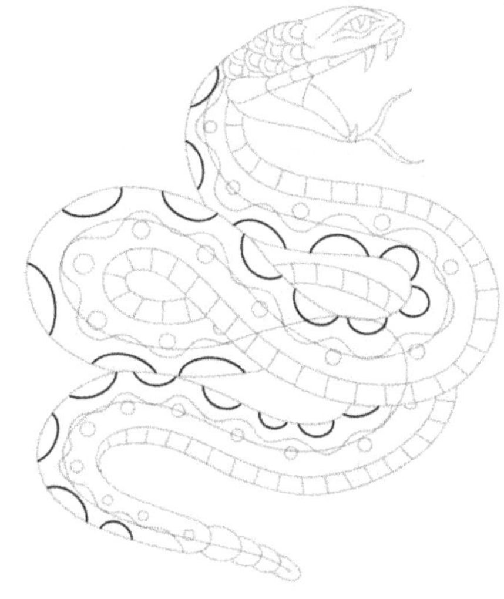

12

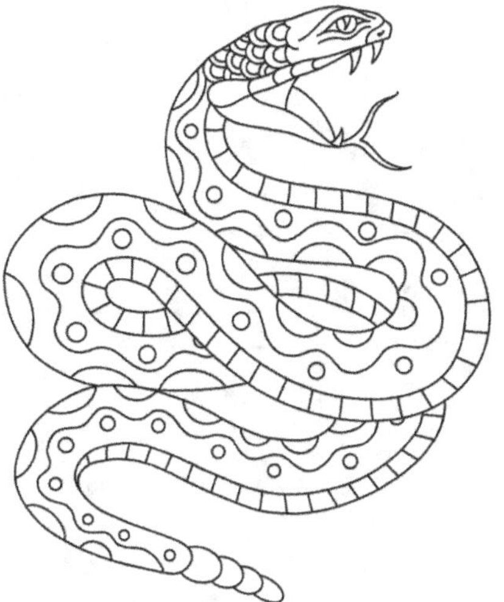

HOW TO DRAW TATTOO FLASH

TIGER

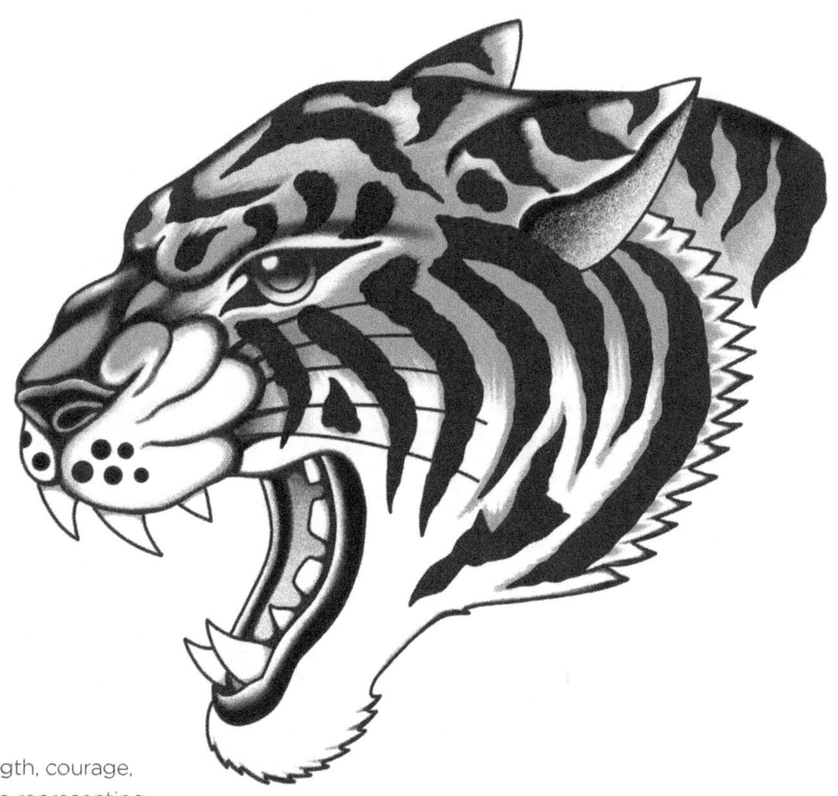

A tiger symbolises strength, courage, and independence, often representing raw power, protection, and primal instincts. It also carries themes of authority and personal willpower.

01

02

03

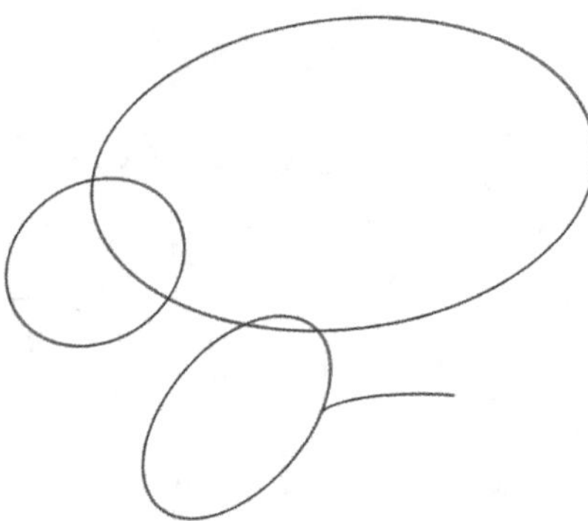

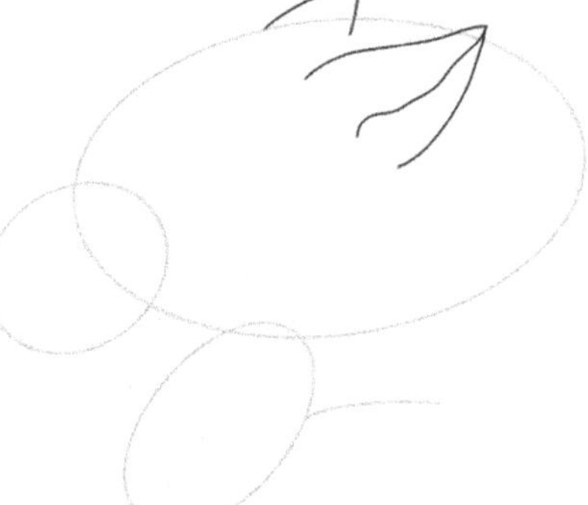

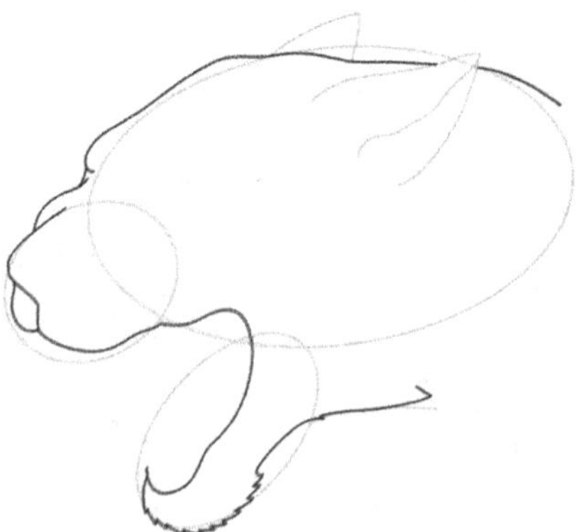

04

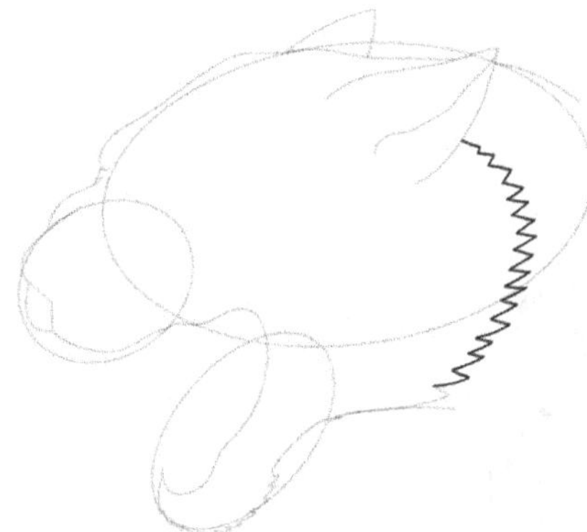

05

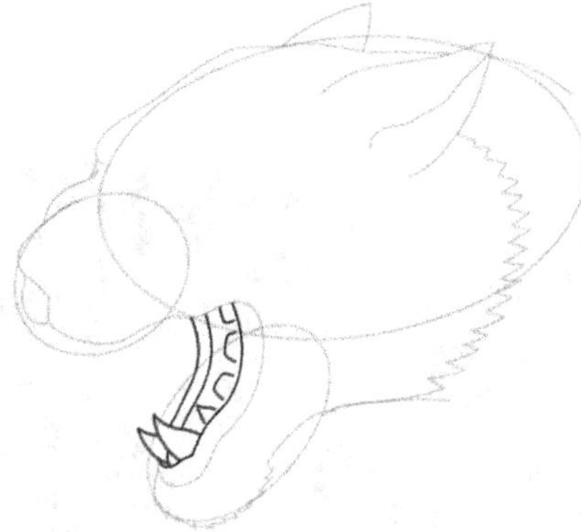

06

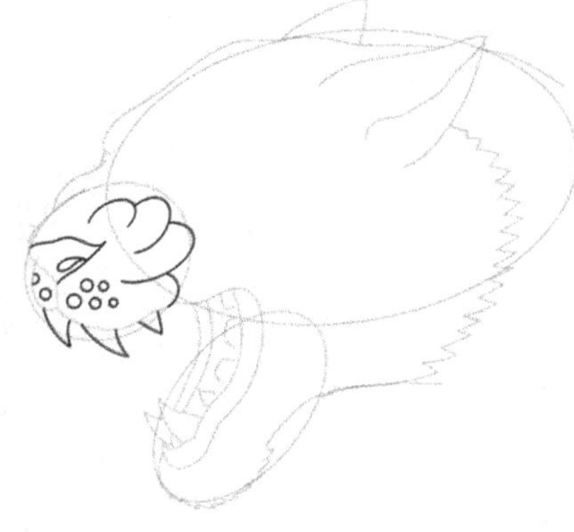

07

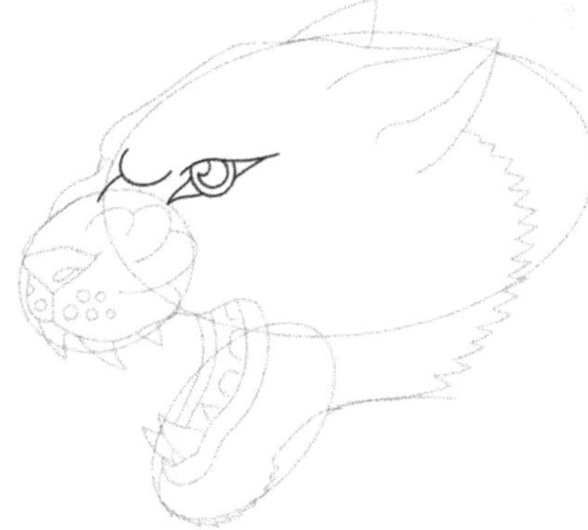

08

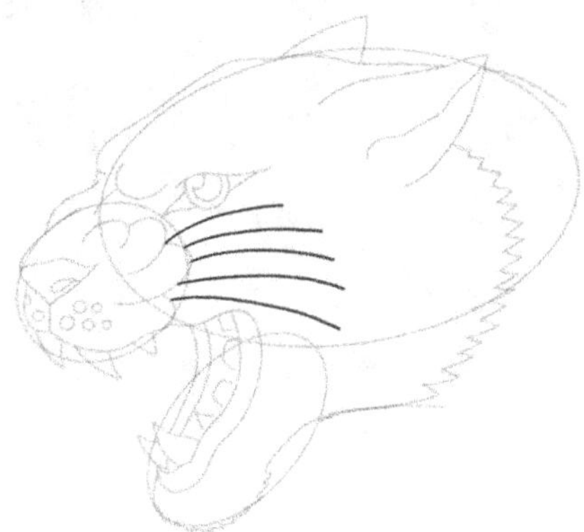

09

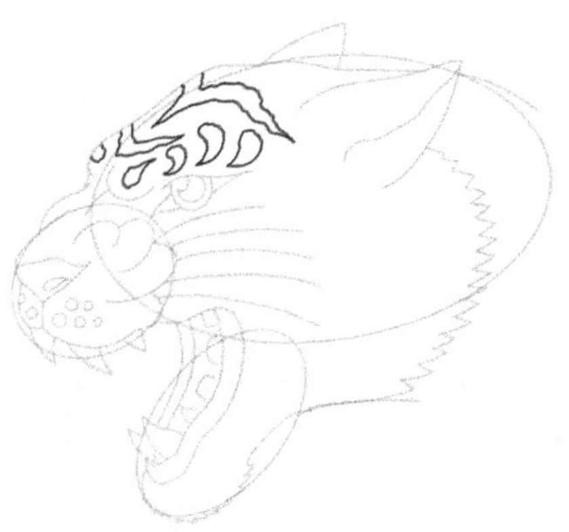

10

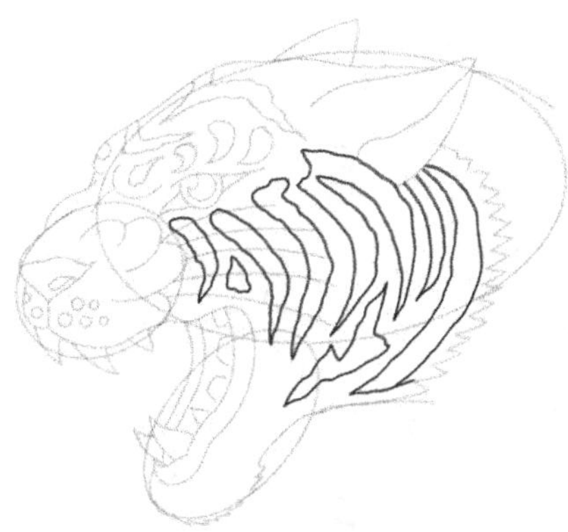

11

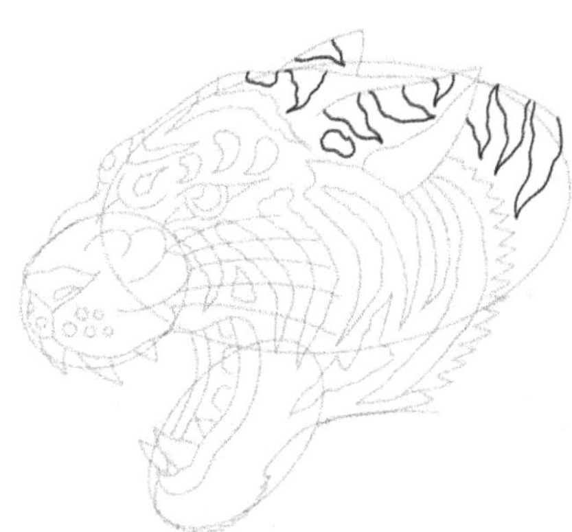

12

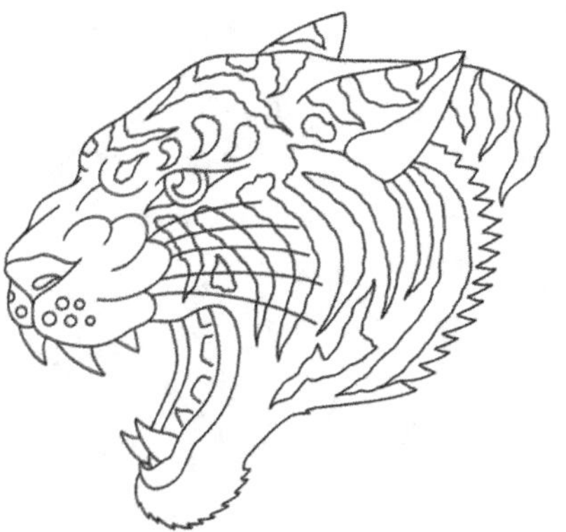

HOW TO DRAW TATTOO FLASH

WITCH

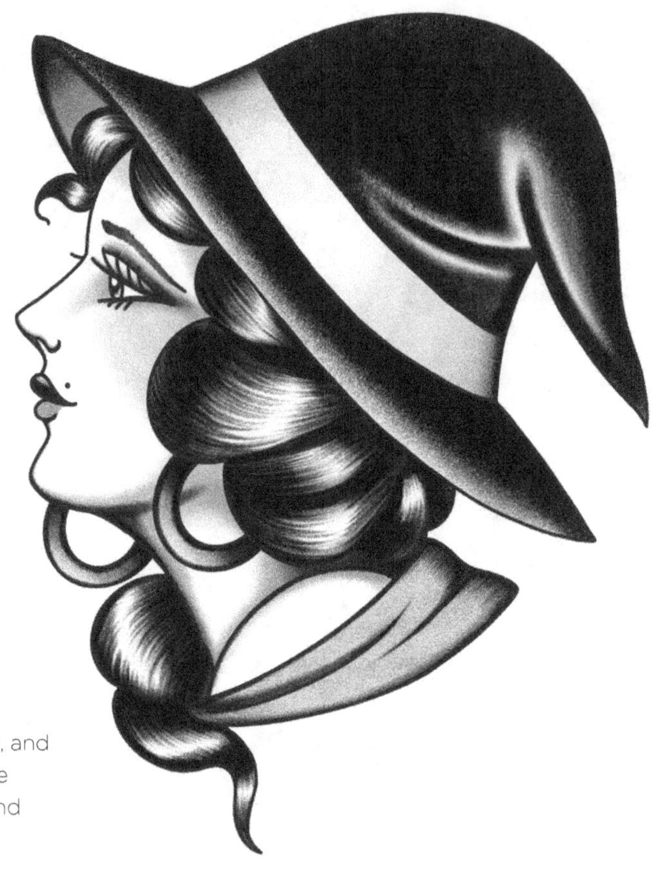

A witch symbolises power, wisdom, and rebellion. This tattoo is for someone who embraces their individuality and inner strength, even if it defies the societal norms.

01

02

03

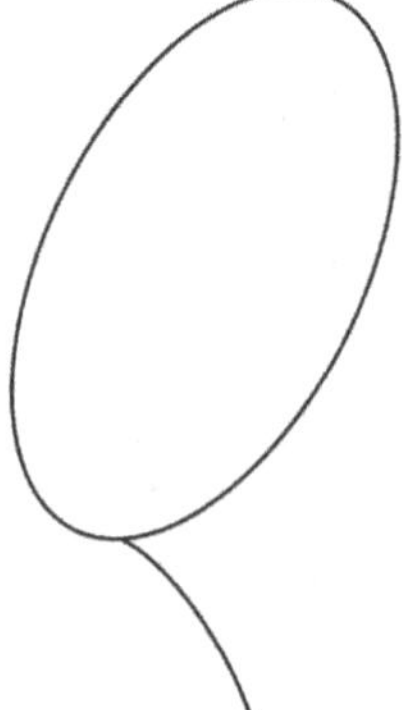

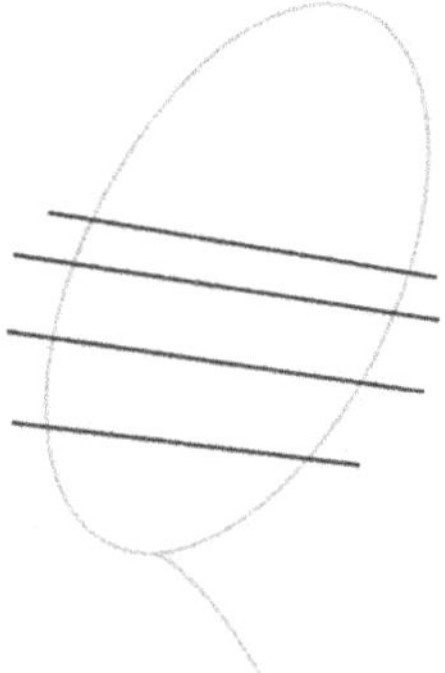

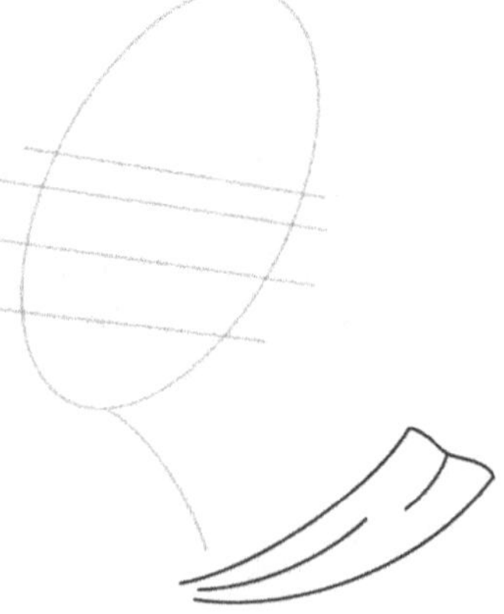

04

05

06

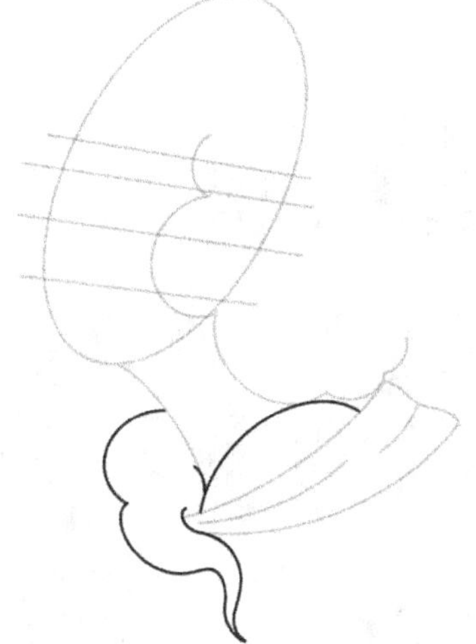

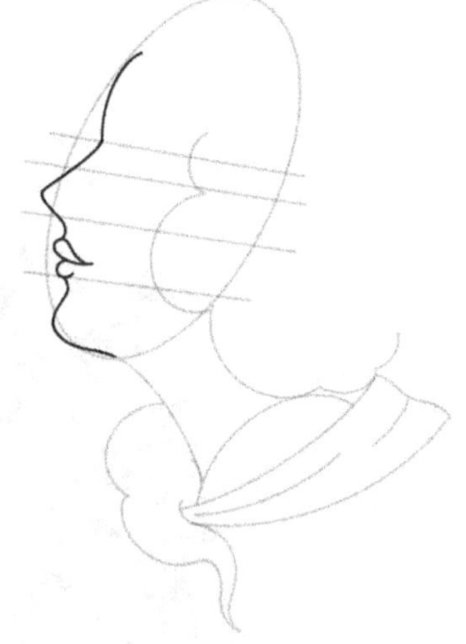

07

08

09

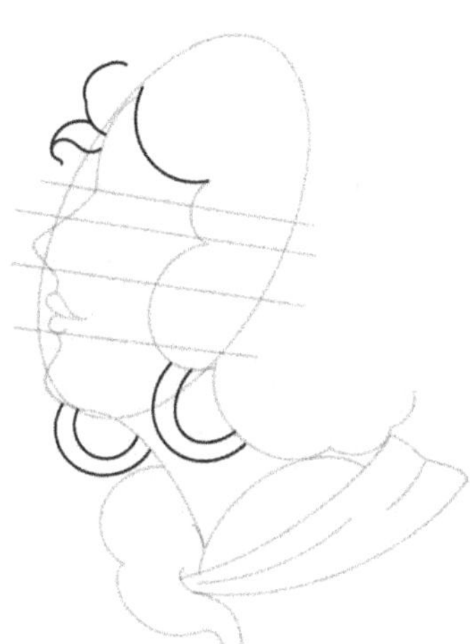

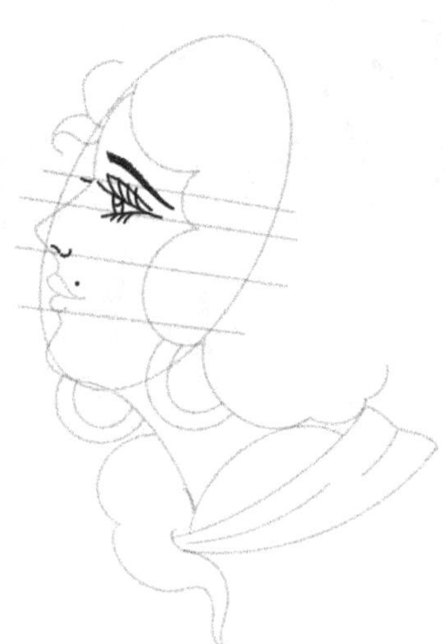

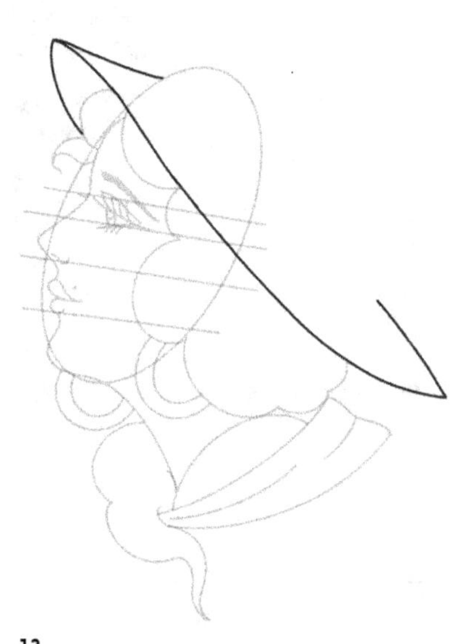

10

11

12

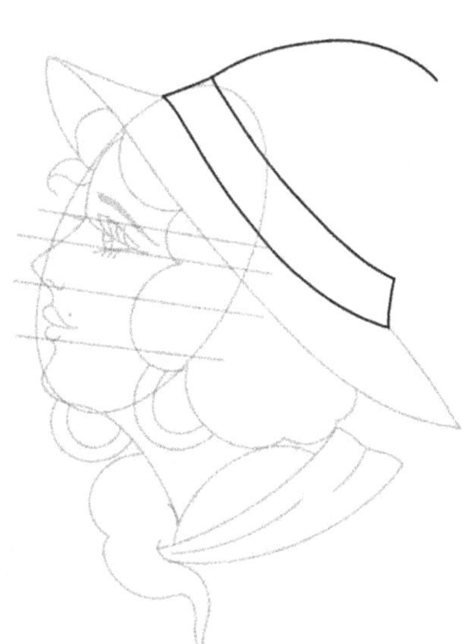

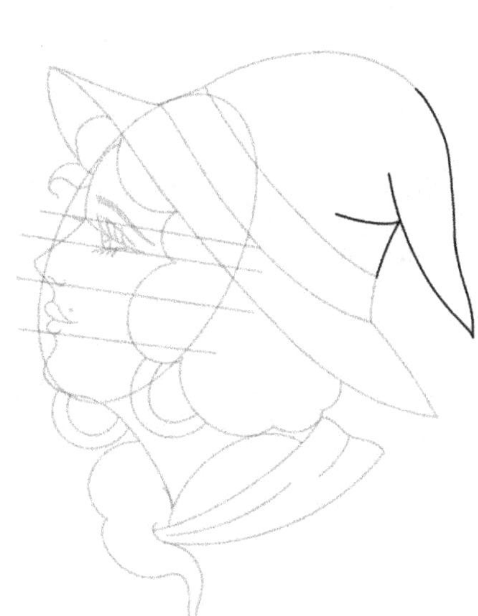

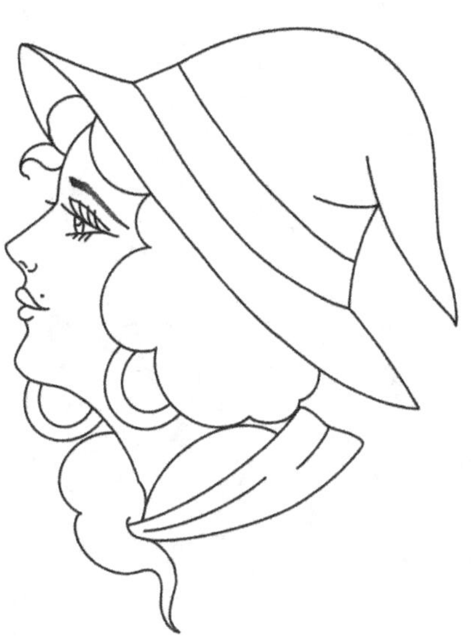

HOW TO DRAW TATTOO FLASH

WOLF

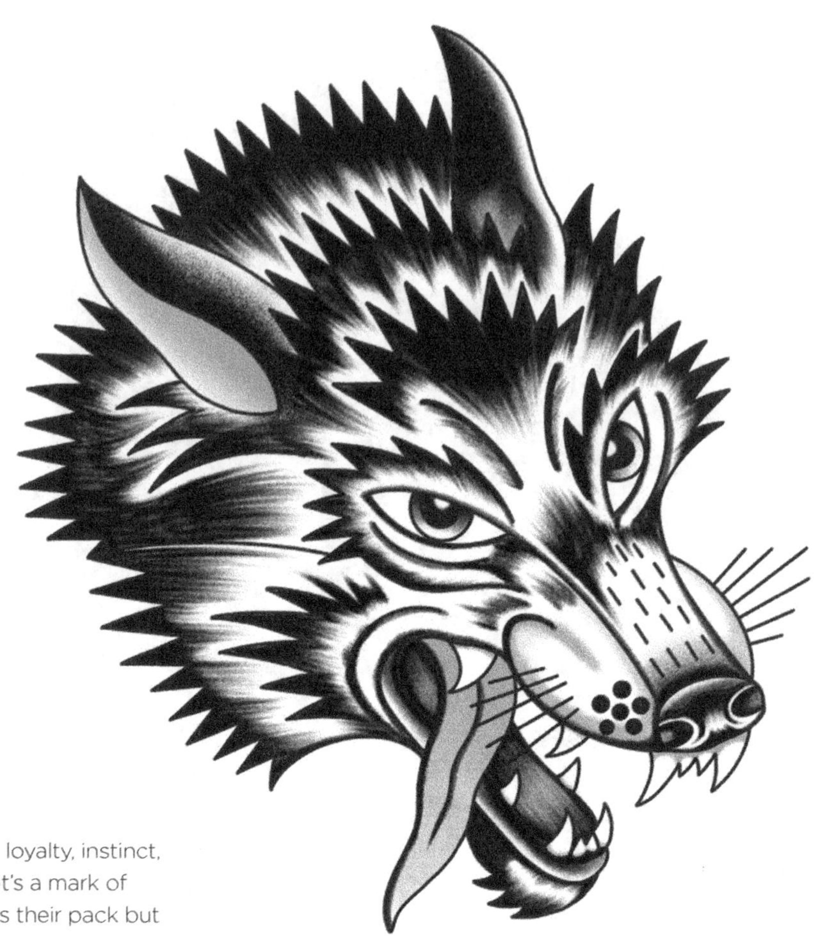

The wolf symbolises loyalty, instinct, and independence. It's a mark of someone who values their pack but thrives in solitude.

01

02

03

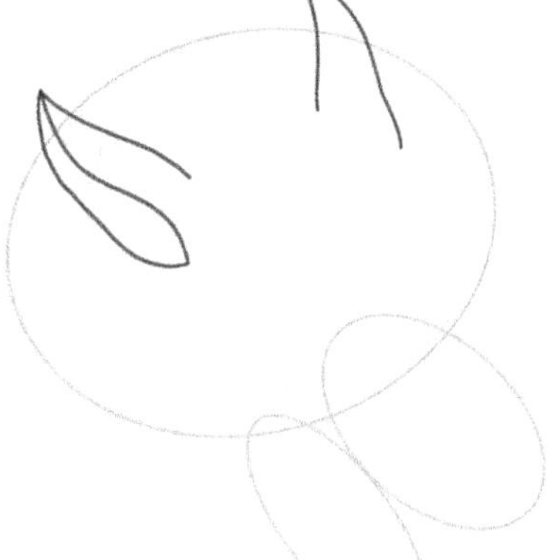

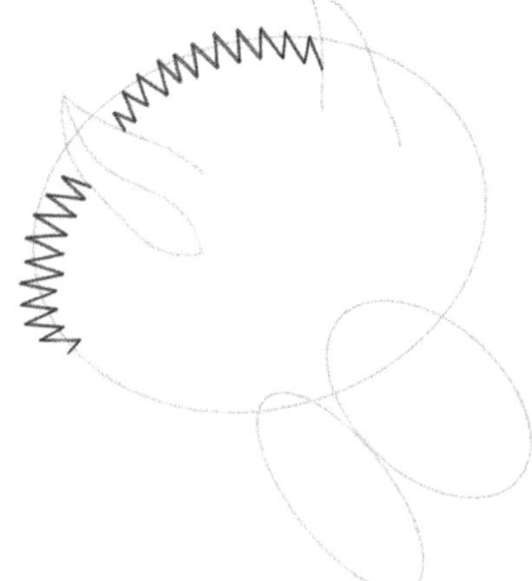

04

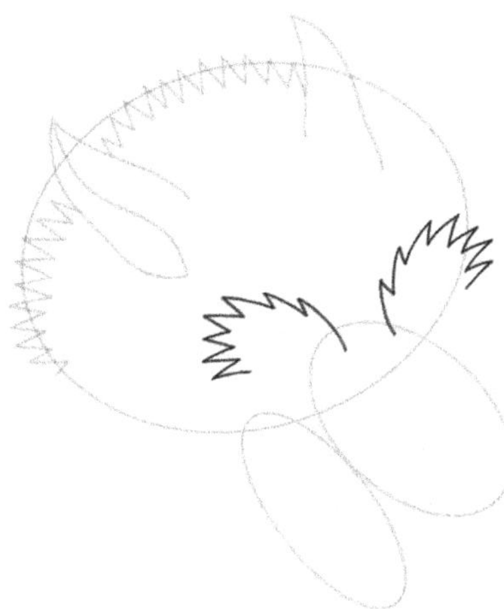

05

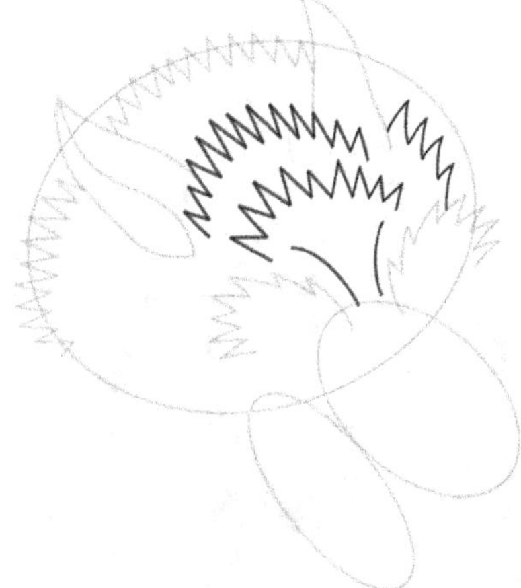

06

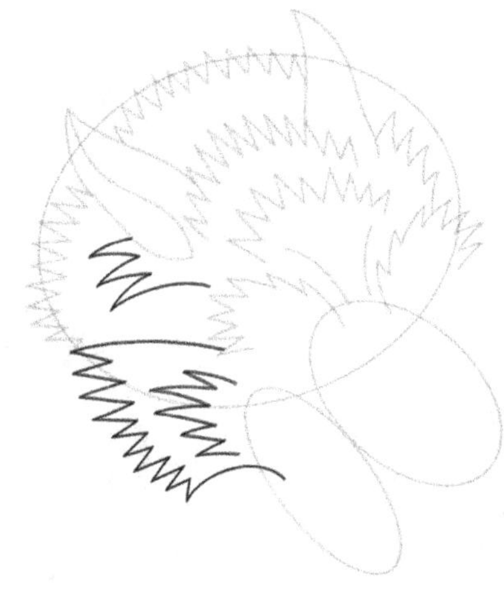

07

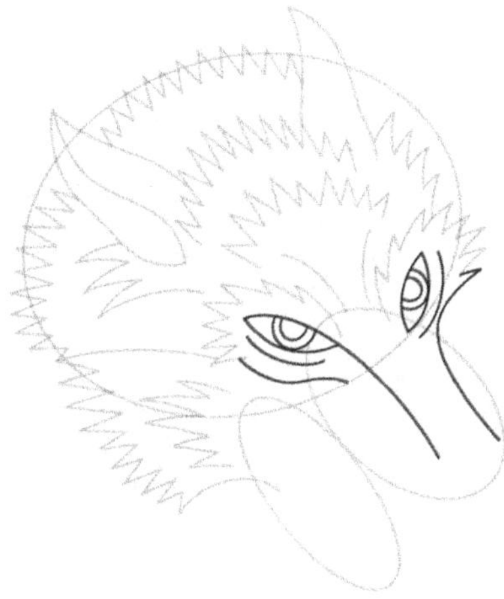

08

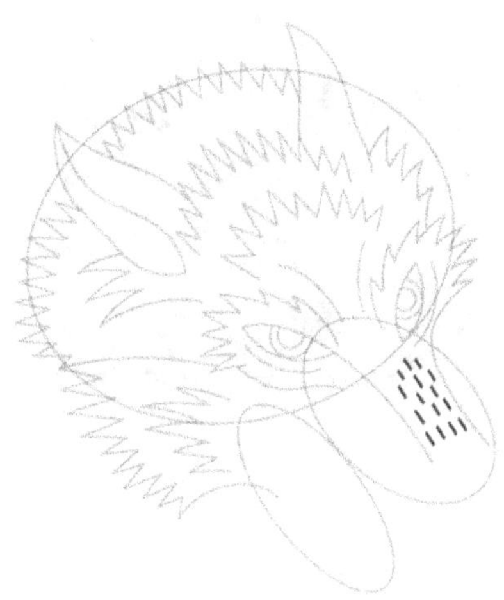

09

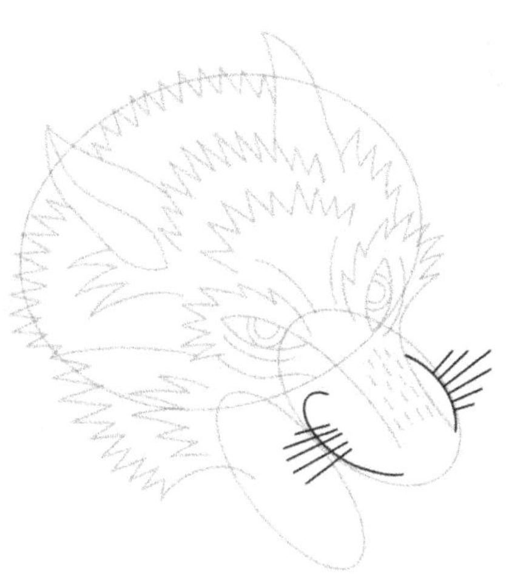

10

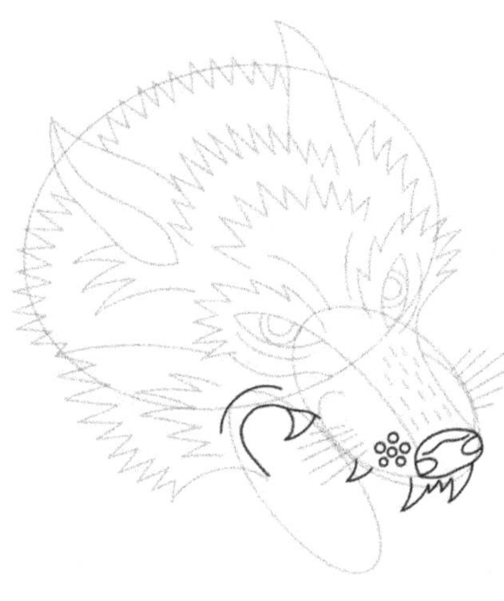

11

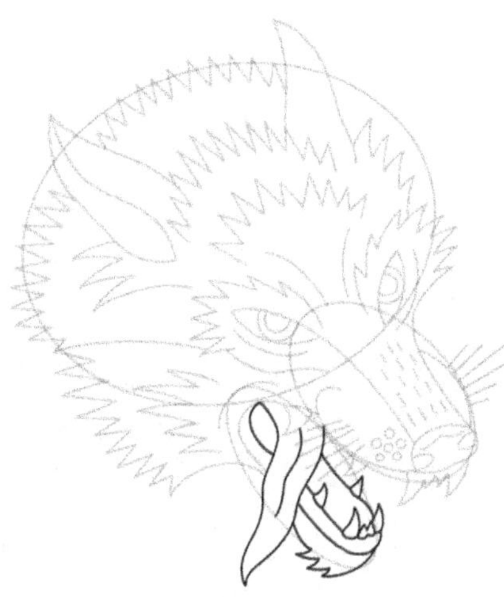

12

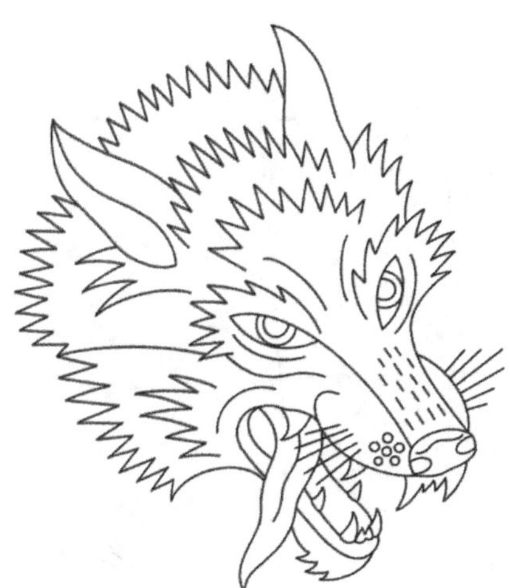

HOW TO DRAW TATTOO FLASH

HOW TO DRAW TATTOO FLASH

ZIPPO LIGHTER

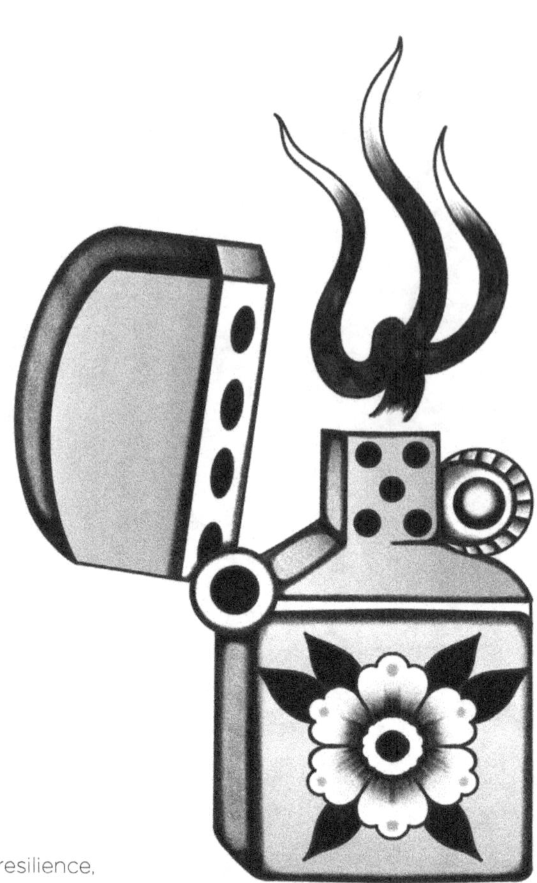

A Zippo lighter symbolises resilience, rebellion, and independence, often representing themes of nostalgia and adventure, with the lighter serving as an iconic tool of rugged individuality.

01   02   03

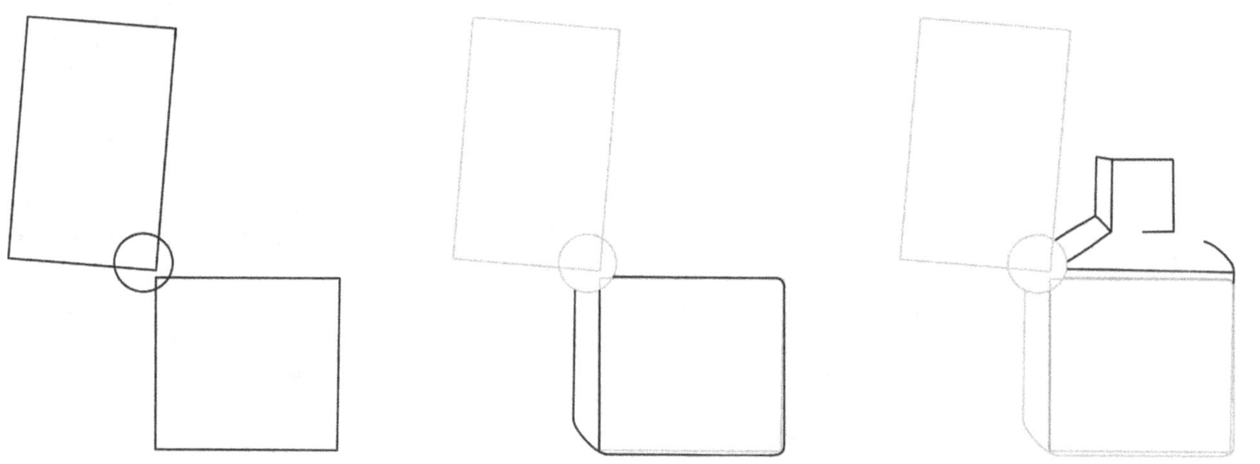

04

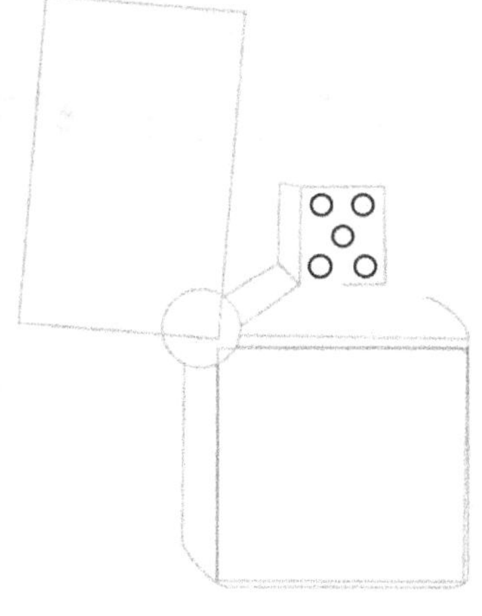

05

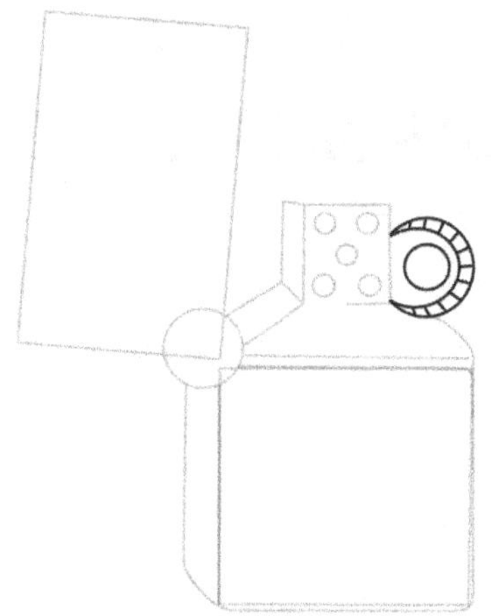

06

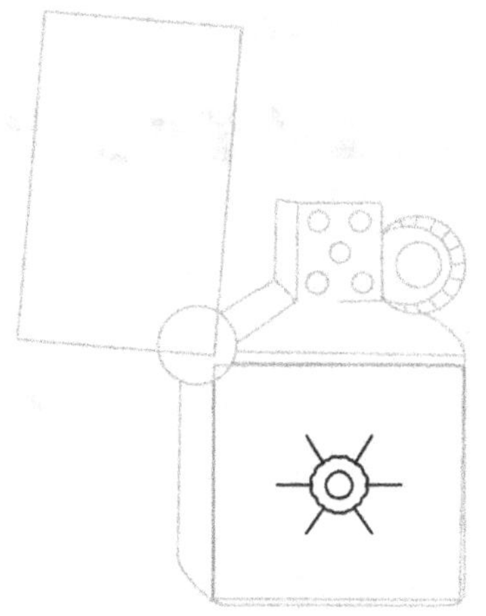

07

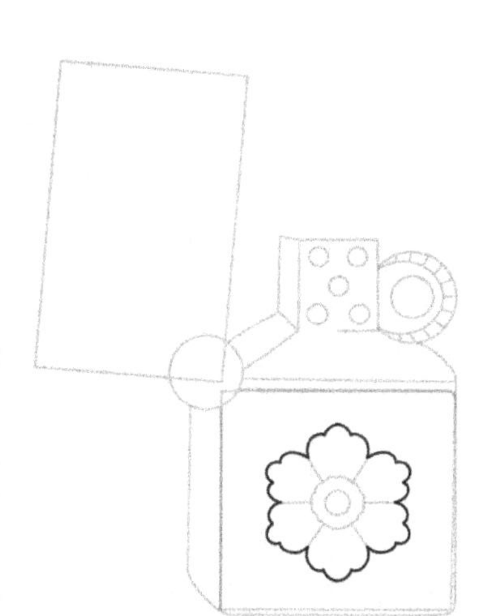

08

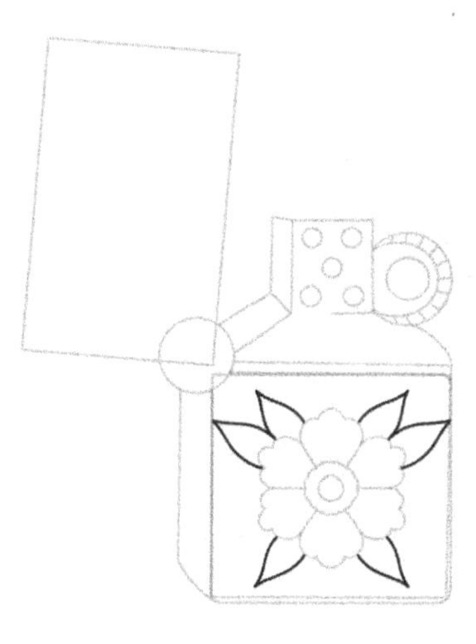

09

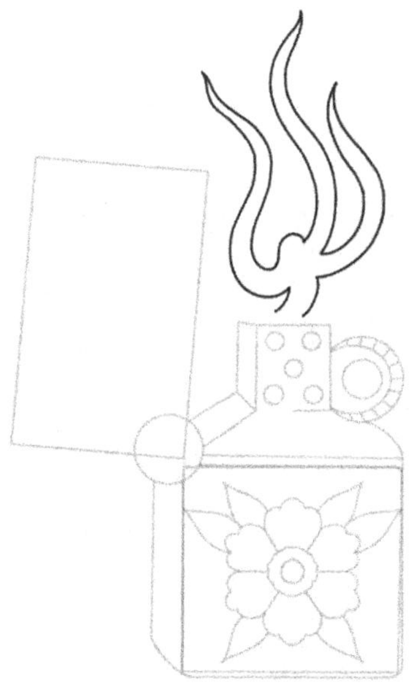

10

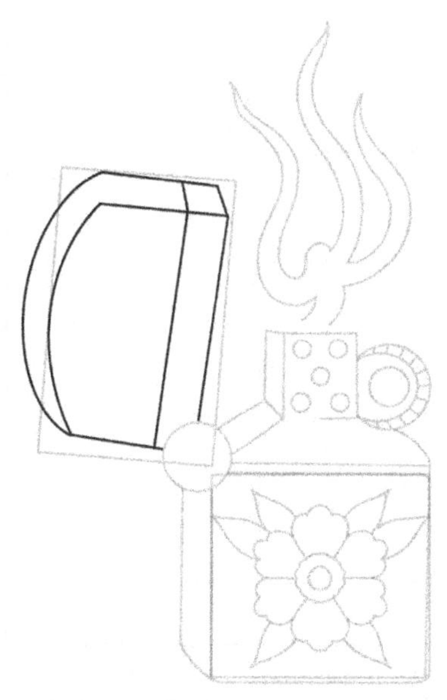

11

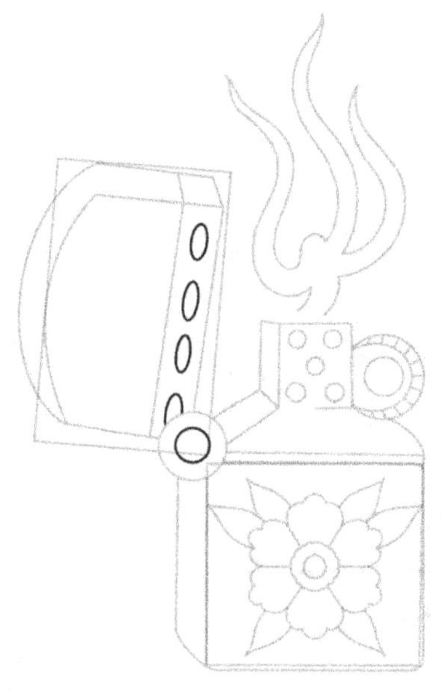

12

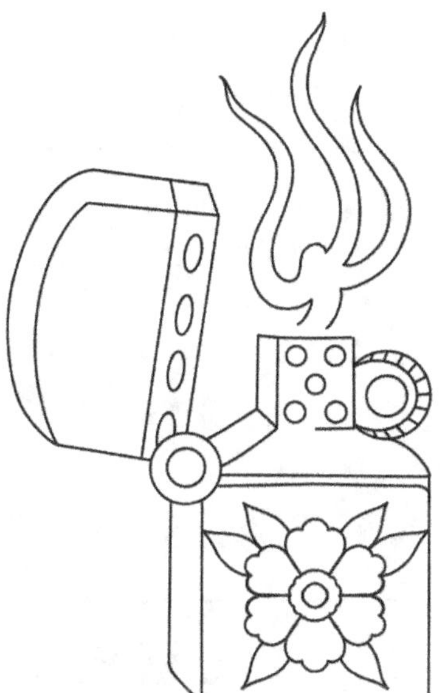

HOW TO DRAW TATTOO FLASH

PRACTICE MAKES PERFECT

T R D   M R K

HOW TO DRAW TATTOOS

PRACTICE MAKES PERFECT

T R D   M R K

Vault Editions Ltd

CREATION AND RESTORATION SERVICES

LEARN MORE

VAULTEDITIONS.COM

PRACTICE
MAKES
PERFECT
T R D   M R K

HOW TO DRAW
TATTOOS

PRACTICE
MAKES
PERFECT
T R D   M R K

Vault Editions Ltd

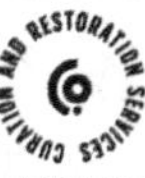

LEARN MORE

VAULTEDITIONS.COM

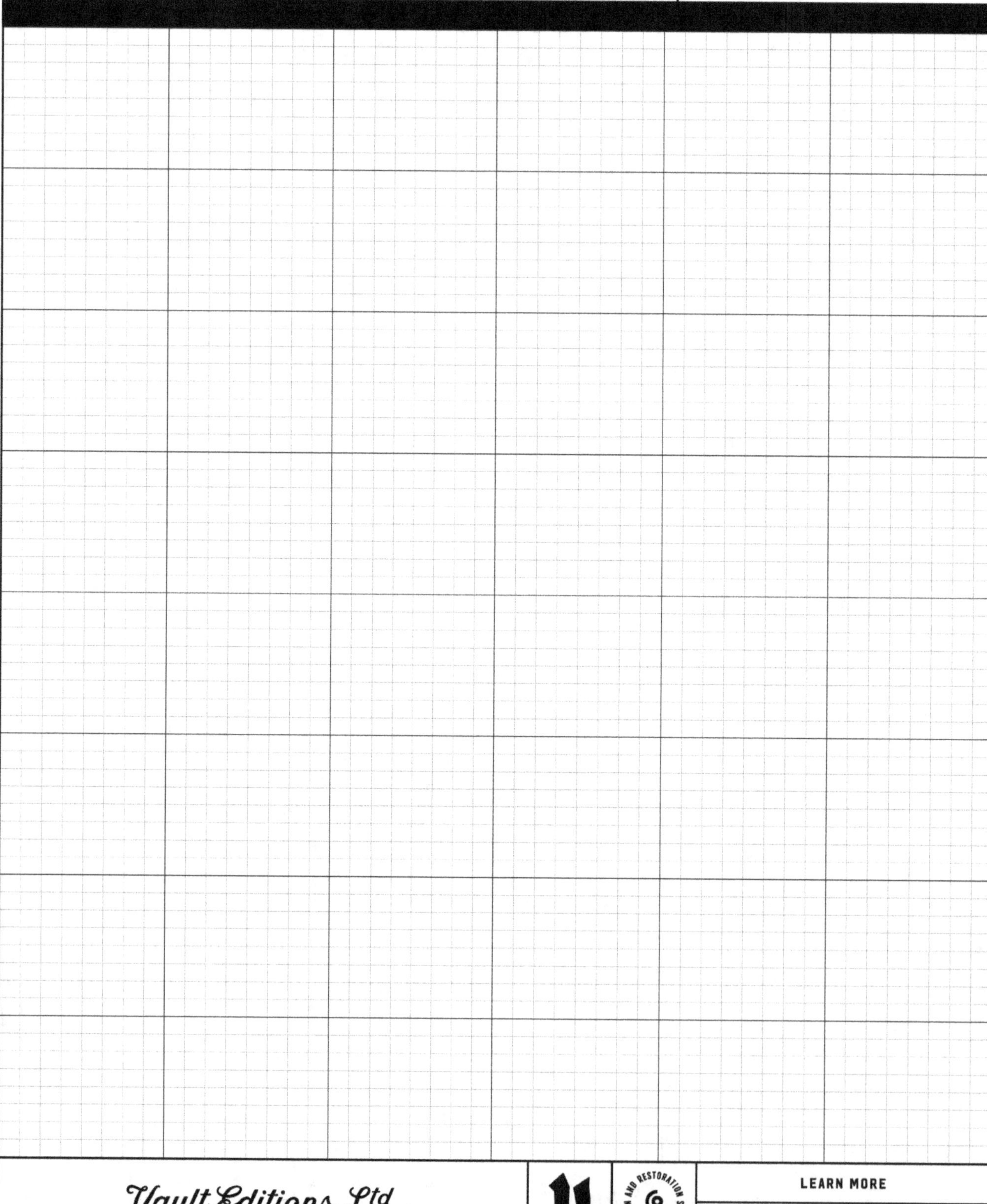
PRACTICE
MAKES
PERFECT
T R D
MRK
HOW TO DRAW
TATTOOS
PRACTICE
MAKES
PERFECT
T R D
MRK

PRACTICE MAKES PERFECT
T R D · M R K

HOW TO DRAW
TATTOOS

PRACTICE MAKES PERFECT
T R D · M R K

Vault Editions Ltd

CURATION AND RESTORATION SERVICES

LEARN MORE

VAULTEDITIONS.COM

PRACTICE MAKES PERFECT
T R D   M R K

HOW TO DRAW
TATTOOS

PRACTICE MAKES PERFECT
T R D   M R K

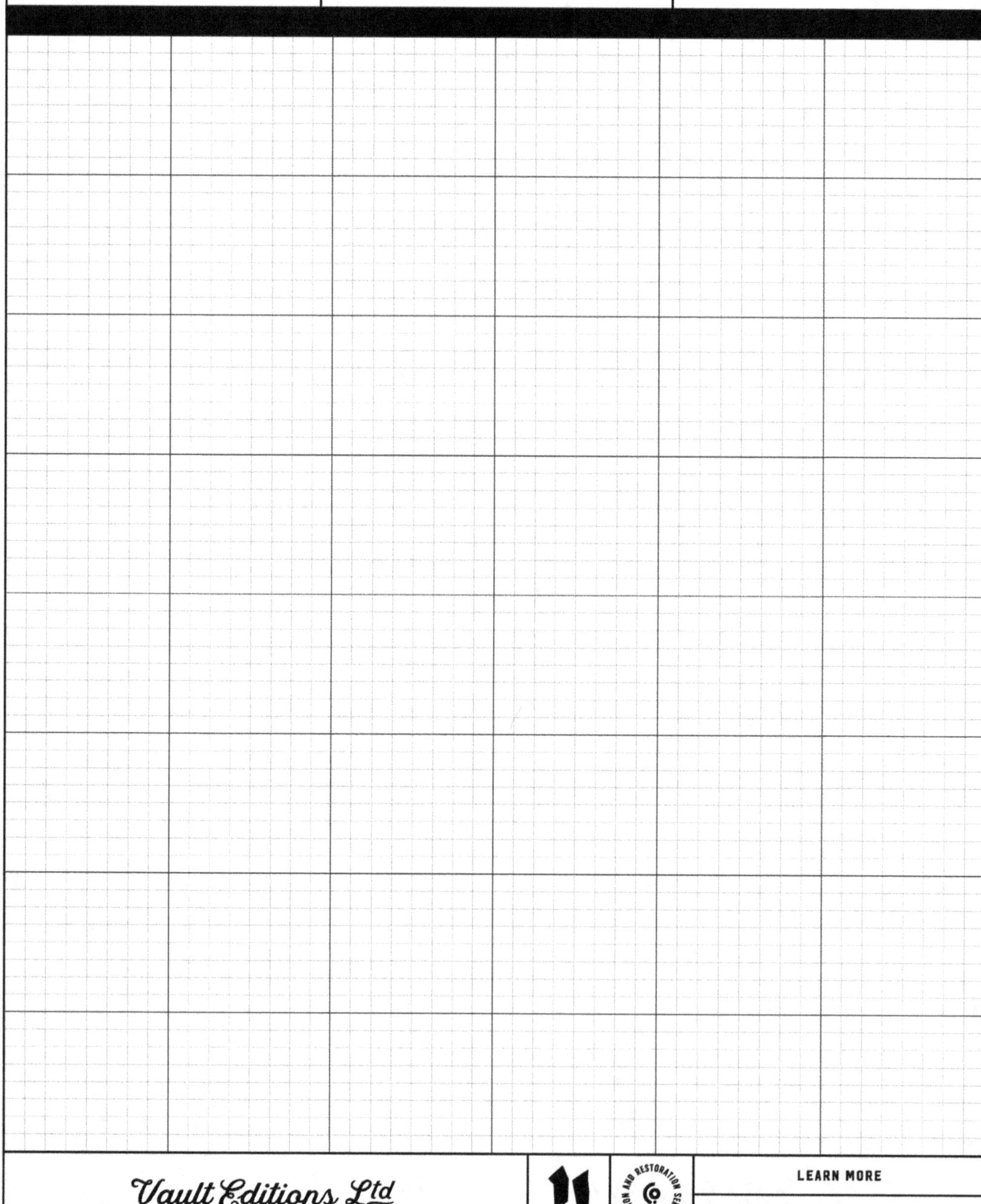

Vault Editions Ltd

SERVICES CURATION AND RESTORATION

LEARN MORE

VAULTEDITIONS.COM

PRACTICE MAKES PERFECT
T R D
M R K

HOW TO DRAW
TATTOOS

PRACTICE MAKES PERFECT
T R D
M R K

Vault Editions Ltd

LEARN MORE

VAULTEDITIONS.COM

PRACTICE
MAKES
PERFECT
T R D
M R K

HOW TO DRAW
TATTOOS

PRACTICE
MAKES
PERFECT
T R D
M R K

HOW TO DRAW TATTOO FLASH

Vault Editions Ltd

CURATION AND RESTORATION SERVICES

LEARN MORE

VAULTEDITIONS.COM

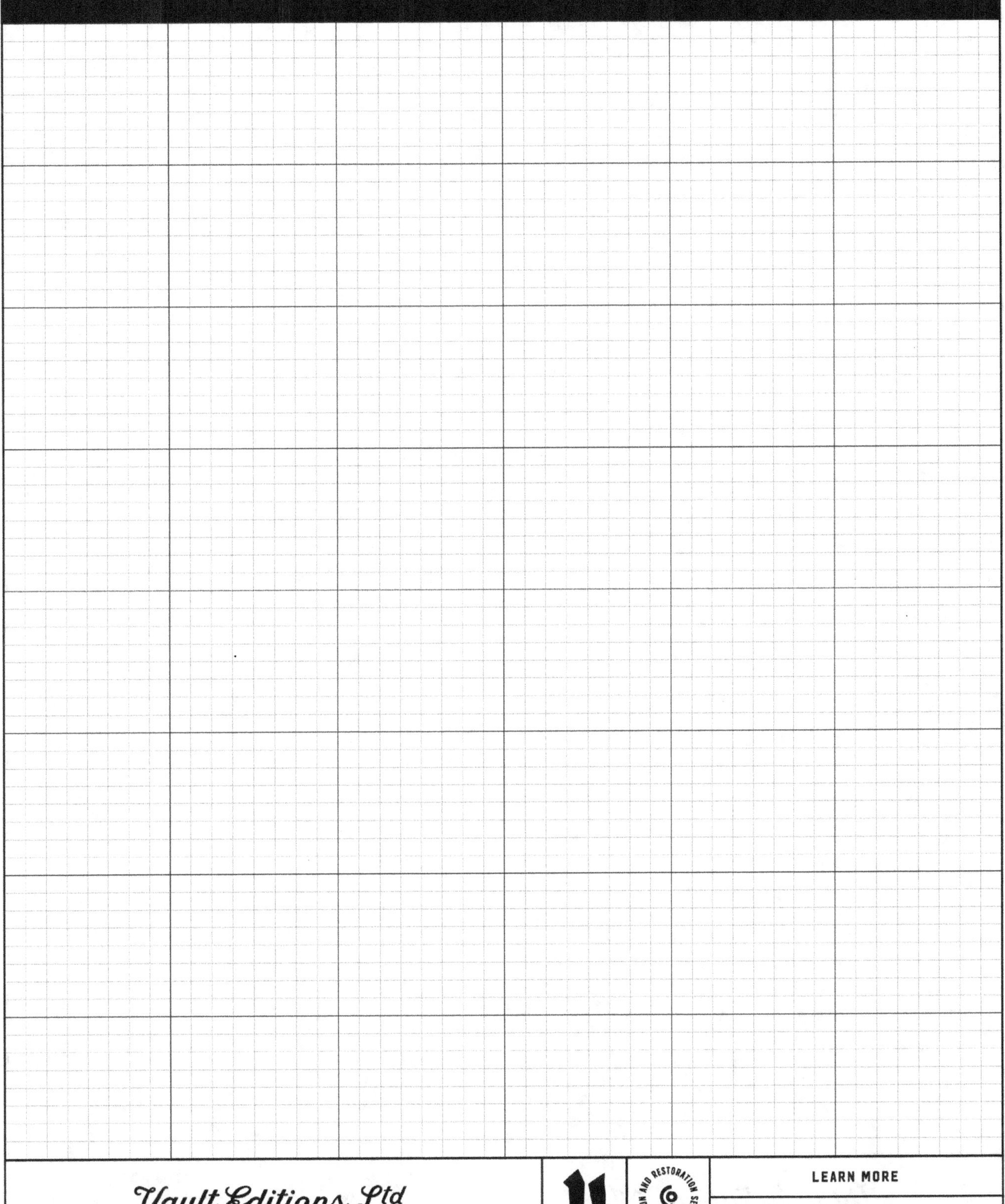
PRACTICE
T R D
MAKES
M R K
PERFECT

HOW TO DRAW
TATTOOS

PRACTICE
T R D
MAKES
M R K
PERFECT

Vault Editions Ltd

LEARN MORE
VAULTEDITIONS.COM

CURATION AND RESTORATION SERVICES

HOW TO DRAW
TATTOOS

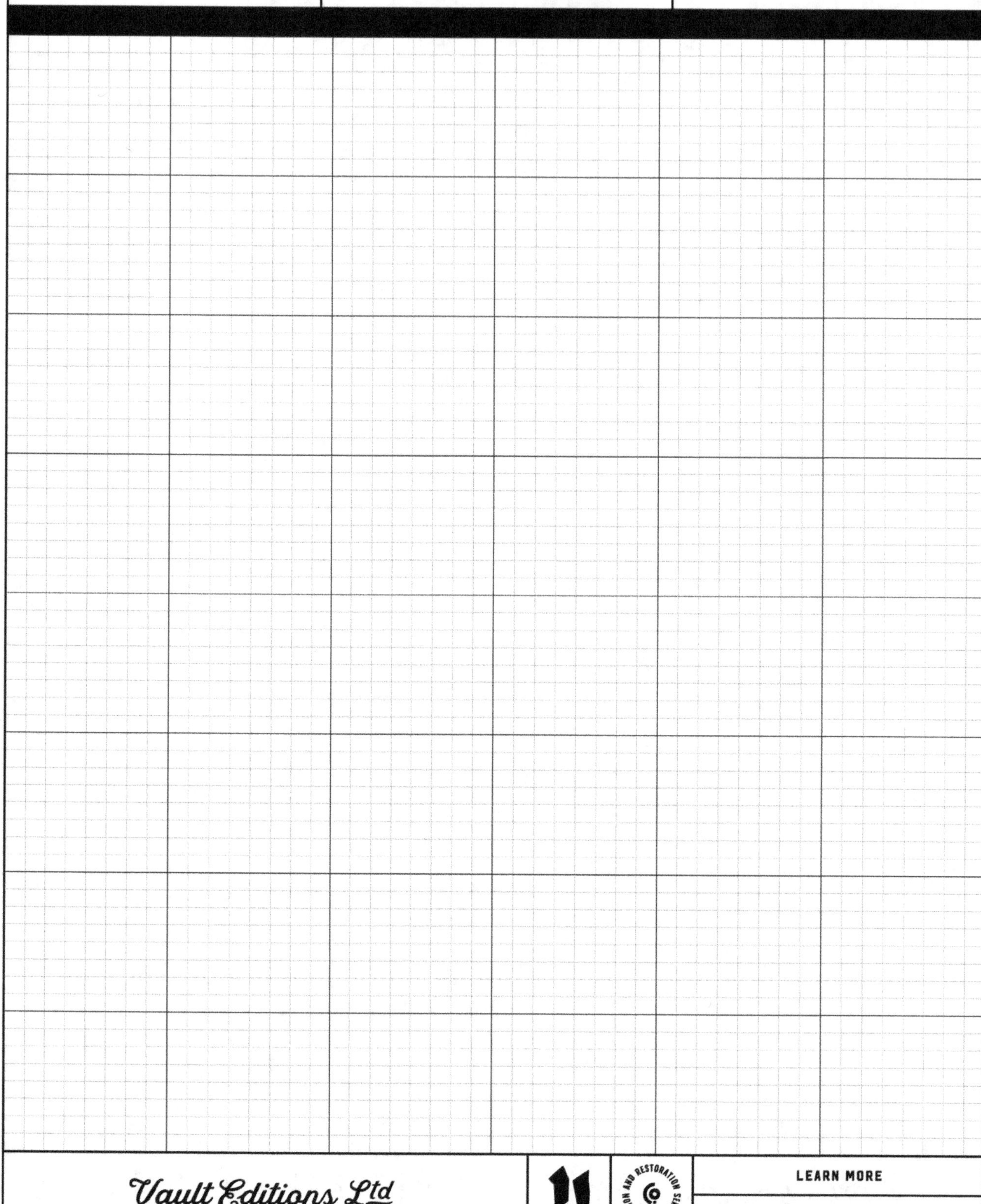

Vault Editions Ltd

LEARN MORE

VAULTEDITIONS.COM

HOW TO DRAW
TATTOOS

Vault Editions Ltd

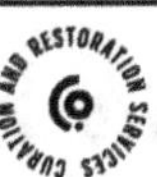

LEARN MORE

VAULTEDITIONS.COM

HOW TO DRAW
TATTOOS

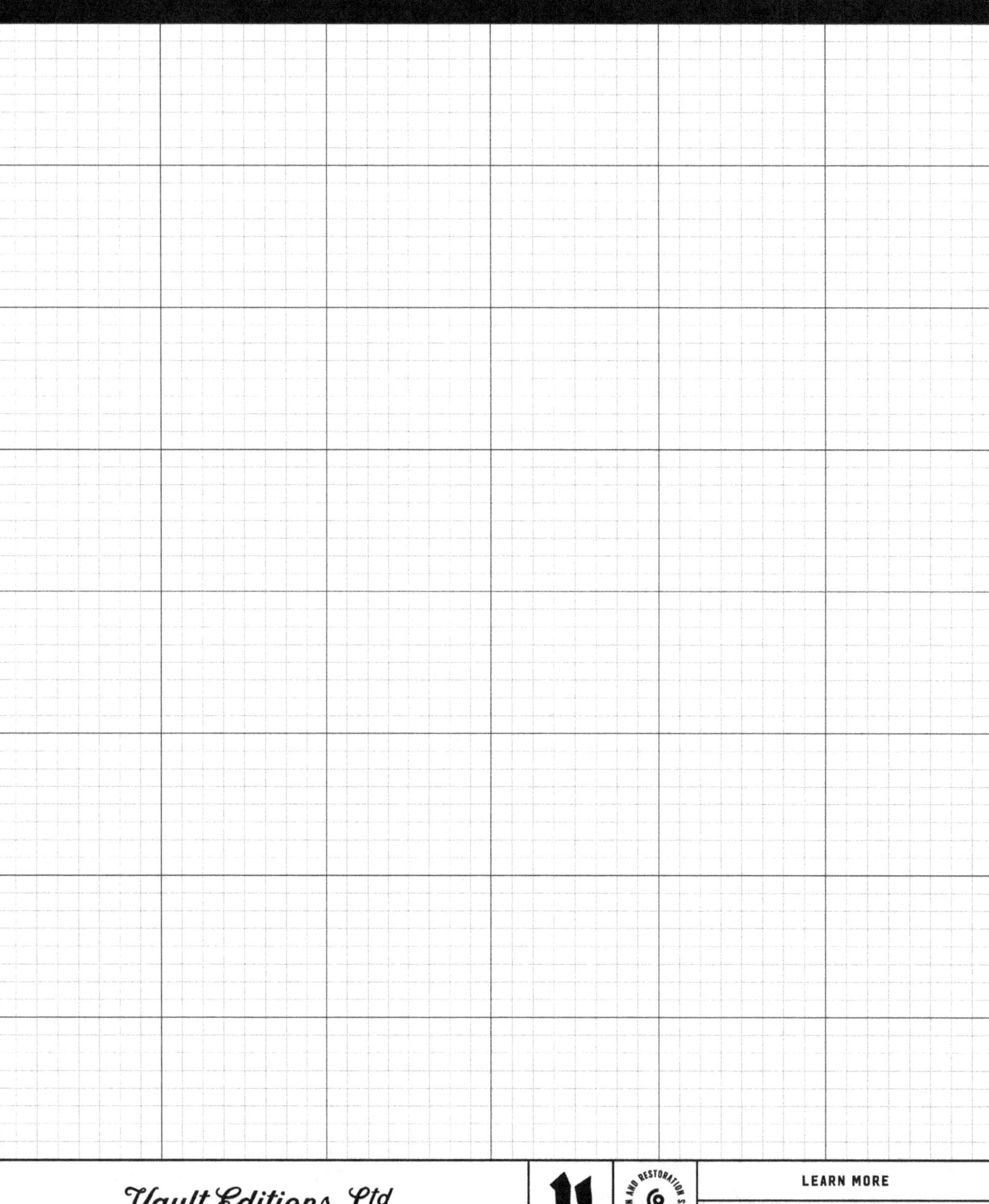

HOW TO DRAW TATTOO FLASH

Vault Editions Ltd

LEARN MORE

VAULTEDITIONS.COM

HOW TO DRAW
TATTOOS

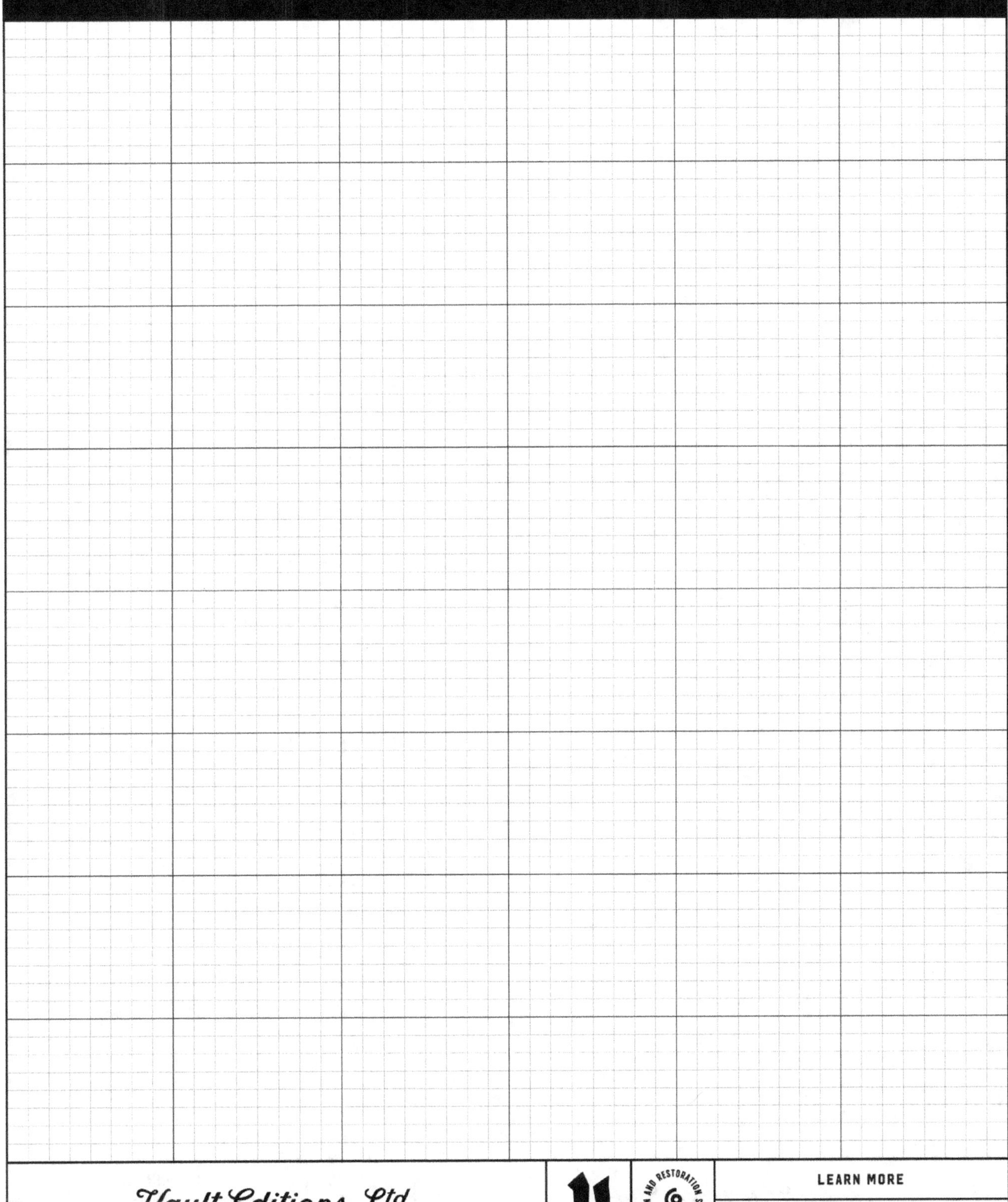

HOW TO DRAW TATTOO FLASH

Vault Editions Ltd

LEARN MORE

VAULTEDITIONS.COM

HOW TO DRAW TATTOO FLASH

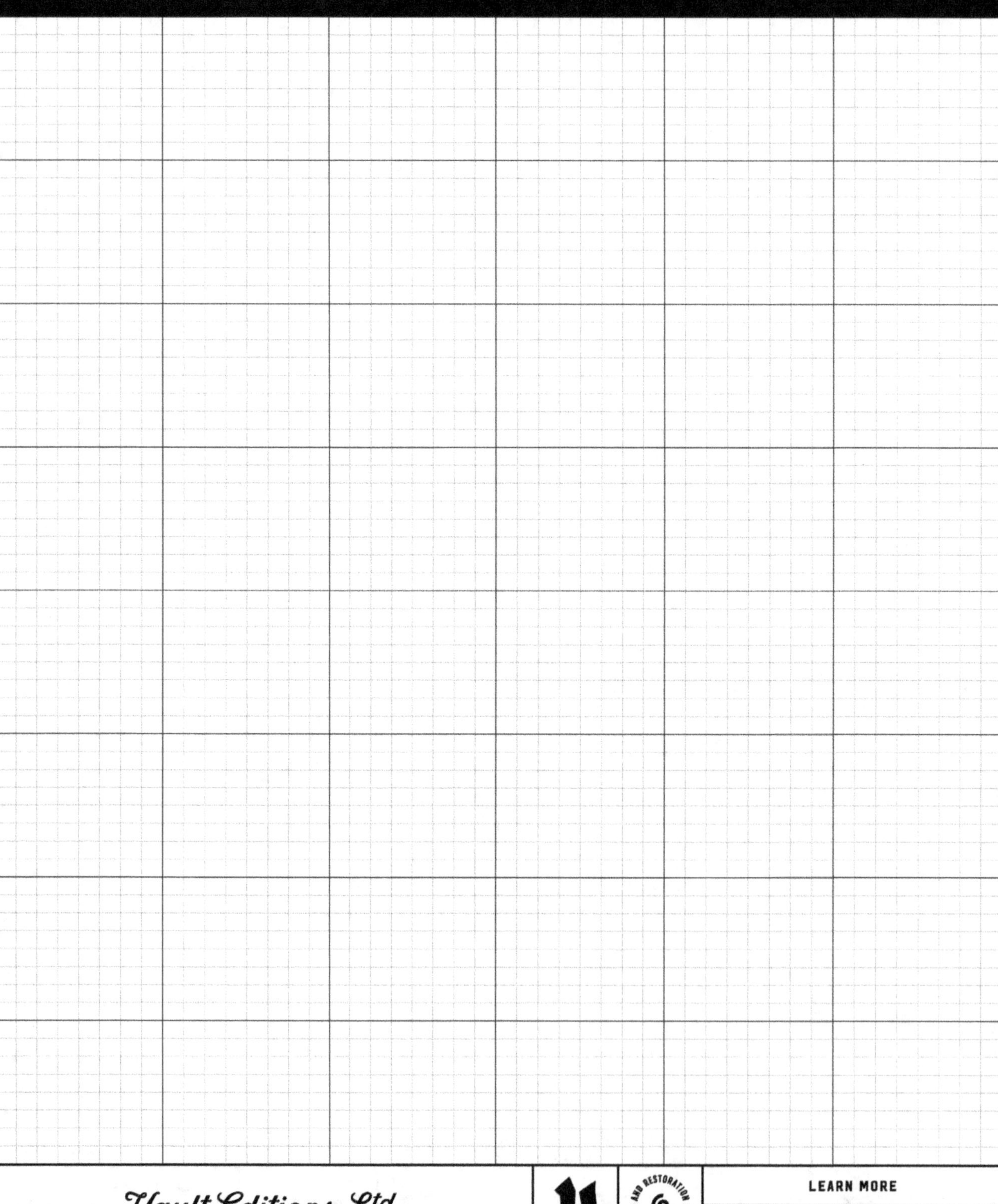

PRACTICE MAKES PERFECT
T R D
M R K

HOW TO DRAW
TATTOOS

PRACTICE MAKES PERFECT
T R D
M R K

HOW TO DRAW TATTOO FLASH

Vault Editions Ltd

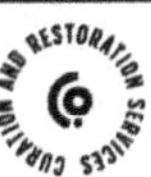

LEARN MORE

VAULTEDITIONS.COM

CONCLUSION

As you reach the end of *How to Draw Tattoo Flash*, you've not only honed your ability to draw iconic designs but have also deepened your understanding of the powerful symbols that define traditional tattoo art. The skills and knowledge you've gained will serve as a foundation for endless creative exploration, whether you're looking to pursue a career in tattooing, design your own meaningful tattoos, or simply appreciate the artistry behind the flash.

Remember, mastering this craft is a continuous journey. The bold lines, timeless motifs, and cultural significance of traditional tattoo flash offer limitless potential for personal expression. With practice, patience, and passion, you have the tools to create designs that resonate deeply with those who wear them and that honour the legacy of tattoo art.

Now, it's time to take what you've learned and push your creativity further. Let each design you create tell its own story, and may your journey into the world of tattoo flash continue to evolve, inspiring you and those around you.

ABOUT THE ARTIST

The designs in this book were produced by Aaron Hingston, a highly skilled tattoo artist whose work brings traditional tattoo designs to life by merging classic artistry with modern techniques. Since starting his career in 2009, Aaron has earned a reputation for precise line work and attention to detail. Based in Victoria, Australia, his creations draw from the rich heritage of tattoo traditions while incorporating fresh, contemporary influences, resulting in designs that are both timeless and personal.

Aaron collaborates closely with clients to craft custom tattoos that tell their unique stories. Whether it's a bold new design or an addition to existing work, his creative process ensures each piece is tailored to the individual. To explore Aaron's portfolio or inquire about bookings and commissions, visit his Instagram profile: @aaron_hingston.

LEARN MORE

At Vault Editions, our mission is to provide the highest quality reference materials for artists and designers, offering meticulously curated resources that inspire and empower creativity. If you've found value in this book, we invite you to explore more of our expertly crafted titles at our website **www.vaulteditions.com**, where you'll discover a world of visual inspiration and practical tools designed to elevate your creative work.

REVIEW THIS BOOK

As a family-owned and operated independent publisher, reviews are essential to the success of our business. Please leave an honest review of this book wherever you purchased it.

JOIN OUR COMMUNITY

Are you the creative and curious type? If so, you will love our community on Instagram. Every day, we share bizarre and beautiful artwork ranging from 17th and 18th-century natural history and scientific illustrations to mythical beasts, ornamental designs, anatomical drawings and more; join our community of 300K+ people today by searching @vault_editions on Instagram.

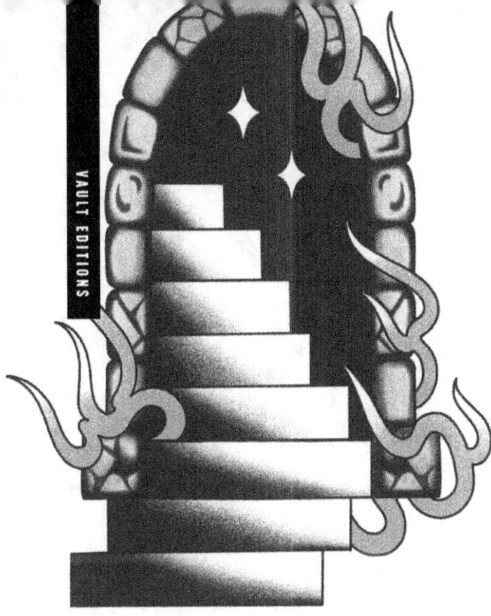

DOWNLOAD YOUR FILES

To enhance your creative journey, *How to Draw Tattoo Flash* comes with a digital PDF version of the book and a specially designed set of Procreate brushes. These resources are tailored to help you refine your skills and streamline your workflow, whether you're working traditionally or digitally.

The digital PDF provides easy access to the book's contents on any device, so you can reference the designs anytime, anywhere. It's perfect for artists on the go, allowing you to study and practice whenever inspiration strikes.

The custom Procreate brushes are designed to replicate the look and feel of traditional tattoo flash designs, from bold outlining to shading techniques. These brushes make it easier for digital artists to create authentic-looking designs in a digital medium, offering precision and flexibility as you sketch, refine, and finalise your artwork. Whether you're experimenting with new ideas or perfecting your final designs, these brushes allow you to bring your creations to life with the same iconic style that defines classic tattoo flash.

Download now and get creating!

STEP ONE

Enter the following web address on a desktop or laptop computer in your web browser.

vaulteditions.com/pages/tfd

STEP TWO

Enter the following password to access the download page:

tfd273646sxda

STEP THREE

Follow the prompts to access your high-resolution files.

CONTACT

For technical support, please email: info@vaulteditions.com

Copyright © 2024
Vault Editions Ltd

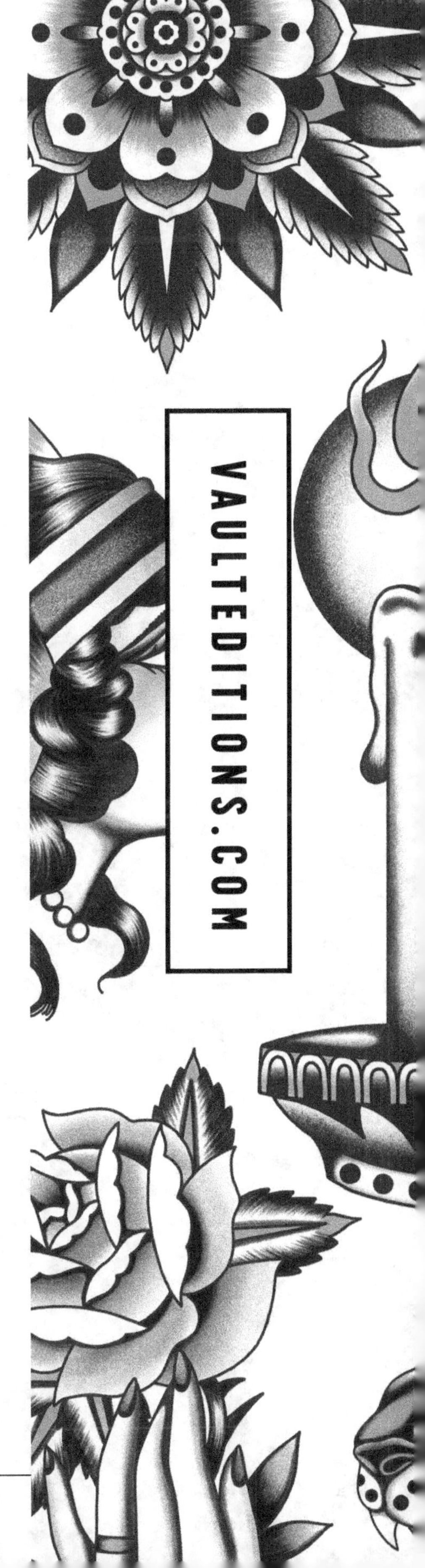

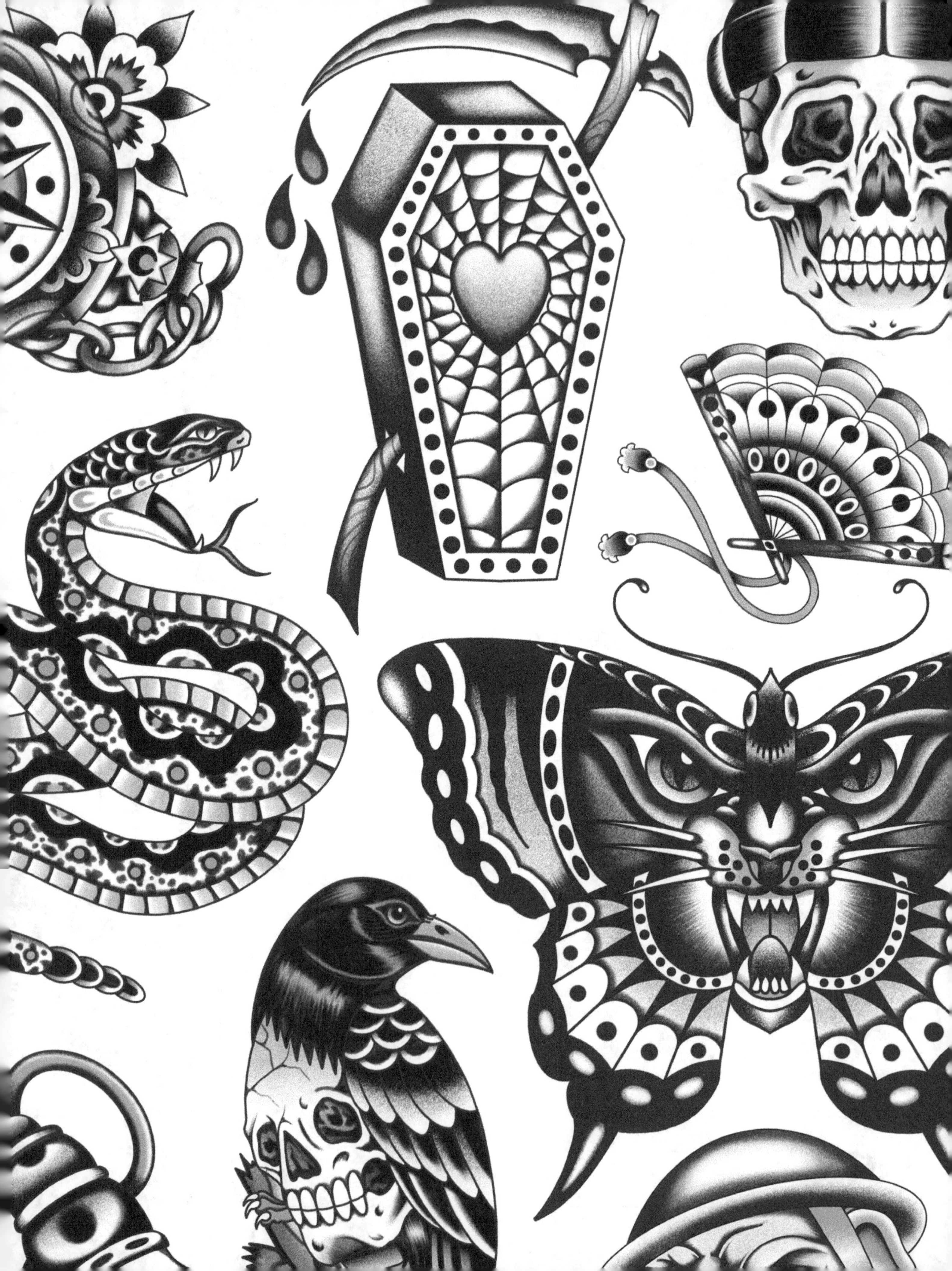

www.ingramcontent.com/pod-product-compliance
Lightning Source LLC
Chambersburg PA
CBHW080521030726

47592CB00012B/3429

9 781922 966483